I0003984

Network Automation Cookbook

Proven and actionable recipes to automate and manage
network devices using Ansible

Karim Okasha

BIRMINGHAM - MUMBAI

Network Automation Cookbook

Copyright © 2020 Packt Publishing

All rights reserved. No part of this book may be reproduced, stored in a retrieval system, or transmitted in any form or by any means, without the prior written permission of the publisher, except in the case of brief quotations embedded in critical articles or reviews.

Every effort has been made in the preparation of this book to ensure the accuracy of the information presented. However, the information contained in this book is sold without warranty, either express or implied. Neither the author, nor Packt Publishing or its dealers and distributors, will be held liable for any damages caused or alleged to have been caused directly or indirectly by this book.

Packt Publishing has endeavored to provide trademark information about all of the companies and products mentioned in this book by the appropriate use of capitals. However, Packt Publishing cannot guarantee the accuracy of this information.

Commissioning Editor: Vijin Boricha
Acquisition Editor: Rohit Rajkumar
Content Development Editor: Ronn Kurien
Senior Editor: Richard Brookes-Bland
Technical Editor: Dinesh Pawar
Copy Editor: Safis Editing
Project Coordinator: Neil Dmello
Proofreader: Safis Editing
Indexer: Tejal Daruwale Soni
Production Designer: Nilesh Mohite

First published: April 2020

Production reference: 1170420

Published by Packt Publishing Ltd.
Livery Place
35 Livery Street
Birmingham
B3 2PB, UK.

ISBN 978-1-78995-648-1

www.packt.com

Packt>

Packt.com

Subscribe to our online digital library for full access to over 7,000 books and videos, as well as industry leading tools to help you plan your personal development and advance your career. For more information, please visit our website.

Why subscribe?

- Spend less time learning and more time coding with practical eBooks and Videos from over 4,000 industry professionals

- Improve your learning with Skill Plans built especially for you

- Get a free eBook or video every month

- Fully searchable for easy access to vital information

- Copy and paste, print, and bookmark content

Did you know that Packt offers eBook versions of every book published, with PDF and ePub files available? You can upgrade to the eBook version at www.packt.com and as a print book customer, you are entitled to a discount on the eBook copy. Get in touch with us at customercare@packtpub.com for more details.

At www.packt.com, you can also read a collection of free technical articles, sign up for a range of free newsletters, and receive exclusive discounts and offers on Packt books and eBooks.

Contributors

About the author

Karim Okasha is a network consultant with over 15 years of experience in the ICT industry. He is specialized in the design and operation of large telecom and service provider networks and has lots of experience in network automation. Karim has a bachelor's degree in telecommunications and holds several expert-level certifications, such as CCIE, JNCIE, and RHCE. He is currently working in Red Hat as a network automation consultant, helping large telecom and service providers to design and implement innovative network automation solutions. Prior to joining Red Hat, he worked for Saudi Telecom Company as well as Cisco and Orange S.A.

I would like to thank my wife and kids for providing me with the freedom and understanding needed to focus on this dream; without their support, this book wouldn't be possible.

I would like to thank the Packt Publishing team and my technical reviewers, for making my dream of writing this book a reality.

Finally, I would like to thank my mentor and best friend, Mohammed Mahmoud, for all his support and encouragement during all these years.

About the reviewers

Mohamed Radwan is a senior network architect with 20 years of experience in designing solutions for telecommunications, global service providers, data centers, the cloud, governments, and Fortune 500 companies in Europe, the Middle East, and the Asia-Pacific. He is the author of *CCDE: The Practical Guide,* he is an award-winning network designer, and he holds bachelor's degree in engineering – computers and systems, in addition to many expert-level certificates. He currently lives in Sydney, Australia, working within the Cisco Advanced Services team. Before that, he worked with Orange S.A, Saudi Telecom Company, Qatar Foundation, and Vodafone.

Bassem Aly is a senior SDN/NFV solution consultant at Juniper Networks and has been working in the telecom industry for the last 10 years. He is focused on designing and implementing next-generation networks by leveraging different automation and DevOps frameworks. Also, he has extensive experience in architecting and deploying telecom applications over OpenStack. Bassem also conducts corporate training on network automation and network programmability using Python and Ansible. Finally, he's an active blogger on different technology areas and is the author of *Hands-On Enterprise Automation with Python*, published by Packt.

Packt is searching for authors like you

If you're interested in becoming an author for Packt, please visit `authors.packtpub.com` and apply today. We have worked with thousands of developers and tech professionals, just like you, to help them share their insight with the global tech community. You can make a general application, apply for a specific hot topic that we are recruiting an author for, or submit your own idea.

Table of Contents

Preface

Network Automation Cookbook provides an overview of the various topics of network automation and how to use software development practices in order to design and operate different networking solutions. We use Ansible as our framework to introduce the topic of network automation and how to manage different vendor equipment using Ansible. In the first section, we outline how to install and configure Ansible specifically for the purpose of network automation. We will explore how we can use Ansible to manage traditional network solutions from various vendors such as Cisco, Juniper, Arista, and F5. Next, we continue to explore how to utilize Ansible to build and scale network solutions from major cloud providers such as AWS, Azure, and **Google Cloud Platform** (**GCP**). Finally, we outline different supporting open source projects in network automation, such as NetBox, Batfish, and AWX. We outline how to integrate all these tools with Ansible in order to build a complete framework for network automation.

By the end of this book, you will have a solid foundation on how to integrate Ansible with different vendor equipment and how to build a network automation solution based on Ansible. Further, you will understand how to use various open source projects and how to integrate all these solutions with Ansible to build a robust and scalable network automation framework.

Who this book is for

This book is ideal for IT professionals and network engineers who are responsible for the design and operation of network devices within an organization and would like to expand their knowledge on using Ansible to automate their network infrastructure. Basic knowledge of networking and Linux is recommended.

What this book covers

Chapter 1, *Building Blocks of Ansible*, focuses on how to install Ansible and describes the main building blocks of Ansible and how to utilize them to build advanced Ansible playbooks.

Chapter 2, *Managing Cisco IOS Devices Using Ansible,* focuses on how to integrate Ansible with Cisco IOS devices and how to use Ansible to configure Cisco IOS devices. We will explore the core Ansible modules developed to interact with Cisco IOS devices. Finally, we will explore how to use the Cisco PyATS library and how to integrate it with Ansible in order to validate the network state on Cisco IOS and Cisco IOS-XE devices.

Chapter 3, *Automating Juniper Devices in the Service Providers Using Ansible,* describes how to integrate Ansible with Juniper devices in **Service Provider** (**SP**) environments and how to manage the configuration of Juniper devices using Ansible. We will explore how to use the core Ansible modules developed to manage Juniper devices. Furthermore, we will explore the PyEZ library, which is used by Juniper custom Ansible modules to extend Ansible functionality in managing Juniper devices.

Chapter 4, *Building Data Center Networks with Arista and Ansible,* outlines how to integrate Ansible with Arista devices to build data center fabrics using EVPN/VXLANs. We will explore how to use the core Ansible modules developed to manage Arista devices and how to use these modules to configure and validate the network state on Arista switches.

Chapter 5, *Automating Application Delivery with F5 LTM and Ansible,* focuses on how to integrate Ansible with F5 BIG-IP LTM devices to onboard new BIG-IP LTM devices and how to set up the BIG-IP system as a reverse proxy for application delivery.

Chapter 6, *Administering Multi-Vendor Network with NAPALM and Ansible,* introduces the NAPALM library and outlines how to integrate this library with Ansible. We will explore how to utilize Ansible and NAPALM to simplify the management of multi-vendor environments.

Chapter 7, *Deploying and Operating AWS Networking Resources with Ansible,* outlines how to integrate Ansible with your AWS environment and how to describe your AWS infrastructure using Ansible. We explore how to utilize the core Ansible AWS modules to manage networking resources in AWS in order to build your AWS network infrastructure using Ansible.

Chapter 8, *Deploying and Operating Azure Networking Resources with Ansible,* outlines how to integrate Ansible with your Azure environment and how to describe your Azure infrastructure using Ansible. We will explore how to utilize the core Ansible Azure modules to manage networking resources in Azure in order to build Azure network solutions using Ansible.

Chapter 9, *Deploying and Operating GCP Networking Resources with Ansible*, describes how to integrate Ansible with your GCP environment and how to describe your GCP infrastructure using Ansible. We explore how to utilize the core Ansible GCP modules to manage networking resources in GCP in order to build GCP network solutions using Ansible.

Chapter 10, *Network Validation with Batfish and Ansible*, introduces the Batfish framework for offline network validation and how to integrate this framework with Ansible in order to perform offline network validation using both Ansible and Batfish.

Chapter 11, *Building a Network Inventory with Ansible and NetBox*, introduces NetBox, which is a complete inventory system to document and describe any network. We outline how to integrate Ansible with NetBox and how to use NetBox data to build Ansible dynamic inventories.

Chapter 12, *Simplifying Automation with AWX and Ansible*, introduces the AWX project, which extends Ansible and provides a powerful GUI and API on top of Ansible to simplify running automation tasks within an organization. We outline the extra features provided by AWX and how to use it to manage network automation within an organization.

Chapter 13, *Advanced Techniques and Best Practices for Ansible*, describes various best practices and advanced techniques that can be used for more advanced playbooks.

To get the most out of this book

Basic knowledge regarding different networking concepts, such as **Open Shortest Path First (OSPF)** and **Border Gateway Protocol (BGP)**, is assumed.

Basic knowledge of Linux is assumed, including knowledge of how to create files and folders and install software on Linux machines.

Software/hardware covered in the book	OS requirements
Ansible 2.9	CentOS 7
Python 3.6.8	

If you are using the digital version of this book, we advise you to type the code yourself or access the code via the GitHub repository (link available in the next section). Doing so will help you avoid any potential errors related to the copying and pasting of code.

Download the example code files

You can download the example code files for this book from your account
at www.packt.com. If you purchased this book elsewhere, you can
visit www.packtpub.com/support and register to have the files emailed directly to you.

You can download the code files by following these steps:

1. Log in or register at www.packt.com.
2. Select the **Support** tab.
3. Click on **Code Downloads**.
4. Enter the name of the book in the **Search** box and follow the onscreen
   instructions.

Once the file is downloaded, please make sure that you unzip or extract the folder using the
latest version of:

- WinRAR/7-Zip for Windows
- Zipeg/iZip/UnRarX for Mac
- 7-Zip/PeaZip for Linux

The code bundle for the book is also hosted on GitHub at https://github.com/
PacktPublishing/Network-Automation-Cookbook. In case there's an update to the code, it
will be updated on the existing GitHub repository.

We also have other code bundles from our rich catalog of books and videos available
at https://github.com/PacktPublishing/. Check them out!

Download the color images

We also provide a PDF file that has color images of the screenshots/diagrams used in this
book. You can download it here: http://www.packtpub.com/sites/default/files/
downloads/9781789956481_ColorImages.pdf.

Code in Action

The code in action videos are based on Ansible version 2.8.5. The code has also been tested
on version 2.9.2 and works fine.

Visit the following link to check out videos of the code being run:
https://bit.ly/34JooNp

Conventions used

There are a number of text conventions used throughout this book.

`CodeInText`: Indicates code words in text, database table names, folder names, filenames, file extensions, pathnames, dummy URLs, user input, and Twitter handles. Here is an example: "Mount the downloaded `WebStorm-10*.dmg` disk image file as another disk in your system."

A block of code is set as follows:

```
$ cat ansible.cfg

[defaults]
 inventory=hosts
 retry_files_enabled=False
 gathering=explicit
 host_key_checking=False
```

When we wish to draw your attention to a particular part of a code block, the relevant lines or items are set in bold:

```
- name: Configure ACL on IOS-XR
  hosts: all
  serial: 1
  tags: deploy
  tasks:
    - name: Backup Config
      iosxr_config:
        backup:
      when: not ansible_check_mode
    - name: Deploy ACLs
      iosxr_config:
        src: acl_conf.cfg
        match: line
      when: not ansible_check_mode
```

Any command-line input or output is written as follows:

```
$ python3 -m venv dev
$ source dev/bin/activate
```

Bold: Indicates a new term, an important word, or words that you see onscreen. For example, words in menus or dialog boxes appear in the text like this. Here is an example: "Select **System info** from the **Administration** panel."

Warnings or important notes appear like this.

Tips and tricks appear like this.

Sections

In this book, you will find several headings that appear frequently (*Getting ready*, *How to do it...*, *How it works...*, *There's more...*, and *See also*).

To give clear instructions on how to complete a recipe, use these sections as follows:

Getting ready

This section tells you what to expect in the recipe and describes how to set up any software or any preliminary settings required for the recipe.

How to do it...

This section contains the steps required to follow the recipe.

How it works...

This section usually consists of a detailed explanation of what happened in the previous section.

There's more...

This section consists of additional information about the recipe in order to make you more knowledgeable about the recipe.

See also

This section provides helpful links to other useful information for the recipe.

Get in touch

Feedback from our readers is always welcome.

General feedback: If you have questions about any aspect of this book, mention the book title in the subject of your message and email us at customercare@packtpub.com.

Errata: Although we have taken every care to ensure the accuracy of our content, mistakes do happen. If you have found a mistake in this book, we would be grateful if you would report this to us. Please visit www.packtpub.com/support/errata, selecting your book, clicking on the Errata Submission Form link, and entering the details.

Piracy: If you come across any illegal copies of our works in any form on the Internet, we would be grateful if you would provide us with the location address or website name. Please contact us at copyright@packt.com with a link to the material.

If you are interested in becoming an author: If there is a topic that you have expertise in and you are interested in either writing or contributing to a book, please visit authors.packtpub.com.

Reviews

Please leave a review. Once you have read and used this book, why not leave a review on the site that you purchased it from? Potential readers can then see and use your unbiased opinion to make purchase decisions, we at Packt can understand what you think about our products, and our authors can see your feedback on their book. Thank you!

For more information about Packt, please visit packt.com.

Building Blocks of Ansible

1

Ansible is an enormously popular automation framework that has been used to automate IT operations for a long time. It simplifies the management of different infrastructure nodes and translates the business logic into well-defined procedures in order to implement this business logic. Ansible is written in Python and it mainly relies on SSH to communicate with infrastructure nodes to execute instructions on them. It started support for networking devices beginning with Ansible 1.9, and with Ansible 2.9, its current support for network devices has grown extensively. It can interact with network devices using either SSH or via API if the network vendors support APIs on their equipment. It also provides multiple advantages, including the following:

- **An easy learning curve:** Writing Ansible playbooks requires knowledge of YAML and Jinja2 templates, which are easy to learn, and its descriptive language is easy to understand.
- **Agentless:** It doesn't require an agent to be installed on the remotely managed device in order to control this device.
- **Extensible:** Ansible comes equipped with multiple modules to execute a variety of tasks on the managed nodes. It also supports writing custom modules and plugins to extend Ansible's core functionality.
- **Idempotent:** Ansible will not change the state of the device unless it needs to in order to change its setting to reach the desired state. Once it is in this desired state, running Ansible Playbooks against the device will not alter its configurations.

In this chapter, we will introduce the main components of Ansible and outline the different features and options that Ansible supports. The following are the main recipes that will be covered:

- Installing Ansible
- Building Ansible's inventory
- Using Ansible's variables
- Building Ansible's playbook
- Using Ansible's conditionals
- Using Ansible's loops
- Securing secrets with Ansible Vault
- Using Jinja2 with Ansible
- Using Ansible's filters
- Using Ansible Tags
- Customizing Ansible's settings
- Using Ansible Roles

The purpose of this chapter is to have a basic understanding of the different Ansible components that we will utilize throughout this book in order to interact with the networking device. Consequently, all the examples in this chapter are not focused on managing networking devices. Instead, we will focus on understanding the different components in Ansible in order to use them effectively in the next chapters.

Technical requirements

Here are the requirements for installing Ansible and running all of our Ansible playbooks:

- A Linux **Virtual Machine** (**VM**) with either of the following distributions:
    - Ubuntu 18.04 or higher
    - CentOS 7.0 or higher
- Internet connectivity for the VM

 Setting up the Linux machine is outside the scope of this recipe. However, the easiest approach to setting up a Linux VM with any OS version is by using *Vagrant* to create and set up the Ansible VM.

Installing Ansible

The machine on which we install Ansible (this is known as the Ansible control machine) should be running on any Linux distribution. In this recipe, we will outline how to install Ansible on both an Ubuntu Linux machine or a CentOS machine.

Getting ready

To install Ansible, we need a Linux VM using either an Ubuntu 18.04+ OS or CentoS 7+ OS. Furthermore, this machine needs to have internet access for Ansible to be installed on it.

How to do it...

Ansible is written in Python and all its modules need Python to be installed on the Ansible control machine. Our first task is to ensure that Python is installed on the Ansible control machine, as outlined in the following steps.

1. Most Linux distributions have Python installed by default. However, if Python is not installed, here are the steps for installing it on Linux:

    - On an Ubuntu OS, execute the following command:

    ```
    # Install python3
    $sudo apt-get install python3

    # validate python is installed
    $python3 --version
    Python 3.6.9
    ```

    - On a CentOS OS, execute the following command:

    ```
    # Install python
    $sudo yum install pytho3

    # validate python is installed
    $python3 --version
    Python 3.6.8
    ```

2. After we have validated that Python is installed, we can start to install Ansible:

- On an Ubuntu OS, execute the following command:

```
# We need to use ansible repository to install the latest
version of Ansible
$ sudo apt-add-repository ppa:ansible/ansible

# Update the repo cache to use the new repo added
$ sudo apt-get update

# We install Ansible
$ sudo apt-get install ansible
```

- On a CentOS OS, execute the following command:

```
# We need to use latest epel repository to get the latest
ansible
$ sudo yum install epel-release

# We install Ansible
$ sudo yum install ansible
```

How it works..

The easiest way to install Ansible is by using the package manager specific to our Linux distribution. We just need to make sure that we have enabled the required repositories to install the latest version of Ansible. In both Ubuntu and CentOS, we need to enable extra repositories that provide the latest version for Ansible. In CentOS, we need to install and enable the **Extra Packages for Enterprise Linux Repository** (**EPEL repo**), which provides extra software packages and has the latest Ansible packages for CentOS.

Using this method, we will install Ansible and all the requisite system packages needed to run the Ansible modules. In both Ubuntu and CentOS, this method will also install Python 2 and run Ansible using Python 2. We can validate the fact that Ansible is installed and which version is used by running the following command:

```
$ ansible --version
ansible 2.9
  config file = /etc/ansible/ansible.cfg
  configured module search path =
[u'/home/vagrant/.ansible/plugins/modules',
u'/usr/share/ansible/plugins/modules']
  ansible python module location = /usr/lib/python2.7/site-packages/ansible
  executable location = /usr/bin/ansible
```

```
python version = 2.7.5 (default, Aug 7 2019, 00:51:29) [GCC 4.8.5
20150623 (Red Hat 4.8.5-39)]
```

Also, we can check that Ansible is working as expected by trying to connect to the local machine using the `ping` module as shown:

```
$ ansible -m ping localhost

localhost | SUCCESS => {
    "changed": false,
    "ping": "pong"
}
```

Using this method, we can see that it has the following issues:

- It uses Python 2 as the execution environment, but we want to use Python 3.
- It updates the Python packages installed on the system, which might not be desirable.
- It doesn't provide us with the granularity needed in order to select which version of Ansible to use. Using this method, we will always install the latest version of Ansible, which might not be what we need.

How it works...

In order to install Ansible in a Python 3 environment and to have more control over the version of Ansible deployed, we are going to use the pip Python program to install Ansible as shown here:

- Install Python 3 if it is not present, as follows:

  ```
  # Ubuntu
  $ sudo apt-get install python3

  # CentOS
  sudo yum install python3
  ```

- Install the `python3-pip` package:

  ```
  # Ubuntu
  $ sudo apt-get install python3-pip

  # CentOS
  $ sudo yum install python3-pip
  ```

- Install Ansible:

```
# Ubuntu and CentOS
# This will install ansible for the current user ONLY
$ pip3 install ansible==2.9 --user

# We Can install ansible on the System Level
$ sudo pip3 install ansible==2.9
```

- We can verify that Ansible has been installed successfully, as shown here:

```
$$ ansible --version
ansible 2.9
 config file = None
 configured module search path =
['/home/vagrant/.ansible/plugins/modules',
'/usr/share/ansible/plugins/modules']
 ansible python module location =
/home/vagrant/.local/lib/python3.6/site-packages/ansible
 executable location = /home/vagrant/.local/bin/ansible
 python version = 3.6.8 (default, Aug 7 2019, 17:28:10) [GCC 4.8.5
20150623 (Red Hat 4.8.5-39)]
```

Installing Ansible using this method ensures that we are using Python 3 as our execution environment and allows us to control which version of Ansible to install, as outlined in the example shown.

We are going to use this method as our Ansible installation method and all the subsequent chapters will be based on this installation procedure.

In Chapter 13, *Advanced Techniques and Best Practices for Ansible,* we will outline yet another method for installing Ansible using Python virtual environments.

See also...

For more information regarding the installation of Ansible, please check the following URL:

https://docs.ansible.com/ansible/latest/installation_guide/intro_installation.html

Building Ansible's inventory

After installing Ansible, we need to define Ansible's inventory, which is a text file that defines the nodes that Ansible will manage. In this recipe, we will outline how to create and structure Ansible's inventory file.

Getting ready

We need to create a folder that will contain all the code that we will outline in this chapter. We create a folder called ch1_ansible, as shown here:

```
$ mkdir ch1_ansible
$ cd ch1_ansible
```

How to do it...

Perform the following steps to create the inventory file:

1. Create a file named hosts:

```
$ touch hosts
```

2. Using any text editor, open the file and add the following content:

```
$ cat hosts

[cisco]
csr1 ansible_host=172.10.1.2
csr2 ansible_host=172.10.1.3

[juniper]
mx1 ansible_host=172.20.1.2
mx2 ansible_host=172.20.1.3

[core]
mx1
mx2

[edge]
csr[1:2]

[network:children]
core
edge
```

The Ansible inventory file can have any name. However, as a best practice, we will use the name `hosts` to describe the devices in our inventory.

How it works...

The Ansible inventory files define the hosts that will be managed by Ansible (in the preceding example, this is `csr1-2` and `mx1-2`) and how to group these devices into custom-defined groups based on different criteria. The groups are defined with `[]`. This grouping helps us to define the variables and simplify the segregation between the devices and how Ansible interacts with them. How we group the devices is based on our use case, so we can group them as per the vendor (Juniper and IOS) or function (core and edge).

We can also build hierarchies for the groups using the children, which is outlined in the inventory file. The following diagram shows how the hosts are grouped and how the group hierarchy is built:

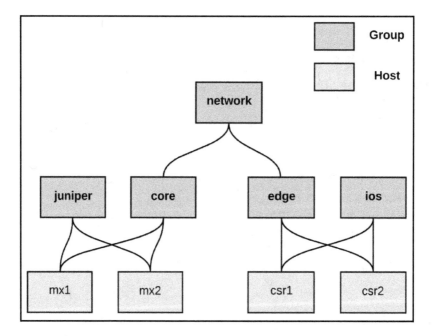

Using Ansible's variables

Ansible stores the information for the nodes that it manages using Ansible variables. Ansible variables can be declared in multiple locations. However, in observing the best practices for Ansible, we will outline the two main parts where Ansible looks for variables for the nodes that are declared in the inventory file.

Getting ready

In order to follow along with this recipe, an Ansible inventory file must be already defined as outlined in the previous recipes.

How to do it...

In the inventory file, we define hosts and we group the hosts into groups. We now define two directories that Ansible searches for group variables and host variables:

1. Create two folders, group_vars and host_vars:

```
$ cd ch1_ansible
$ mkdir group_vars host_vars
```

2. Create ios.yml and junos.yml files inside group_vars:

```
$ touch group_vars/cisco.yml group_vars/juniper.yml
```

3. Create mx1.yml and csr1.yml inside host_vars:

```
$ touch host_vars/csr1.yml host_vars/mx1.yml
```

4. Populate variables in all the files, as shown here:

```
$echo 'hostname: core-mx1' >> host_vars/mx1.yml
$echo 'hostname: core-mx2' >> host_vars/mx2.yml
$echo 'hostname: edge-csr1' >> host_vars/csr1.yml
$echo 'hostname: edge-csr2' >> host_vars/csr2.yml
$echo 'os: ios' >> group_vars/cisco.yml
$echo 'os: junos' >> group_vars/juniper.yml
```

How it works...

We created the following structure of directories and files to host our variables, as shown in the following diagram:

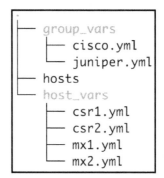

All files inside the `group_vars` directory contain the group variables for the groups that we have defined in our inventory and they apply to all the hosts within this group. As for the files within `host_vars`, they contain variables for each host. Using this structure, we can group variables from multiple hosts into a specific group file and variables that are host-specific will be placed in a separate file specific to this host.

There's more...

In addition to `host_vars` and `group_vars`, Ansible supports the definition of variables using other techniques, including the following:

- Using the `vars` keyword within the play to specify multiple variables
- Using `vars_files` to define variables in a file and having Ansible read these variables from this file while running the playbook
- Specifying variables at the command line using the `--e` option

In addition to the user-defined variables that we can specify, Ansible has some default variables that it builds dynamically for its inventory. The following table captures some of the most frequently used variables:

inventory_hostname	The name of the hosts as defined in the inventory (for example, csr1 and mx1)
play_hosts	A list of all the hosts included in the play
group_names	A list of all the groups that a specific host is a part of (for example, for csr1 this will be [edge, Cisco, network])

Building Ansible's playbook

An Ansible playbook is the fundamental element in Ansible that declares what actions we would like to perform on our managed hosts (specified in the inventory). An Ansible playbook is a YAML-formatted file that defines a list of tasks that will be executed on our managed devices. In this recipe, we will outline how to write an Ansible playbook and how to define the hosts that will be targeted by this playbook.

Getting ready

In order to follow along with this recipe, an Ansible inventory file must already be defined, along with all the group- and host-specific variable files created in accordance with previous recipes.

How to do it...

1. Create a new file called `playbook.yml` inside the `ch1_ansible` folder and incorporate the following lines in this file:

```
$  cat playbook.yml

---

 - name: Initial Playbook
   hosts: all
   gather_facts: no
   tasks:
     - name: Display Hostname
       debug:
         msg: "Router name is {{ hostname }}"
     - name: Display OS
```

```
        debug:
          msg: "{{ hostname }} is running {{ os }}"
```

2. Run the playbook as shown here:

```
$ ansible-playbook -i hosts playbook.yml
```

How it works...

The Ansible playbook is structured as a list of plays and each play targets a specific group of hosts (defined in the inventory file). Each play can have one or more tasks to execute against the hosts in this play. Each task runs a specific Ansible module that has a number of arguments. The general structure of the playbook is outlined in the following screenshot:

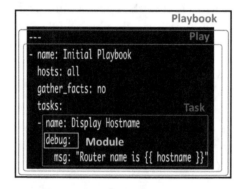

In the preceding playbook, we reference the variables that we defined in the previous recipe inside the {{ }} brackets. Ansible reads these variables from either group_vars or host_vars, and the module that we used in this playbook is the debug module, which displays as a custom message specified in the msg parameter to the Terminal output. The playbook run is shown here:

```
PLAY [Initial Playbook] *********************

TASK [Display Hostname] *********************
ok: [mx1] => {
    "msg": "Router name is core-mx1"
}
ok: [mx2] => {
    "msg": "Router name is core-mx2"
}
ok: [csr1] => {
    "msg": "Router name is edge-csr1"
}
ok: [csr2] => {
    "msg": "Router name is edge-csr2"
}

TASK [Display OS] ***************************
ok: [mx1] => {
    "msg": "core-mx1 is running junos"
}
ok: [mx2] => {
    "msg": "core-mx2 is running junos"
}
ok: [csr1] => {
    "msg": "edge-csr1 is running ios"
}
ok: [csr2] => {
    "msg": "edge-csr2 is running ios"
}
```

We use the `-i` option in the `ansible-playbook` command in order to point to the Ansible inventory file, which we will use as our source to construct our inventory.

> In this playbook, I have used the `all` keyword to specify all the hosts within the inventory. This is a well-known group name that Ansible dynamically constructs for all hosts within the inventory.

Using Ansible's conditionals

One of the core features of Ansible is conditional task execution. This provides us with the ability to control which tasks to run on a given host based on a condition/test that we specify. In this recipe, we will outline how to configure conditional task execution.

Getting ready

In order to follow along with this recipe, an Ansible inventory file must be present and configured as outlined in the previous recipes. Furthermore, the Ansible variables for all our hosts should be defined as outlined in the previous recipes.

How to do it...

1. Create a new playbook called `ansible_cond.yml` inside the `ch1_ansible` folder.
2. Place the following content in the new playbook as shown here:

```
---
- name: Using conditionals
  hosts: all
  gather_facts: no
  tasks:
    - name: Run for Edge nodes Only
      debug:
        msg: "Router name is {{ hostname }}"
      when: "'edge' in group_names"

    - name: Run for Only MX1 node
      debug:
        msg: "{{ hostname }} is running {{ os }}"
      when:
        - inventory_hostname == 'mx1'
```

3. Run the playbook as shown here:

```
$ ansible-playbook -i hosts ansible_cond.yml
```

How it works...

Ansible uses the `when` statement to provide conditional execution for the tasks. The `when` statement is applied at the task level and if the condition in the `when` statement evaluates to `true`, the task is executed for the given host. If `false`, the task is skipped for this host. The output as a result of running the preceding playbook is shown here:

```
PLAY [Using conditionals] **********************************************

TASK [Run for Edge nodes Only] *****************************************
skipping: [mx1]
skipping: [mx2]
ok: [csr1] => {
    "msg": "Router name is edge-csr1"
}
ok: [csr2] => {
    "msg": "Router name is edge-csr2"
}

TASK [Run for Only MX1 node] *******************************************
ok: [mx1] => {
    "msg": "core-mx1 is running junos"
}
skipping: [mx2]
skipping: [csr1]
skipping: [csr2]

PLAY RECAP *************************************************************
csr1                       : ok=1    changed=0   unreachable=0   failed=0
csr2                       : ok=1    changed=0   unreachable=0   failed=0
mx1                        : ok=1    changed=0   unreachable=0   failed=0
mx2                        : ok=0    changed=0   unreachable=0   failed=0
```

The when statement can take a single condition as seen in the first task, or can take a list of conditions as seen in the second task. If when is a list of conditions, all the conditions need to be true in order for the task to be executed.

 In the first task, the when statement is enclosed in "" since the statement starts with a string. However, in the second statement, we use a normal when statement with no "" since the when statement starts with a variable name.

See also...

For more information regarding Ansible's conditionals, please check the following URL:

`https://docs.ansible.com/ansible/latest/user_guide/playbooks_conditionals.html`

Using Ansible's loops

In some cases, we need to run a task inside an Ansible playbook to loop over some data. Ansible's loops allow us to loop over a variable (a dictionary or a list) multiple times in order to achieve this behavior. In this recipe, we will outline how to use Ansible's loops.

Getting ready

In order to follow along with this recipe, an Ansible inventory file must be present and configured, as outlined in the previous recipes.

How to do it...

1. Create a new playbook called `ansible_loops.yml` inside the `ch1_ansible` folder.

2. Inside the `group_vars/cisco.yml` file, incorporate the following content:

    ```
    snmp_servers:
      - 10.1.1.1
      - 10.2.1.1
    ```

3. Inside the `group_vars/juniper.yml` file, incorporate the following content:

    ```
    users:
      admin: admin123
      oper: oper123
    ```

4. Inside the `ansible_loops.yml` file, incorporate the following content:

    ```
    ---
    - name: Ansible Loop over a List
      hosts: cisco
      gather_facts: no
      tasks:
        - name: Loop over SNMP Servers
          debug:
            msg: "Router {{ hostname }} with snmp server {{ item }}"
          loop: "{{ snmp_servers}}"

    - name: Ansible Loop over a Dictionary
      hosts: juniper
      gather_facts: no
      tasks:
        - name: Loop over Username and Passowrds
          debug:
            msg: "Router {{ hostname }} with user {{ item.key }}
    password {{ item.value }}"
          with_dict: "{{ users}}"
    ```

5. Run the playbook as shown here:

```
$ ansible-playbook ansible_loops.yml -i hosts
```

How it works..

Ansible supports looping over two main iterable data structures: lists and dictionaries. We use the `loops` keyword when we need to iterate over lists (`snmp_servers` is a list data structure) and we use `with_dicts` when we loop over a dictionary (`users` is a dictionary data structure where the username is the key and the passwords are the values). In both cases, we use the `item` keyword to specify the value in the current iteration. In the case of `with_dicts`, we get the key using `item.key` and we get the value using `item.value`.

The output of the preceding playbook run is shown here:

```
PLAY [Ansible Loop over a List] ******************************************

TASK [Loop over SNMP Servers] *******************************************
ok: [csr1] => (item=10.1.1.1) => {
    "msg": "Router edge-csr1 with snmp server 10.1.1.1"
}
ok: [csr1] => (item=10.2.1.1) => {
    "msg": "Router edge-csr1 with snmp server 10.2.1.1"
}
ok: [csr2] => (item=10.1.1.1) => {
    "msg": "Router edge-csr2 with snmp server 10.1.1.1"
}
ok: [csr2] => (item=10.2.1.1) => {
    "msg": "Router edge-csr2 with snmp server 10.2.1.1"
}

PLAY [Ansible Loop over a Dictionary] ***********************************

TASK [Loop over Username and Passowrds] *********************************
ok: [mx1] => (item={'value': u'admin123', 'key': u'admin'}) => {
    "msg": "Router core-mx1 with user admin password admin123"
}
ok: [mx1] => (item={'value': u'oper123', 'key': u'oper'}) => {
    "msg": "Router core-mx1 with user oper password oper123"
}
ok: [mx2] => (item={'value': u'admin123', 'key': u'admin'}) => {
    "msg": "Router core-mx2 with user admin password admin123"
}
ok: [mx2] => (item={'value': u'oper123', 'key': u'oper'}) => {
    "msg": "Router core-mx2 with user oper password oper123"
}

PLAY RECAP *************************************************************
csr1                       : ok=1    changed=0    unreachable=0    failed=0
csr2                       : ok=1    changed=0    unreachable=0    failed=0
mx1                        : ok=1    changed=0    unreachable=0    failed=0
mx2                        : ok=1    changed=0    unreachable=0    failed=0
```

See also...

For more information regarding the different Ansible *looping constructs,* please consult the following URL:

```
https://docs.ansible.com/ansible/latest/user_guide/playbooks_loops.html
```

Securing secrets with Ansible Vault

When we are dealing with sensitive material that we need to reference in our Ansible playbooks, such as passwords, we shouldn't save this data in plain text. Ansible Vault provides a method to encrypt this data and therefore be safely decrypted and accessed while the playbook is running. In this recipe, we will outline how to use Ansible Vault in order to secure sensitive information in Ansible.

How to do it...

1. Create a new file called `decrypt_passwd` as shown:

    ```
    $ echo 'strong_password' > decrypt_passwd
    ```

2. Using `ansible-vault` creates a new file called `secrets`, as shown here:

    ```
    $ ansible-vault create --vault-id=decrypt_passwd secrets
    ```

3. Add the following variables to this new `secrets` file:

    ```
    ospf_password: ospf_P@ssw0rD
    bgp_password: BGP_p@ssw0rd
    ```

4. Create a new playbook called `ansible_vault.yml`, as shown here:

    ```
    ---
    - name: Using Ansible vault
      hosts: all
      gather_facts: no
      vars_files:
        - secrets
      tasks:
        - name: Output OSPF passowrd
          debug:
            msg: "Router {{ hostname }} ospf Password {{
    ospf_password }}"
    ```

```
            when: inventory_hostname == 'csr1'

      - name: Output BGP passowrd
        debug:
           msg: "Router {{ hostname }} BGP Password {{ bgp_password
}}"
            when: inventory_hostname == 'mx1'
```

5. Run the playbook as shown here:

```
$ ansible-playbook --vault-id=decrypt_passwd ansible_vault.yml -i
hosts
```

How it works..

We use the `ansible-vault` command to create a new file that is encrypted using a key
specified by `-- vault-id`. We place this key/password in another file (which is called
`decrypt_passwd` in our example) and we pass this file as an argument to `vault-id`.
Inside this file, we can place as many variables as we need. Finally, we include this file as a
variable file in the playbook using `vars_files`. The following is the content of the secret
file in case we try to read it without decryption:

```
$ cat secrets
$ANSIBLE_VAULT;1.1;AES256
61383264326363373336383839643834386661343630393965656135666336383837633439383
13963
35383762306135343238333562376635326663636246264640a66383939623064663435383396
26461
31336461386361616261336534663137326265363261626536663564623764663861623735 6
33865
30333565363936313203a64356162363536383065323663383338353313661663265666231396
33838
32633335616663623761313363061313463663566386536356336656431336537643133 34616
23232
34633838333383636386531323836396630346637306535656135363836373161613 53861643
73263
66653065333346431333832396633237653034
```

In order for Ansible to decrypt this file, we must supply the decryption password (stored in a `decrypt_passwd` file in this example) via the `--vault-id` option. When we run `ansible-playbook`, we must supply this decryption password, otherwise the `ansible-playbook` fails, as shown here:

```
### Running the Ansible playbook without --vault-id
$ansible-playbook ansible_vault.yml -i hosts
ERROR! Attempting to decrypt but no vault secrets found
```

There's more...

In case we don't want to specify the encryption/decryption password in the text file, we can use `--ask-vault-pass` with the `ansible-playbook` command in order to input the password while running the playbook, as shown here:

```
### Running the Ansible playbook with --ask-vault-pass
$ansible-playbook ansible_vault.yml -i hosts --ask-vault-pass
Vault password:
```

Using Jinja2 with Ansible

Jinja2 is a powerful templating engine for Python and is supported by Ansible. It is also used to generate any text-based files, such as HTML, CSV, or YAML. We can utilize Jinja2 with Ansible variables in order to generate custom configuration files for network devices. In this recipe, we will outline how to use Jinja2 templates with Ansible.

Getting ready

In order to follow along with this recipe, an Ansible inventory file must be present and configured as outlined in the previous recipes.

How to do it...

1. Create a new file inside the `group_vars` directory called `network.yml`:

```
$ cat group_vars/network.yml

---
ntp_servers:
```

```
- 172.20.1.1
- 172.20.2.1
```

2. Create a new `templates` directory and create a new `ios_basic.j2` file with the following content:

```
$ cat templates/ios_basic.j2
hostname {{ hostname }}
!
{% for server in ntp_servers %}
ntp {{ server }}
{% endfor %}
!
```

3. Create a new `junos_basic.j2` file within the `templates` directory with the following content:

```
$ cat templates/junos_basic.j2
set system host-name {{ hostname }}
{% for server in ntp_servers %}
set system ntp server {{ server }}
{% endfor %}
```

4. Create a new playbook called `ansible_jinja2.yml` with the following content:

```
---
- name: Generate Cisco config from Jinja2
  hosts: localhost
  gather_facts: no
  tasks:
    - name: Create Configs Directory
      file: path=configs state=directory

- name: Generate Cisco config from Jinja2
  hosts: cisco
  gather_facts: no
  tasks:
    - name: Generate Cisco Basic Config
      template:
        src: "templates/ios_basic.j2"
        dest: "configs/{{inventory_hostname}}.cfg"
      delegate_to: localhost

- name: Generate Juniper config from Jinja2
  hosts: juniper
  gather_facts: no
  tasks:
    - name: Generate Juniper Basic Config
```

```
template:
  src: "templates/junos_basic.j2"
  dest: "configs/{{inventory_hostname}}.cfg"
delegate_to: localhost
```

5. Run the Ansible playbook as shown here:

```
$ ansible-playbook -i hosts ansible_jinja2.yml
```

How it works...

We created the `network.yml` file in order to group all the variables that will apply to all devices under this group. After that, we create two Jinja2 files, one for Cisco IOS devices, and the other for Juniper devices. Inside each Jinja2 template, we reference the Ansible variables using `{{}}`. We also use the `for` loop construct, `{% for server in ntp_servers %}`, supported by the Jinja2 templating engine in order to loop over the `ntp_servers` variable (which is a list) to access each item within this list.

Ansible provides the `template` module that takes two parameters:

- `src`: This references the Jinja2 template file.
- `dest`: This specifies the output file that will be generated.

In our case, we use the `{{inventory_hostname}}` variable in order to make the output configuration file unique for each router in our inventory.

By default, the `template` modules create the output file on the remotely managed nodes. However, this is not possible in our case since the managed devices are network nodes. Consequently, we use the `delegate_to: localhost` option in order to run this task locally on the Ansible control machine.

The first play in the playbook creates the `configs` directory to store the configuration files for the network devices. The second play runs the template module on Cisco devices, and the third play runs the `template` task on Juniper devices.

The following is the configuration file for one of the Cisco devices:

```
$ cat configs/csr1.cfg
hostname edge-csr1
!
ntp 172.20.1.1
ntp 172.20.2.1
!
```

This is the configuration file for one of the Juniper devices:

```
$ cat configs/mx1.cfg
set system host-name core-mx1
set system ntp server 172.20.1.1
set system ntp server 172.20.2.1
```

See also...

For more information regarding the Ansible template module, please consult the following URL:

```
https://docs.ansible.com/ansible/latest/modules/template_module.html
```

Using Ansible's filters

Ansible's filters are mainly derived from Jinja2 filters, and all Ansible filters are used to transform and manipulate data (Ansible's variables). In addition to Jinja2 filters, Ansible implements its own filters to augment Jinja2 filters, while also allowing users to define their own custom filters. In this recipe, we will outline how to configure and use Ansible filters to manipulate our input data.

How to do it...

1. Install `python3-pip` and Python's `netaddr` library, since we will be using the Ansible IP filter, which requires Python's `netaddr` library:

```
# On ubuntu
$ sudo apt-get install python3-pip

# On CentOS
$ sudo yum install python3-pip

$ pip3 install netaddr
```

2. Create a new Ansible playbook called `ansible_filters.yml`, as shown here:

```
---
 - name: Ansible Filters
   hosts: csr1
   vars:
```

```
                interfaces:
                  - { port: FastEthernet0/0, prefix: 10.1.1.0/24 }
                  - { port: FastEthernet1/0, prefix: 10.1.2.0/24 }
                tasks:
                  - name: Generate Interface Config
                    blockinfile:
                      block: |
                        hostname {{ hostname | upper }}
                        {% for intf in interfaces %}
                        !
                        interface {{ intf.port }}
                           ip address {{intf.prefix | ipv4(1) | ipv4('address')
}} {{intf.prefix | ipv4('netmask') }}
                        !
                        {% endfor %}
                      dest: "configs/csr1_interfaces.cfg"
                      create: yes
                    delegate_to: localhost
```

How it works...

First of all, we are using the `blockinfile` module to create a new configuration file on the Ansible control machine. This module is very similar to the `template` module. However, we can write the Jinja2 expressions directly in the module in the `block` option. We define a new variable called `interfaces` using the `vars` parameter in the playbook. This variable is a list data structure where each item in the list is a dictionary data structure. This nested data structure specifies the IP prefix used on each interface.

In the Jinja2 expressions, we can see that we have used a number of filters as shown here:

- `{{ hostname | upper}}`: `upper` is a Jinja2 filter that transforms all the letters of the input string into uppercase. In this way, we pass the value of the hostname variable to this filter and the output will be the uppercase version of this value.
- `{{intf.prefix | ipv4(1) | ipv4('address') }}`: Here, we use the Ansible IP address filter twice. `ipv4(1)` takes an input IP prefix and outputs the first IP address in this prefix. We then use another IP address filter, `ipv4('address')`, in order to only get the IP address part of an IP prefix. So in our case, we take `10.1.1.0/24` and we output `10.1.1.1` for the first interface.
- `{{intf.prefix | ipv4('netmask') }}`: Here, we use the Ansible IP address filter to get the netmask of the IP address prefix, so in our case, we get the `/24` subnet and transform it to `255.255.255.0`.

The output file for the `csr1` router after this playbook run is shown here:

```
$ cat configs/csr1_interfaces.cfg
# BEGIN ANSIBLE MANAGED BLOCK
hostname EDGE-CSR1
!
interface FastEthernet0/0
  ip address 10.1.1.1 255.255.255.0
!
!
interface FastEthernet1/0
  ip address 10.1.2.1 255.255.255.0
!
# END ANSIBLE MANAGED BLOCK
```

Using Ansible Tags

Ansible Tags is a powerful tool that allows us to tag specific tasks within a large Ansible playbook and provides us with the flexibility to choose which tasks will run within a given playbook based on the tags we specify. In this recipe, we will outline how to configure and use Ansible Tags.

How to do it...

1. Create a new Ansible playbook called `ansible_tags.yml`, as shown here:

```
---

- name: Using Ansible Tags
  hosts: cisco
  gather_facts: no
  tasks:
    - name: Print OSPF
      debug:
        msg: "Router {{ hostname }} will Run OSPF"
      tags: [ospf, routing]

   - name: Print BGP
     debug:
       msg: "Router {{ hostname }} will Run BGP"
     tags:
       - bgp
       - routing
```

```
      - name: Print NTP
        debug:
          msg: "Router {{ hostname }} will run NTP"
        tags: ntp
```

2. Run the playbook as shown here:

```
$ ansible-playbook ansible_tags.yml -i hosts --tags routing
```

3. Run the playbook again, this time using tags, as shown here:

```
$ ansible-playbook ansible_tags.yml -i hosts --tags ospf
```

```
$ ansible-playbook ansible_tags.yml -i hosts --tags routing
```

How it works...

We can use tags to mark both tasks and plays with a given tag in order to use it to control which tasks or plays get executed. This gives us more control when developing playbooks to allow us to run the same playbook. However, with each run, we can control what we are deploying. In the example playbook in this recipe, we have tagged the tasks as OSPF, BGP, or NTP and have applied the `routing` tag to both the OSPF and BGP tasks. This allows us to selectively run the tasks within our playbook as shown here:

- With no tags specified, this will run all the tasks in the playbook with no change in the behavior, as shown in the following screenshot:

```
PLAY [Using Ansible Tags] **********************

TASK [Print OSPF] ******************************
ok: [csr1] => {
    "msg": "Router edge-csr1 will Run OSPF"
}
ok: [csr2] => {
    "msg": "Router edge-csr2 will Run OSPF"
}

TASK [Print BGP] *******************************
ok: [csr1] => {
    "msg": "Router edge-csr1 will Run BGP"
}
ok: [csr2] => {
    "msg": "Router edge-csr2 will Run BGP"
}

TASK [Print NTP] *******************************
ok: [csr1] => {
    "msg": "Router edge-csr1 will run NTP"
}
ok: [csr2] => {
    "msg": "Router edge-csr2 will run NTP"
}
```

- Using the `ospf` tag, we will only run any task marked with this tag, as shown here:

```
PLAY [Using Ansible Tags] ********************

TASK [Print OSPF] ***************************
ok: [csr1] => {
    "msg": "Router edge-csr1 will Run OSPF"
}
ok: [csr2] => {
    "msg": "Router edge-csr2 will Run OSPF"
}
```

- Using the `routing` tag, we will run all tasks marked with this tag, as shown here:

```
PLAY [Using Ansible Tags] ********************

TASK [Print OSPF] ***************************
ok: [csr1] => {
    "msg": "Router edge-csr1 will Run OSPF"
}
ok: [csr2] => {
    "msg": "Router edge-csr2 will Run OSPF"
}

TASK [Print BGP] ****************************
ok: [csr1] => {
    "msg": "Router edge-csr1 will Run BGP"
}
ok: [csr2] => {
    "msg": "Router edge-csr2 will Run BGP"
}
```

See also...

For more information regarding Ansible Tags, please consult the following URL:

https://docs.ansible.com/ansible/latest/user_guide/playbooks_tags.html

Customizing Ansible's settings

Ansible has many setting that can be adjusted and controlled using a configuration file called `ansible.cfg`. This file has multiple options that control many aspects of Ansible, including how Ansible looks and how it connects to managed devices. In this recipe, we will outline how to adjust some of these default settings.

How to do it...

1. Create a new file called `ansible.cfg`, as shown here:

```
[defaults]
inventory=hosts
vault_password_file=decryption_password
gathering=explicit
```

How it works...

By default, Ansible's settings are controlled by the `ansible.cfg` file located in the `/etc/ansible` directory. This is the default configuration file for Ansible that controls how Ansible interacts with managed nodes. We can edit this file directly. However, this will impact any playbook that we will use on the Ansible control machine, as well as any user on this machine. A more flexible and customized option is to include a file named `ansible.cfg` in the project directory and this includes all the options that you need to modify from their default parameters. In the preceding example, we outline only a small subset of these options, as shown here:

- `inventory`: This option modifies the default inventory file that Ansible searches in order to find its inventory (by default, this is `/etc/ansible/hosts`). We adjust this option in order to let Ansible use our inventory file and stop using the `-i` operator to specify our inventory during each playbook run.
- `vault_password_file`: This option sets the file that has the secret password for encrypting and decrypting `ansible-vault` secrets. This option removes the need to run Ansible playbooks with the `--vault-id` operator when using `ansible-vault`-encrypted variables.

- `gathering = explicit`: By default, Ansible runs a setup module to gather facts regarding the managed nodes while the playbook is running. This setup module is not compatible with network nodes since this module requires a Python interpreter on the managed nodes. By setting fact gathering to `explicit`, we disable this default behavior.

See also...

For more information regarding Ansible's configuration settings, please consult the following URL:

```
https://docs.ansible.com/ansible/latest/reference_appendices/config.
html#ansible-configuration-settings
```

Using Ansible Roles

Ansible Roles promotes code reusability and provides a simple method for packaging Ansible code in a simple way that can be shared and consumed. An Ansible role is a collection of all the required Ansible tasks, handlers, and Jinja2 templates that are packaged together in a specific structure. A role should be designed in order to deliver a specific function/task. In this recipe, we will outline how to create an Ansible role and how to use it in our playbooks.

How to do it...

1. Inside the `ch1_ansible` folder, create a new folder called `roles` and create a new role called `basic_config`, as shown here:

   ```
   $ mkdir roles
   $ cd roles
   $ ansible-galaxy init basic_config
   ```

2. Update the `basic_config/vars/main.yml` file with the following variable:

   ```
   $ cat roles/basic_config/vars/main.yml


   ---
   config_dir: basic_config
   ```

3. Update the `basic_config/tasks/main.yml` file with the following tasks:

```
$ cat roles/basic_config/tasks/main.yml

---
  - name: Create Configs Directory
    file:
      path: "{{ config_dir }}"
      state: directory
    run_once: yes

  - name: Generate Cisco Basic Config
    template:
      src: "{{os}}.j2"
      dest: "{{config_dir}}/{{inventory_hostname}}.cfg"
```

4. Inside the `basic_config/templates` folder, create the following structure:

```
$ tree roles/basic_config/templates/

roles/basic_config/templates/
├── ios.j2
└── junos.j2

$ cat roles/basic_config/templates/ios.j2
hostname {{ hostname }}
!
{% for server in ntp_servers %}
ntp {{ server }}
{% endfor %}
```

5. Create a new playbook, `pb_ansible_role.yml`, with the following content to use our role:

```
$ cat pb_ansible_role.yml
---
  - name: Build Basic Config Using Roles
    hosts: all
    connection: local
    roles:
      - basic_config
```

How it works...

In this recipe, we start by creating the `roles` directory within our main folder. By default, when using roles, Ansible will look for roles in the following location in this order:

- The `roles` folder within the current working directory
- `/etc/ansible/roles`

Consequently, we create the `roles` folder within our current working directory (`ch1_ansible`) in order to host all the roles that we will create in this folder. We create the role using the `ansible-galaxy` command with the `init` option and the role name (`basic_config`), which will create the following role structure inside our `roles` folder:

```
$ tree roles/
roles/
└── basic_config
    ├── defaults
    │   └── main.yml
    ├── files
    ├── handlers
    │   └── main.yml
    ├── meta
    │   └── main.yml
    ├── README.md
    ├── tasks
    │   └── main.yml
    ├── templates
    ├── tests
    │   ├── inventory
    │   └── test.yml
    └── vars
        └── main.yml
```

As can be seen from the preceding output, this folder structure is created using the `ansible-galaxy` command and this command builds the role in keeping with the best practice role layout. Not all these folders need to have a functional role that we can use, and the following list outlines the main folders that are commonly used:

- The `tasks` folder: This contains the `main.yml` file, which lists all the tasks that should be executed when we use this role.
- The `templates` folder: This contains all the Jinja2 templates that we will use as part of this role.

- The `vars` folder: This contains all the variables that we want to define and that we will use in our role. The variables inside the `vars` folder have very high precedence when evaluating the variables while running the playbook.
- The `handlers` folder: This contains the `main.yml` file, which includes all the handlers that should run as part of this role.

The role that we created has a single purpose, which is to build the basic configuration for our devices. In order to accomplish this task, we need to define some Ansible tasks as well as use a number of Jinja2 templates in order to generate the basic configuration for the devices. We list all the tasks that we need to run in the `tasks/main.yml` file and we include all the necessary Jinja2 templates in the `templates` folder. We define any requisite variable that we will use in our role in the `vars` folder.

We create a new playbook that will use our new role in order to generate the configuration for the devices. We call all the roles that we want to run as part of our playbook in the `roles` parameter. In our case, we have a single role that we want to run, which is the `basic_config` role.

Once we run our playbook, we can see that a new directory called `basic_config` is created with the following content:

```
$ tree basic_config/
basic_config/
├── csr1.cfg
├── csr2.cfg
├── mx1.cfg
└── mx2.cfg
```

See also

For more information regarding Ansible Roles, please consult the following URL:

https://docs.ansible.com/ansible/latest/user_guide/playbooks_reuse_roles.html

2
Managing Cisco IOS Devices Using Ansible

In this chapter, we will outline how to automate Cisco IOS-based devices using Ansible. We will explore the different modules available in Ansible to automate configuration and collect network information from Cisco IOS devices. This chapter will be based on the following sample network diagram, and we will walk through how we can implement this network design using Ansible:

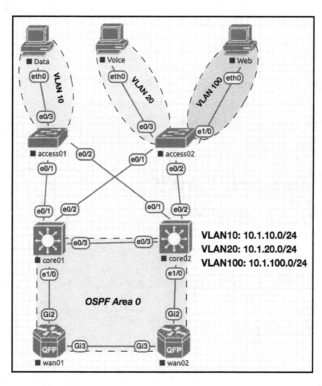

The following table outlines the management IP addresses on the Cisco nodes, which Ansible will use to connect to the devices:

Device	Role	Vendor	MGMT Port	MGMT IP
access01	Access switch	Cisco IOS 15.1	Ethernet0/0	172.20.1.18
access02	Access switch	Cisco IOS 15.1	Ethernet0/0	172.20.1.19
core01	Core switch	Cisco IOS 15.1	Ethernet0/0	172.20.1.20
core02	Core switch	Cisco IOS 15.1	Ethernet0/0	172.20.1.21
wan01	WAN router	Cisco IOS–XE 16.6.1	GigabitEthernet1	172.20.1.22
wan02	WAN router	Cisco IOS–XE 16.6.1	GigabitEthernet1	172.20.1.23

The main recipes covered in this chapter are as follows:

- Building an Ansible network inventory
- Connecting to Cisco IOS devices
- Configuring basic system information
- Configuring interfaces on IOS devices
- Configuring L2 VLANS on IOS devices
- Configuring trunk and access interfaces
- Configuring interface IP addresses
- Configuring OSPF on IOS devices
- Collecting IOS device facts
- Validating network reachability on IOS devices
- Retrieving operational data from IOS devices
- Validating network states with pyATS and Ansible

Technical requirements

The code files for this chapter can be found here:

```
https://github.com/PacktPublishing/Network-Automation-Cookbook/tree/master/ch2_
ios
```

The software releases that this chapter is based on are as follows:

- Cisco IOS 15.1
- Cisco IOS–XE 16.6.1
- Ansible 2.9
- Python 3.6.8

Check out the following video to see the Code in Action:
`https://bit.ly/34F8xPW`

Building an Ansible network inventory

In this recipe, we will outline how to build and structure the Ansible inventory to describe the network setup outlined in the previous section.

Getting ready

Make sure that Ansible is already installed on the control machine.

How to do it...

1. Create a new directory with the following name: `ch2_ios`.
2. Inside this new folder, create the `hosts` file with the following content:

```
$ cat hosts
 [access]
 access01 Ansible_host=172.20.1.18
 access02 Ansible_host=172.20.1.19

 [core]
 core01 Ansible_host=172.20.1.20
 core02 Ansible_host=172.20.1.21

 [wan]
 wan01 Ansible_host=172.20.1.22
 wan02 Ansible_host=172.20.1.23

 [lan:children]
 access
 core

 [network:children]
 lan
 wan
```

3. Create the `Ansible.cfg` file with the following content:

```
$ cat Ansible.cfg

[defaults]
 inventory=hosts
 retry_files_enabled=False
 gathering=explicit
```

How it works...

We built the Ansible inventory using the `hosts` file, and we defined multiple groups in order to group the different devices in our topology in the following manner:

- We created the `access` group, which has both access switches (`access01` and `access02`) in our topology.
- We created the `core` group, which groups all core switches that will act as the L3 termination for all the VLANs on the access switches.
- We created the `wan` group, which groups all our Cisco IOS–XE routes, which will act as our wan routers.
- We created another group called `lan`, which groups both access and core groups.
- We created the `network` group, which groups both `lan` and `wan` groups.

Finally, we created the `Ansible.cfg` file and configured it to point to our `hosts` file to be used as an Ansible inventory file. We disabled the setup module, which is not required when running Ansible against network nodes.

Connecting to Cisco IOS devices

In this recipe, we will outline how to connect to Cisco IOS devices from Ansible via SSH in order to start managing devices from Ansible.

Getting ready

In order to follow along with this recipe, an Ansible inventory file should be constructed as per the previous recipe. IP reachability between the Ansible control machine and all the devices in the network must be configured.

How to do it...

1. Inside the `ch2_ios` directory, create the `groups_vars` folder.

2. Inside the `group_vars` folder, create the `network.yml` file with the following content:

```
$cat network.yml
Ansible_network_os: ios
Ansible_connection: network_cli
Ansible_user: lab
Ansible_password: lab123
Ansible_become: yes
Ansible_become_password: admin123
Ansible_become_method: enable
```

3. On all IOS devices, ensure that the following is configured to set up SSH access:

```
!
hostname <device_hostname>
!
ip domain name <domain_name>
!
username lab secret 5 <password_for_lab_user>.
!
enable secret 5 <enable_password>.
!
line vty 0 4
login local
transport input SSH
!
```

4. Generate SSH keys on the Cisco IOS devices from the config mode, as shown in the following code snippet:

```
(config)#crypto key generate rsa
 Choose the size of the key modulus in the range of 360 to 4096 for
your
 General Purpose Keys. Choosing a key modulus greater than 512 may
take
 a few minutes.
How many bits in the modulus [512]: 2048
 % Generating 2048 bit RSA keys, keys will be non-exportable...
 [OK] (elapsed time was 0 seconds)
```

5. Update the `Ansible.cfg` file with the following highlighted parameters:

```
$ cat Ansible.cfg
[defaults]
 host_key_checking=False
```

How it works...

In our sample network, we will use SSH to set up the connection between Ansible and our Cisco devices. In this setup, Ansible will use SSH in order to establish the connection to our Cisco devices with a view to start managing it. We will use username/password authentication in order to authenticate our Ansible control node with our Cisco devices.

On the Cisco devices, we must ensure that SSH keys are present in order to have a functional SSH server on the Cisco devices. The following code snippet outlines the status of the SSH server on the Cisco device prior to generating the SSH keys:

```
wan01#show ip SSH
SSH Disabled - version 2.0
%Please create RSA keys to enable SSH (and of atleast 768 bits for SSH v2).
Authentication methods:publickey,keyboard-interactive,password
Authentication Publickey Algorithms:x509v3-SSH-rsa,SSH-rsa
Hostkey Algorithms:x509v3-SSH-rsa,SSH-rsa
Encryption Algorithms:aes128-ctr,aes192-ctr,aes256-ctr
MAC Algorithms:hmac-sha2-256,hmac-sha2-512,hmac-sha1,hmac-sha1-96
KEX Algorithms:diffie-hellman-group-exchange-sha1,diffie-hellman-group14-
sha1
Authentication timeout: 120 secs; Authentication retries: 3
Minimum expected Diffie Hellman key size : 2048 bits
IOS Keys in SECSH format(SSH-rsa, base64 encoded): NONE
```

Once we create the SSH keys, the SSH server on the Cisco device is operational, and is ready to accept an SSH connection from the Ansible control node.

On the Ansible machine, we include all the variables required to establish the SSH connection to the managed devices in the `network.yml` file. As per our inventory file, the network group includes all the devices within our topology, and so all the attributes that we configure in this file will apply to all the devices in our inventory. The following is a breakdown of the attributes that we included in the file:

- `Ansible_connection`: This establishes how Ansible connects to the device. In this scenario, we set it to `network_cli` to indicate that we will use SSH to connect to a network device.

- `Ansible_network_os`: When using `network_cli` as the connection plugin to connect to the network device, we must indicate which network OS Ansible will be connecting to, so as to use the correct SSH parameters with the devices. In this scenario, we will set it to `ios`, since all the devices in our topology are IOS-based devices.
- `Ansible_user`: This parameter specifies the username that Ansible will use to establish the SSH session with the network device.
- `Ansible_password`: This parameter specifies the password that Ansible will use to establish the SSH session with the network device.
- `Ansible_become`: This instructs Ansible to use the `enable` command to enter privileged mode when configuring or executing `show` commands on the managed device. We set this to `yes` in our context, since we will require privileged mode to configure the devices.
- `Ansible_become_password`: This specifies the `enable` password to use in order to enter privileged mode on the managed IOS device.
- `Ansible_become_method`: This option specifies the method to use in order to enter privileged mode. In our scenario, this is the `enable` command on IOS devices.

> In this recipe, I have defined the SSH password and the `enable` passwords as plain text just for simplicity; however, this is highly discouraged. We should use `Ansible-vault` to secure the passwords, as outlined in the *Ansible Vault* recipe in the previous chapter.

On the Cisco devices, we set up the required username and password so that Ansible can open an SSH connection to the managed Cisco IOS devices. We also configure an `enable` password to be able to enter privileged mode, and to make configuration changes. Once we apply all of these configurations to the devices, we are ready to set up Ansible.

In any SSH connection, when an SSH client (Ansible control node in our case) connects to an SSH server (Cisco devices in our case), the server sends a copy of its public key to the client before the client logs in. This is used to establish the secure channel between the client and the server, and to authenticate the server to the client in order to prevent any man-in-the-middle attacks. So, at the start of a new SSH session involving a new device, we see the following prompt:

```
$SSH lab@172.20.1.18
The authenticity of host '172.20.1.18 (172.20.1.18)' can't be established.
RSA key fingerprint is SHA256:KnWOalnENZfPokYYdIG3Ogm9HDnXIwjh/it3cqdiRRQ.
RSA key fingerprint is MD5:af:18:4b:4e:84:19:a6:8d:82:17:51:d5:ee:eb:16:8d.
Are you sure you want to continue connecting (yes/no)?
```

When the SSH client initiates the SSH connection to the client, the SSH server sends its public key to the client in order to authenticate itself to the client. The client searches for the public key in its local known `hosts` files (in the `~/.SSH/known_hosts` or `/etc/SSH/SSH_known_hosts` files). In the event that it does not find the public key for this machine in its local known `hosts` file, it will prompt the user to add this new key to its local database, and this is the prompt that we see when we initiate the SSH connection.

In order to simplify the SSH connection setup between the Ansible control node and its remotely managed `hosts`, we can disable this host checking. We can do this by telling Ansible to ignore host keys and not to add them to the known `hosts` files by setting `host_key_checking` to `False` in the `Ansible.cfg` configuration file.

 Disabling host key checking is not a best practice, and we are only showing it as it is a lab setup. In the next section, we will outline an alternative method to establish the SSH connection between Ansible and its remote managed devices.

There's more...

If we need to verify the identity of the SSH `hosts` that we will connect to, and thereby enable `host_key_checking`, we can automate the addition of the SSH public key of the remote managed `hosts` to the `~/.SSH/known_hosts` file using Ansible. We create a new Ansible playbook that will run on the Ansible control machine to connect to the remote devices using the `ssk-keyscan` command. We then collect the SSH public keys for the remote machines and add them to the `~/.SSH/known_hosts` file. The method is outlined here:

1. Create a new `playbook pb_gather_SSH_keys.yml` file and add the following play:

```
- name: "Play2: Record Keys in Known Hosts file"
  hosts: localhost
  vars:
  - hosts_file: "~/.SSH/known_hosts"
  tasks:
  - name: create know hosts file
    file:
    path: "{{ hosts_file }}"
    state: file
    changed_when: false
```

2. Update the playbook and add another play within the same playbook to save and store the SSH public keys for the remote managed nodes:

```
- name: "Play2: Record Keys in Known Hosts file"
  hosts: localhost
  vars:
    - hosts_file: "~/.SSH/known_hosts"
  tasks:
    - name: create know hosts file
      file:
        path: "{{ hosts_file }}"
        state: file
      changed_when: false
    - name: Populate the known_hosts file
      blockinfile:
        block: |
          {% for host in groups['all'] if
hostvars[host].SSH_keys.stdout != ''
%}
          {{ hostvars[host].SSH_keys.stdout}}
          {% endfor %}
        path: "{{ hosts_file }}"
        create: yes
```

In our new playbook, we have a play that targets all our managed devices by setting the `hosts` parameter to `all`. In this play, we have a single task, which we run on the Ansible control node (using the `delegate_to` localhost) to issue the `SSH-keyscan` command, which returns the SSH public key for the remote device, as shown in the following code:

```
$ SSH-keyscan 172.20.1.22

# 172.20.1.22:22 SSH-2.0-Cisco-1.25
 172.20.1.22 SSH-rsa
AAAAB3NzaC1yc2EAAAADAQABAAAABAQDTwrH4phzRnW/RsC8eXMh/accIErRfkgffDWBGSdEX0r9
EwAa6p2uFMWj8dq6kvrREuhqpgFyMoWmpgdx5Cr+10kEonr8So5yHhOhqG1SJO9RyzAb93H0P0r
o5DXFK8A/Ww+m++avyZ9dShuWGxKj9CDM6dxFLg9ZU/9vlzkwtyKF/+mdWNGoSiCbcBg7LrOgZ7
Id7oxnhEhkrVIa+IxxGa5Pwc73eR45Uf7QyYZXPC0RTOm6aH2f9+8oj+vQMsAzXmeudpRgAu151
qUH3nEG9HIgUxwhvmi4MaTC+psmsGg2x26PKTOeX9eLs4RHquVS3nySwv4arqVzDqWf6aruJ
```

 In this task, we are using `delegate_to` as being equal to `localhost`, as Ansible will try to connect to the remote devices and issue the command on the remote device by default. In our case, this is not what we need; we need to issue this command from the Ansible control node. So, we use `delegate_to` as being equal to `localhost` in order to enforce this behavior.

We run the second play on the Ansible control host by setting `hosts` to `localhost,` and we execute tasks to create the known hosts file (if not already present) and to populate this file with the data that we captured in the first play using the `SSH_keys` variable. We run this playbook on the Ansible control machine to store the SSH keys from the remotely managed nodes prior to running any of our playbooks.

Configuring basic system information

In this recipe, we will outline how we can configure basic system parameters on Cisco IOS devices, such as setting the hostname, DNS server, and NTP servers. Following the network setup that we outlined at the start of this chapter, we will configure the following information on all the Cisco IOS devices:

- DNS servers 172.20.1.250 and 172.20.1.251
- NTP server 172.20.1.17

Getting ready

An Ansible inventory file must be present, as well as the configuration for Ansible to connect to the Cisco IOS devices via SSH.

How to do it...

1. To the `group_vars/network.yml` file, add the following system parameters:

```
$ cat group_vars/network.yml
<-- Output Trimmed for brevity ------>
name_servers:
 - 172.20.1.250
 - 172.20.1.251
ntp_server: 172.20.1.17
```

2. Create a new playbook called `pb_build_network.yml` with the following information:

```
$ cat pb_build_network.yml
---
- name: "PLAY 1: Configure All Lan Switches"
  hosts: lan
  tags: lan
  tasks:
  - name: "Configure Hostname and Domain Name"
    ios_system:
      hostname: "{{ inventory_hostname }}"
      domain_name: "{{ domain_name }}"
      lookup_enabled: no
      name_servers: "{{ name_servers }}"
  - name: "Configure NTP"
    ios_ntp:
      server: "{{ ntp_server }}"
      logging: true
      state: present
```

How it works...

In the `network.yml` file, we define the `name_servers` variable as a list of DNS servers, and we also define the `ntp_servers` variable, which defines the NTP servers that we want to configure on the IOS devices. Defining these parameters in the `network.yml` file applies these variables to all the devices within the network group.

We create a playbook and the first play targets all the `hosts` in the `lan` group (this includes both access and core devices) and, within this play, we reference two tasks:

- `ios_system`: This sets the hostname and the DNS servers on the devices.
- `ios_ntp`: This configures the NTP on the IOS devices and enables logging for NTP events.

Both these modules are declarative Ansible modules in which we just identify the state pertaining to our infrastructure. Ansible converts this declaration into the necessary IOS commands. The modules retrieve the configuration of the devices and compare the current state with our intended state (to have DNS and NTP configured on them) and then, if the current state does not correspond to the intended state defined by these modules, Ansible will apply the needed configuration to the devices.

When we run these tasks on all the LAN devices, the following configuration is pushed to the devices:

```
!
ip name-server 172.20.1.250 172.20.1.251
no ip domain lookup
ip domain name lab.net
!
ntp logging
ntp server 172.20.1.17
!
```

See also...

For more information regarding the `ios_system` and `ios_ntp` modules, as well as the different parameters supported by these modules, please consult the following URLs:

- https://docs.Ansible.com/Ansible/latest/modules/ios_system_module.html
- https://docs.Ansible.com/Ansible/latest/modules/ios_ntp_module.html

Configuring interfaces on IOS devices

In this recipe, we will outline how to configure the basic interface properties on Cisco IOS-based devices, such as setting the interface description, the interface **maximum transmission unit** (**MTU**), and enabling `interfaces`. We will configure all the links within our topology as having a link MTU of 1,500 and to be fully duplex.

Getting ready

To follow along with this recipe, an Ansible inventory is assumed to be already set up, as is IP reachability between the Ansible control node with the Cisco devices in place.

How to do it...

1. In the `group_vars/network.yml` file, add the following content to define the generic interface parameters:

   ```
   $ cat group_vars/network.yml
   <-- Output Trimmed for brevity ------>
   ```

```
intf_duplex: full
intf_mtu: 1500
```

2. Create a new file, `lan.yml`, under the `group_vars` folder, with the following data to define the `interfaces` on our Cisco devices:

```
$ cat group_vars/lan.yaml

interfaces:
  core01:
    - name: Ethernet0/1
      description: access01_e0/1
      mode: trunk
    - name: Ethernet0/2
      description: access02_e0/1
      mode: trunk
    - name: Ethernet0/3
      description: core01_e0/3
      mode: trunk
  <--    Output Trimmed for brevity ------>
  access01:
    - name: Ethernet0/1
      description: core01_e0/1
      mode: trunk
    - name: Ethernet0/2
      description: core02_e0/1
      mode: trunk
    - name: Ethernet0/3
      description: Data_vlan
      mode: access
      vlan: 10
```

3. Update the `pb_build_network.yml` playbook file with the following task to set up the `interfaces`:

```
- name: "P1T3: Configure Interfaces"
  ios_interface:
    name: "{{ item.name }}"
    description: "{{ item.description }}"
    duplex: "{{ intf_duplex }}"
    mtu: "{{ intf_mtu }}"
    state: up
  loop: "{{ interfaces[inventory_hostname] }}"
  register: ios_intf
```

How it works...

In this recipe, we outline how to configure the physical interfaces on IOS devices. We first declare the generic parameters (interface duplex and MTU) that apply to all the interfaces. These parameters are defined under the network.yml file. Next, we define all the interface-specific parameters for all our LAN devices under the lan.yml file to be applied to all devices. All these parameters are declared in the interfaces dictionary data structure.

We update our playbook with a new task to configure the physical parameters for all of our LAN devices in our network. We use the ios_interface module to provision all the interface parameters, and we loop over all the interfaces in each node using the interfaces data structure. We set the state to up in order to indicate that the interface should be present and operational.

See also...

For more information regarding the ios_interface module, and the different parameters supported by these modules, please consult the following URL: https://docs.Ansible.com/Ansible/latest/modules/ios_interface_module.html

Configuring L2 VLANs on IOS devices

In this recipe, we will outline how to configure L2 VLANs on Cisco IOS devices, as per the network topology discussed in the introduction to this chapter. We will outline how to declare VLANs as Ansible variables, and how to use suitable Ansible modules to provision these VLANs on the network.

Getting ready

We will be building on the previous recipes discussed in this chapter to continue to configure the L2 VLANs on all the LAN devices within our sample topology.

How to do it...

1. Update the `group_vars/lan.yml` file with the VLAN definition, as outlined in the following code:

```
$ cat group_vars/lan.yaml

vlans:
  - name: Data
    vlan_id: 10
  - name: Voice
    vlan_id: 20
  - name: Web
    vlan_id: 100
```

2. Update the `pb_build.yml` playbook with the following task to provision the VLANs:

```
- name: "P1T4: Create L2 VLANs"
  ios_vlan:
    vlan_id: "{{ item.vlan_id }}"
    name: "{{ item.name  }}"
  loop: "{{ vlans }}"
  tags: vlan
```

How it works...

In the `group_vars/lan.yml` file, we define a `vlans` list data structure that holds the VLAN definition that we need to apply to all our core and access switches. This variable will be available for all the core and access switches, and Ansible will use this variable in order to provision the required VLANs on the remote devices.

We use another declarative module, `ios_vlan`, which takes the VLAN definition (its name and the VLAN ID) and configures these VLANs on the remote managed device. It pulls the existing configuration from the device and compares it with the list of devices that need to be present, while only pushing the delta.

We use the `loop` construct to go through all the items in the `vlans` list, and configure all the respective VLANs on all the devices.

After running this task on the devices, the following is the output from one of the access switches:

```
access01#sh vlan
VLAN Name                             Status    Ports
---- -------------------------------- --------- ---------------------------
----
1    default                          active    Et1/0, Et1/1, Et1/2, Et1/3
10   Data                             active    Et0/3
20   Voice                            active
100  Web                              active
```

Configuring trunk and access interfaces

In this recipe, we will show how to configure access and trunk interfaces on Cisco IOS-based devices, and how to map interfaces to an access VLAN, as well as how to allow specific VLANs on the trunks.

Getting ready

Following our sample topology, we will configure the interfaces on the devices. As shown in this table, we are only showing the VLANs for `access01` and `core01`— the other devices are exact replicas:

Device	Interface	Mode	VLANs
Core01	Ethernet0/1	Trunk	10,20,100
Core01	Ethernet0/2	Trunk	10,20,100
Core01	Ethernet0/3	Trunk	10,20,100,200
Access01	Ethernet0/1	Trunk	10,20,100
Access01	Ethernet0/2	Trunk	10,20,100
Access01	Ethernet0/3	Access	10

How to do it...

1. Create a new `core.yml` file under `group_vars` and include the following `core_vlans` definition:

```
core_vlans:
  - name: 13_core_vlan
    vlan_id: 200
    interface: Ethernet0/3
```

2. Update the `pb_build_network.yml` playbook with the following tasks to configure all trunk ports:

```
- name: "Configure L2 Trunks"
  ios_l2_interface:
    name: "{{ item.name }}"
    mode: "{{ item.mode }}"
    trunk_allowed_vlans: "{{ vlans | map(attribute='vlan_id') |
join(',') }}"
    state: present
  loop: "{{ interfaces[inventory_hostname] |
selectattr('mode','equalto','trunk') | list }}"
- name: "Enable dot1q Trunks"
  ios_config:
    lines:
      - switchport trunk encapsulation dot1q
    parents: interface {{item.name}}
  loop: "{{ interfaces[inventory_hostname] |
selectattr('mode','equalto','trunk') | list }}"
  tags: dot1q
```

3. Update the playbook with the following task to configure all access ports:

```
- name: "Configure Access Ports"
  ios_l2_interface:
    name: "{{ item.name }}"
    mode: "{{ item.mode}}"
    access_vlan: "{{ item.vlan }}"
    state: present
  loop: "{{ interfaces[inventory_hostname] |
selectattr('mode','equalto','access') | list }}"
```

How it works...

We are using the same data structure in the `lan.yml` file that defines all the interfaces within the LAN network and describes their type (access/trunk). In the case of access ports, we define which access interface is part of which VLAN. We will reference this list data structure to configure the access and trunk ports on all the devices within the `lan` group. The interfaces within our `layer2` network are one of the following two options:

Access:

- We use `ios_l2_interface` with the `access_vlan` parameter to configure the correct access VLAN on the interface.
- We select only the access interfaces for each device using the `selectattr` `jinja2` filter, and we match only one interface with a mode equal to `access`, and we loop over this list for each device.

Trunk:

- We use `ios_l2_interface` with the `trunk_allowed_vlans` parameter to add all the VLANs to the trunk ports, on both access and core switches.
- We create the permitted VLAN list using the Jinja2 `map` and `join` filters and we apply this filter to the `vlans` list data structure. This outputs a string similar to the following: `10,20,100`.
- We select only the trunk ports using the `selectattr` Jinja2 filter from the interface's data structure per node.
- We need to configure these trunks as `dot1q` ports; however, this attribute is still not enabled on `ios_l2_interface`. Hence, we use another module, `ios_config`, to send the required Cisco IOS command to set up the `dot1q` trunks.

The following output outlines the configuration applied to the `access01` device as an example for both access and trunk ports:

```
!
interface Ethernet0/3    >> Access Port
 description Data_vlan
 switchport access vlan 10
 switchport mode access


 !
interface Ethernet0/1    >> Trunk Port
 description core01_e0/1
 switchport trunk encapsulation dot1q
```

```
switchport trunk allowed vlan 10,20,100
switchport mode trunk
```

See also...

For more information regarding `ios_l2_interface` and the different parameters supported by these modules, please consult the following URL:

```
https://docs.Ansible.com/Ansible/latest/modules/ios_l2_interface_module.html
```

Configuring interface IP addresses

In this recipe, we will explore how to configure the interface IP address on Cisco IOS devices. We will use the sample topology to configure the VLAN interfaces on both the core switches. We will outline how to configure VRRP between the core switches for all the VLAN interfaces. We will configure the following IP addresses:

Interface	Prefix	VRRP IP address
VLAN10	10.1.10.0/24	10.1.10.254
VLAN20	10.1.20.0/24	10.1.20.254
VLAN100	10.1.100.0/24	10.1.100.254

Getting ready

This recipe assumes that the interface and VLANs are configured as per the previous recipes in this chapter.

How to do it...

1. Update the `group_vars/core.yml` file with following data to define the SVI interfaces:

```
$ cat group_vars/core.yml
<-- Output Trimmed for brevity ------>
svi_interfaces:
  - name: Vlan10
    ipv4: 10.1.10.0/24
    vrrp: yes
    ospf: passive
  - name: Vlan20
```

```
    ipv4: 10.1.20.0/24
    vrrp: yes
    ospf: passive
  - name: Vlan100
    ipv4: 10.1.100.0/24
    vrrp: yes
    ospf: passive
```

2. Create `core01.yml` and `core02.yml` files under the `host_vars` folder and add the following content:

```
$ cat host_vars/core01.yml
 hst_svi_id: 1
 hst_vrrp_priority: 100
$ cat host_vars/core02.yml
 hst_svi_id: 2
 hst_vrrp_priority: 50
```

3. Update the `pb_build_network.yml` playbook with the following tasks to create and enable the L3 SVI interfaces:

```
- name: "PLAY 2: Configure Core Switches"
  hosts: core
  tags: l3_core
  tasks:
<-- Output Trimmed for brevity ------>
   - name: "Create L3 VLAN Interfaces"
     ios_l3_interface:
       name: "{{item.name }}"
       ipv4: "{{item.ipv4 | ipv4(hst_svi_id)}}"
     loop: "{{svi_interfaces}}"
     tags: l3_svi
   - name: "Enable the VLAN Interfaces"
     ios_interface:
       name: "{{ item.name }}"
       state: up
     loop: "{{ svi_interfaces }}"
```

4. Update the playbook with the following task to set up VRRP configuration on the SVI interfaces:

```
   - name: "Create VRRP Configs"
     ios_config:
       parents: interface {{ item.name }}
       lines:
         - vrrp {{item.name.split('Vlan')[1]}} priority {{
hst_vrrp_priority }}
         - vrrp {{item.name.split('Vlan')[1]}} ip {{item.ipv4 |
```

```
    ipv4(254)|ipaddr('address')}}
        loop: "{{svi_interfaces | selectattr('vrrp','equalto',true) |
list }}"
```

How it works...

In this section, we are configuring the IP addresses for the L3 VLAN interfaces on the core switches, as well as configuring VRRP on all the L3 VLAN interfaces to provide L3 redundancy.

We are using a new list data structure called `svi_interfaces`, which describes all the SVI interfaces with L3 IP addresses, and also some added parameters to control both the VRRP and OSPF configured on these interfaces. We also set up two new variables on each core router, `hst_svi_id` and `hst_vrrp_priority`, which we will use in the playbook to control the IP address on each core switch, as well as the VRPP priority.

We use the `ios_l3_interface` Ansible module to set the IPv4 addresses on the VLAN interfaces. On each core switch, we loop over the `svi_interfaces` data structure, and for each VLAN we configure the IPv4 address on the corresponding VLAN interface. We determine which IP address is configured on each router using the Ansible `ipaddr` filter, along with the `hst_svi_id` parameter `{{item.ipv4 | ipv4(hst_svi_id)}}`. So, for example, for VLAN10, we will assign `10.1.10.1/24` for `core01` and `10.1.10.2/24` for `core02`.

 When first creating the VLAN interface on Cisco IOS devices, they are in a state of shutdown, so we need to enable them. We use the `ios_interface` module to enable the interfaces.

For the VRRP part, we return to using the `ios_config` module to set up the VRRP configuration on all the VLAN interfaces, and we use `hst_vrrp_priority` to correctly set up `core01` as the master VRRP for all VLANs.

The following is a sample of the configuration that is pushed on the devices after running the playbook:

```
Core01
========
!
interface Vlan10
ip address 10.1.10.1 255.255.255.0
vrrp 10 ip 10.1.10.254
!
```

```
Core02
=======
!
interface Vlan10
ip address 10.1.10.2 255.255.255.0
vrrp 10 ip 10.1.10.254
vrrp 10 priority 50
```

See also...

For more information regarding `ios_l3_interface` and the different parameters supported by these modules, please consult the following URL:

```
https://docs.Ansible.com/Ansible/latest/modules/ios_l3_interface_module.html
```

Configuring OSPF on IOS devices

In this recipe, we will outline how to configure OSPF on Cisco IOS devices with Ansible. Using our sample network topology, we will set up OSPF between core switches and WAN routers, as well as advertising the SVI interface via OSPF.

Getting ready

This recipe assumes that all the interfaces are already configured with the correct IP addresses and are following the same procedures outlined in previous recipes.

How to do it...

1. Update the `group_vars/core.yml` file with the following data to define core links between core switches and WAN routers:

```
core_l3_links:
  core01:
    - name: Ethernet1/0
      description: wan01_Gi2
      ipv4: 10.3.1.0/30
      ospf: yes
      ospf_metric: 100
      peer: wan01
  core02:
```

```
    - name: Ethernet1/0
      description: wan02_Gi2
      ipv4: 10.3.1.4/30
      ospf: yes
      ospf_metric: 200
      peer: wan02
```

2. Update the `pb_build_network.yml` playbook with the following tasks to set up OSPF:

```
- name: "PLAY 2: Configure Core Switches"
  hosts: core
  tags: l3_core
  tasks:
< -------- Snippet -------- >
    - name: "P2T9: Configure OSPF On Interfaces"
      ios_config:
        parents: interface {{ item.name }}
        lines:
          - ip ospf {{ ospf_process }} area {{ ospf_area }}
          - ip ospf network point-to-point
          - ip ospf cost {{item.ospf_metric |
default(ospf_metric)}}
        loop: "{{ (svi_interfaces +
core_l3_links[inventory_hostname]) | selectattr('ospf') | list }}"
    - name: "P2T10: Configure OSPF Passive Interfaces"
      ios_config:
        parents: router ospf {{ ospf_process }}
        lines: passive-interface {{item.name}}
        loop: "{{ (svi_interfaces +
core_l3_links[inventory_hostname]) |
selectattr('ospf','equalto','passive') | list }}"
```

How it works...

We created another dictionary data structure in the `core.yml` file that describes the L3 links between the core switches and the WAN routers. We specified whether they will run OSPF and what the OSPF metric is on these links.

Currently, Ansible doesn't provide a declarative module to manage OSPF configuration on IOS-based devices. Therefore, we need to push the required configuration using the `ios_config` module. We created two separate tasks using `ios_config` in order to push the OSPF-related configuration on each device. In the first task, we configured the interface-related parameters under each interface, and we looped over both the `svi_interface` and `core_l3_interfaces` data structures to enable OSPF on all the OSPF-enabled interfaces. We used the Jinja2 `selectattr` filter to select all the interfaces that have the OSPF attribute set to `yes`/`true`.

In the last task, we applied the passive interface configuration to all the interfaces that have the passive flag enabled on them. We used the Jinja2 `selectattr` filter to select only those interfaces with the passive parameter set to `yes`/`true`.

Collecting IOS device facts

In this recipe, we will outline how to collect device facts from Cisco devices with Ansible. This information includes the serial number, IOS version, and all the interfaces on the devices. Ansible executes several commands on managed IOS devices in order to collect this information.

Getting ready

The Ansible controller must have IP connectivity with the managed network devices, and SSH must be enabled on the IOS devices.

How to do it...

1. Create a new playbook called `pb_collect_facts.yml` in the same `ch2_ios` folder with the following information:

```
---
- name: "PLAY 1: Collect Device Facts"
  hosts: core,wan
  tasks:
    - name: "P1T1: Gather Device Facts"
      ios_facts:
      register: device_facts
    - debug: var=device_facts
```

How it works...

We run this new playbook against all nodes within the core and wan group, and we use the ios_facts module to collect the information from the managed IOS devices. In this recipe, we use the debug module to print out the information that was collected from the ios_facts module. The following is a subset of the information that was discovered:

```
ok: [core01 -> localhost] => {
  "Ansible_facts": {
    "net_all_ipv4_addresses": [
      "172.20.1.20",
< ---------- Snippet ------------ >
      "10.1.100.1"
    ],
    "net_hostname": "core01",
    "net_interfaces": {
< ---------- Snippet ------------ >
      "Vlan10": {
        "bandwidth": 1000000,
        "description": null,
        "duplex": null,
        "ipv4": [
          {
            "address": "10.1.10.1",
            "subnet": "24"
          }
        ],
        "lineprotocol": "up",
        "macaddress": "aabb.cc80.e000",
        "mediatype": null,
        "mtu": 1500,
        "operstatus": "up",
        "type": "Ethernet SVI"
      },

    },
    "net_iostype": "IOS",
    "net_serialnum": "67109088",
    "net_system": "ios",
    "net_version": "15.1",
  }
< ------------ Snippet ------------ >
}
```

From the preceding output, we can see some of the main facts that the `ios_facts` module has captured from the devices, including the following:

- `net_all_ipv4_addresses`: This list data structure contains all the IPv4 addresses that are configured on all the `interfaces` on the IOS device.
- `net_interfaces`: This dictionary data structure captures the status of all of the `interfaces` on this device and their operational state, as well as other important information, such as a description and their operational state.
- `net_serialnum`: This captures the serial number of the device.
- `net_version`: This captures the IOS version running on this device.

There's more...

Using the information that is collected from the `ios_facts` module, we can generate structured reports for the current state of the network and use these reports in further tasks. In this section, we will outline how to modify our playbook to build this report.

Add a new task to the `pb_collect_facts.yml` playbook, as shown in the following code:

```
- name: "P1T2: Write Device Facts"
  blockinfile:
    path: ./facts.yml
    create: yes
    block: |
      device_facts:
      {% for host in play_hosts %}
      {% set node = hostvars[host] %}
        {{ node.Ansible_net_hostname }}:
          serial_number: {{ node.Ansible_net_serialnum }}
          ios_version: {{ node.Ansible_net_version }}
      {% endfor %}
      all_loopbacks:
      {% for host in play_hosts %}
      {% set node = hostvars[host] %}
      {% if node.Ansible_net_interfaces is defined %}
      {% if node.Ansible_net_interfaces.Loopback0 is defined %}
        - {{ node.Ansible_net_interfaces.Loopback0.ipv4[0].address }}
      {% endif %}
      {% endif %}
      {% endfor %}
  run_once: yes
  delegate_to: localhost
```

We use the `blockinfile` module to build a YAML file called `facts.yml`. We use Jinja2 expressions within the `blockinfile` module to customize and select the information we want to capture from the Ansible facts that were captured from the `ios_facts` task. When we run the `pb_collect_facts.yml` playbook, we generate the `facts.yml` file, which has the following data:

```
device_facts:
  wan01:
    serial_number: 90L4XVVPL7V
    ios_version: 16.06.01
  wan02:
    serial_number: 9UOFOO7FH19
    ios_version: 16.06.01
  core01:
    serial_number: 67109088
    ios_version: 15.1
  core02:
    serial_number: 67109104
    ios_version: 15.1
all_loopbacks:
  - 10.100.1.3
  - 10.100.1.4
  - 10.100.1.1
  - 10.100.1.2
```

See also...

For more information regarding `ios_facts` and the different parameters supported by these modules, please consult the following URL:

```
https://docs.Ansible.com/Ansible/latest/modules/ios_facts_module.html
```

Validating network reachability on IOS devices

In this recipe, we will outline how to validate network reachability via `ping` using Ansible. ICMP allows us to validate proper forwarding across our network. Using Ansible to perform this task provides us with a robust tool to validate proper traffic forwarding, since we can perform this task from each node simultaneously and collect all the results for further inspection.

Getting ready

This recipe is built based on the network setup that was outlined in the chapter introduction, and I am assuming that the network has already been built in accordance with all the previous recipes in this chapter.

How to do it...

1. Create a new playbook called `pb_net_validate.yml` and add the following task to store all SVI IP addresses:

```
---
- name: "PLay 1: Validate Network Reachability"
  hosts: core,wan
  vars:
    host_id: 10
    packet_count: 10
  tasks:
    - name: "Get all SVI Prefixes"
      set_fact:
        all_svi_prefixes: "{{ svi_interfaces | selectattr('vrrp')
                                    map(attribute='ipv4') | list }}"
      run_once: yes
      delegate_to: localhost
      tags: svi
```

2. Update the `pb_net_validate.yml` playbook with the following task to ping all the SVI `interfaces`:

```
    - name: "Ping Hosts in all VLANs"
      ios_ping:
        dest: "{{ item | ipaddr(10) | ipaddr('address') }}"
      loop: "{{ all_svi_prefixes }}"
      ignore_errors: yes
      tags: svi
```

How it works...

In this playbook, we are using the `ios_ping` module, which logs into each node defined in our Ansible inventory, and pings the destination specified by the `dest` attribute. In this sample playbook, we would like to validate network reachability to a single host within the data, voice, and web VLANs, and we choose the tenth host in all these VLANs (just as an example). In order to build all the VLAN prefixes we set in the first task, we add a new variable called `all_svi_prefixes` and use multiple `jinja2` filters to collect only those prefixes that are running VRRP (so as to remove any core VLANs). We get only the IPv4 attributes for these SVI `interfaces`. The following are the contents of this new variable after running the first task:

```
ok: [core01 -> localhost] => {
  "all_svi_prefixes": [
    "10.1.10.0/24",
    "10.1.20.0/24",
    "10.1.100.0/24"
  ]
}
```

We supply this new list data structure to the `ios_ping` module and we specify that we need to ping the tenth host within each subnet. As long as the ping succeeds, the task will succeed. However, if there is a connectivity problem from the router/switch to this host, the task will fail. We are using the `ignore_errors` parameter in order to ignore any failure that might occur owing to the fact that the host is unreachable/down, and to run any subsequent tasks. The following code snippet outlines the successful run:

```
TASK [P1T2: Ping Hosts in all VLANs] ****************************
 ok: [core01] => (item=10.1.10.0/24)
 ok: [core02] => (item=10.1.10.0/24)
 ok: [wan01] => (item=10.1.10.0/24)
 ok: [wan02] => (item=10.1.10.0/24)
 ok: [core01] => (item=10.1.20.0/24)
 ok: [core02] => (item=10.1.20.0/24)
 ok: [core01] => (item=10.1.100.0/24)
 ok: [wan01] => (item=10.1.20.0/24)
 ok: [wan02] => (item=10.1.20.0/24)
 ok: [core02] => (item=10.1.100.0/24)
 ok: [wan01] => (item=10.1.100.0/24)
 ok: [wan02] => (item=10.1.100.0/24)
```

Retrieving operational data from IOS devices

In this recipe, we will outline how to execute operational commands on IOS devices and store these outputs to text files for further processing. This allows us to capture any operational commands from IOS devices during pre- or post-validation after we perform any deployment so that we can compare the results.

Getting ready

In order to follow along with this recipe, an Ansible inventory file should be in place and the network should already be set up as per the previous recipes.

How to do it...

1. Create a new playbook called `pb_op_cmds.yml` and populate it with the following tasks to create the directory structure to save the output from the devices:

```
---
- name: "Play 1: Execute Operational Commands"
  hosts: network
  vars:
    config_folder: "configs"
    op_folder: "op_data"
    op_cmds:
      - show ip ospf neighbor
      - show ip route
  tasks:
    - name: "P1T1: Build Directories to Store Data"
      block:
        - name: "Create folder to store Device config"
          file:
            path: "{{ config_folder }}"
            state: directory
        - name: "Create Folder to store operational commands"
          file:
            path: "{{ op_folder }}"
            state: directory
      run_once: yes
      delegate_to: localhost
```

2. Update the `pb_op_cmds.yml` playbook and populate it with the following tasks to retrieve the running configuration from the devices:

```
- name: "P1T2: Get Running configs from Devices"
  ios_command:
    commands: show running-config
  register: show_run
- name: "P1T3: Save Running Config per Device"
  copy:
    content: "{{ show_run.stdout[0] }}"
    dest: "{{ config_folder }}/{{ inventory_hostname }}.cfg"
```

3. Update the playbook and populate it with the following tasks to retrieve the operational commands from the devices and save it:

```
- name: "P1T4: Create Folder per Device"
  file:
    path: "{{ op_folder}}/{{ inventory_hostname }}"
    state: directory
  delegate_to: localhost
- name: "P1T5: Get Operational Data from Devices"
  ios_command:
    commands: "{{ item }}"
  register: op_output
  loop: "{{ op_cmds }}"
- name: "P1T6: Save output per each node"
  copy:
    content: "{{ item.stdout[0] }}"
    dest: "{{ op_folder}}/{{ inventory_hostname }}/{{item.item | replace(' ', '_')}}.txt"
  loop: "{{ op_output.results }}"
```

How it works...

In this recipe, we are using the `ios_command` module in order to execute operational commands on the IOS devices, and saving them to text files. In order to achieve this goal, we perform the following steps:

- We create the folders that we will store the output to, and we create a folder called `configs` to store the running config of all the devices. We also create an `op_data` file to store the output of the operational commands that we will get from the devices.

- We then execute the `show running` command on all the IOS devices in our inventory and we register the output in a new variable called `show_run`.
- We use the copy module to save the output from the previous task to a file for each device. The output from the command run is saved in the `stdout` variable. As we executed a single command, the `stdout` variable only has a single item (`stdout[0]`).

Once we execute this task, we can see that the `configs` folder is populated as shown in the following output:

```
$ tree configs/
 configs/
 ├── access01.cfg
 ├── access02.cfg
 ├── core01.cfg
 ├── core02.cfg
 ├── isp01.cfg
 ├── wan01.cfg
 └── wan02.cfg
```

For the next part, we create a folder for each node to store the output from the multiple `show` commands that we will execute on the IOS devices.

We use the `ios_command` module to execute the `show` commands on the devices, and save all the output in a new variable called `op_output`. We use the copy execute command, `show ip route`, and we create a file for the output of this command with the name `show_ip_route.txt`.

After running this task, we can see that this is the current structure of the `op_data` folder:

```
$ tree op_data/
 op_data/
 ├── access01
 │   ├── show_ip_ospf_neighbor.txt
 │   └── show_ip_route.txt
 ├── access02
 │   ├── show_ip_ospf_neighbor.txt
 │   └── show_ip_route.txt
 ├── core01
 │   ├── show_ip_ospf_neighbor.txt
 │   └── show_ip_route.txt
 ├── core02
 │   ├── show_ip_ospf_neighbor.txt
 │   └── show_ip_route.txt
 ├── isp01
 │   ├── show_ip_ospf_neighbor.txt
```

```
|    └── show_ip_route.txt
├── wan01
|    ├── show_ip_ospf_neighbor.txt
|    └── show_ip_route.txt
└── wan02
    ├── show_ip_ospf_neighbor.txt
    └── show_ip_route.txt
```

We can check the content of one of the files to confirm that all the data has been stored:

```
$ head op_data/core01/show_ip_ospf_neighbor.txt
```

```
Neighbor ID     Pri   State           Dead Time   Address        Interface
10.100.1.3        0   FULL/  -        00:00:37    10.3.1.2
Ethernet1/0
10.100.1.2        0   FULL/  -        00:00:36    10.1.200.2     Vlan200
```

Validating network states with pyATS and Ansible

In this recipe, we will outline how to use Ansible and the Cisco pyATS Python library to execute and parse operational commands on Cisco devices. Using these parsed commands, we can validate various aspects of the network.

Getting ready

This recipe assumes that the network has already been built and configured as outlined in all the previous recipes.

How to do it...

1. Install the Python libraries needed for pyATS:

```
$ sudo pip3 install pyats genie
```

2. Create the `roles` directory and then create the `requirements.yml` file with the following data:

```
$ cat roles/requirements.yml
- src: https://github.com/CiscoDevNet/Ansible-pyats
  scm: git
  name: Ansible-pyats
```

3. Install the `Ansible-pyats` role as shown in the following code:

```
$ Ansible-galaxy install -r requirements.yml
```

4. Create a new playbook called `pb_validate_pyats.yml` and populate it with the following task to collect the `ospf neighbor` from the `wan` devices.

```
---

- name: Network Validation with pyATS
  hosts: wan
  roles:
    - Ansible-pyats
  vars:
    Ansible_connection: local
  tasks:
    - pyats_parse_command:
        command: show ip ospf neighbor
      register: ospf_output
      vars:
        Ansible_connection: network_cli
```

5. Update the playbook with the following tasks to extract the data for OSPF peer information:

```
    - name: "FACT >> Pyats OSPF Info"
      set_fact:
        pyats_ospf_data: "{{ ospf_output.structured.interfaces
}}"

    - name: " FACT >> Set OSPF peers"
      set_fact:
        OSPF_PEERS: "{{ wan_13_links[inventory_hostname] |
selectattr('ospf','equalto',true) | list }}"
```

6. Update the playbook with the following tasks to validate OSPF peers and the OSPF peer state:

```
- name: Validate Number of OSPF Peers
  assert:
    that:
      - pyats_ospf_data | length == OSPF_PEERS | length
  loop: "{{ OSPF_PEERS }}"

- name: Validate All Peers are in Full State
  assert:
    that:
      - pyats_ospf_data[item.name] |
json_query('neighbors.*.state') | first == 'FULL/ -'
  loop: "{{ OSPF_PEERS }}"
```

How it works...

In this recipe, we are exploring how to use the `pyATS` framework to perform network validation. `pyATS` is an open source Python library developed by Cisco as a testing framework for network testing. `Genie` is another Python library that provides parsing capabilities for transforming CLI-based output to Python data structures that we can consume in our automation scripts. Cisco released an Ansible role that uses the pyATS and Genie libraries. Within this role, there are multiple modules that we can use in order to build more robust Ansible validation playbooks to validate the network state. In order to start working with this role, we need to perform the following steps:

1. Install `pyats` and `enie` Python packages using `python-pip`.
2. Install the `Ansible-pyats` role using Ansible-galaxy.

In this recipe, we are using one of the modules within the `Ansible-pyats` role, which is `pyats_parse_command`. This module executes an operational command on the remote managed device and returns both the CLI output for this command and the parsed structured output for this command. The following code snippet outlines the structured data returned by this module for `ip ospf neigbor` on the `wan01` device:

```
"structured": {
  "interfaces": {
    "GigabitEthernet2": {
      "neighbors": {
        "10.100.1.1": {
          "address": "10.3.1.1",
          "dead_time": "00:00:37",
```

```
                    "priority": 0,
                    "state": "FULL/ -"
                }
            }
        }
      }
    }
```

We save the data returned by this module to the `ospf_output` variable and we use the `set_fact` module to capture the structured data returned by this module, before saving it to a new variable – `pyats_ospf_data`. Then, we use the `set_fact` module to filter the links defined in `wan_l3_interfaces` to just the ports that are enabled for OSPF.

Using the structured data returned by `pyats_parse_command`, we can validate this data and compare it with our OSPF peer definition using the `assert` module so as to validate the correct number of OSPF peers and their states.

To extract the OSPF peer state, we use the `json_query` filter to filter the returned data and provide just the OSPF state for each neighbor.

 We are setting `Ansible_connection` to `local` on the play level, and setting it to `network_cli` on the `pyats_parse_command` task level, since we only need to connect to the device in this task. All the other tasks can run locally on the Ansible machine.

See also...

For more information regarding the PyATS and Genie libraries and how to use them for network testing, please consult the following URL:

```
https://developer.cisco.com/docs/pyats/#!introduction/pyats-genie
```

For more information regarding `json_query` and its syntax, please consult the following URLs:

```
https://docs.Ansible.com/Ansible/latest/user_guide/playbooks_filters.html#json-
query-filter
http://jmespath.org/tutorial.html
```

3
Automating Juniper Devices in the Service Providers Using Ansible

In this chapter, we will outline how to automate Juniper devices running the Junos OS software in a typical **service provider** (**SP**) environment. We will explore how to interact with Juniper devices using Ansible, and how to provision different services and protocols on Juniper devices using various Ansible modules. We will base our illustration on the following sample network diagram of a basic SP network:

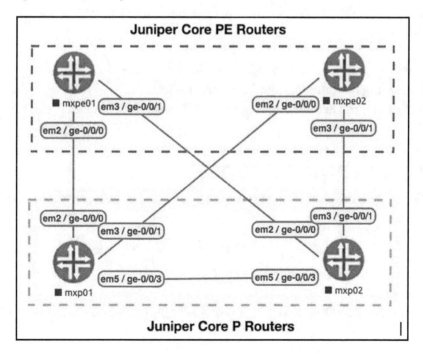

The following table outlines the devices in our sample topology and their respective management **Internet Protocols (IPs)**:

Device	Role	Vendor	Management (MGMT) Port	MGMT IP
mxp01	P Router	Juniper vMX 14.1	fxp0	172.20.1.2
mxp02	P Router	Juniper vMX 14.1	fxp0	172.20.1.3
mxpe01	PE Router	Juniper vMX 14.1	fxp0	172.20.1.4
mxpe02	PE Router	Juniper vMX 17.1	fxp0	172.20.1.5

The main recipes covered in this chapter are as follows:

- Building the network inventory
- Connecting and authenticating to Juniper devices
- Enabling the **Network Configuration Protocol (NETCONF)** on Junos OS devices
- Configuring generic system options on Juniper devices
- Configuring interfaces on Juniper devices
- Configuring **Open Shortest Path First (OSPF)** on Juniper devices
- Configuring **Multiprotocol Label Switching (MPLS)** on Juniper devices
- Configuring the **Border Gate Protocol (BGP)** on Juniper devices
- Deploying configuration on Juniper devices
- Configuring the **Layer 3 virtual private network (L3VPN)** service on Juniper devices
- Gathering Juniper device facts using Ansible
- Validating network reachability on Juniper devices
- Retrieving operational data from Juniper devices
- Validating the network state using PyEZ operational tables

Technical requirements

The code files for this chapter can be found here: `https://github.com/PacktPublishing/Network-Automation-Cookbook/tree/master/ch3_junos`.

The following are the software releases on which this chapter is based:

- Ansible machine running CentOS 7
- Ansible 2.9
- Juniper **Virtual MX (vMX)** running Junos OS 14.1R8 and Junos OS 17.1R1 release

Check out the following video to see the Code in Action:
`https://bit.ly/3ajF4Mp`

Building the network inventory

In this recipe, we will outline how to build and structure the Ansible inventory to describe the sample SP network setup outlined previously. The Ansible inventory is a pivotal part in Ansible, as it defines and groups devices that should be managed by Ansible.

Getting ready

We create a new folder that will host all the files that we will create in this chapter. The new folder is named ch3_junos.

How to do it...

1. Inside the new folder, ch3_junos, we create a hosts file with the following content:

```
$ cat hosts

[pe]
mxpe01 Ansible_host=172.20.1.3
mxpe02 Ansible_host=172.20.1.4

[p]
mxp01 Ansible_host=172.20.1.2
mxp02 Ansible_host=172.20.1.6

[junos]
mxpe[01:02]
mxp[01:02]

[core:children]
pe
p
```

2. Create an `Ansible.cfg` file, as shown in the following code:

```
$ cat Ansible.cfg

[defaults]
inventory=hosts
retry_files_enabled=False
gathering=explicit
host_key_checking=False
```

How it works...

We build the Ansible inventory using the `hosts` file and we define multiple groups in order to group the different devices in our network infrastructure, as follows:

- We create the `PE` group, which references all the MPLS **Provider Edge** (**PE**) nodes in our topology.
- We create the `P` group, which references all the MPLS **Provider** (**P**) nodes in our topology.
- We create the `junos` group, which references all the devices running Junos OS as the OS.
- We create the `core parent` group, which references both the `PE` and `P` groups.

Finally, we create the `Ansible.cfg` file and configure it to point to our `hosts` file, to be used as the Ansible inventory file. We set the `gathering` to `explicit` in order to disable the setup module, which runs by default to discover facts for the managed hosts. Disabling the setup module is mandatory since the setup module will fail when run against network devices.

We can validate that our Ansible inventory is structured and written correctly by typing the following command:

```
$ Ansible-inventory --list
    "all": {
        "children": [
            "core",
            "junos",
            "ungrouped"
        ]
    },
    "core": {
        "children": [
```

```
                "p",
                "pe"
            ]
        },
        "junos": {
            "hosts": [
                "mxp01",
                "mxp02",
                "mxpe01",
                "mxpe02"
            ]
        },
        "p": {
            "hosts": [
                "mxp01",
                "mxp02"
            ]
        },
        "pe": {
            "hosts": [
                "mxpe01",
                "mxpe02"
            ]
        }
    }
```

Connecting and authenticating to Juniper devices

In this recipe, we will outline how to connect and authenticate to Juniper devices from Ansible via **Secure Shell** (**SSH**), in order to start managing the Juniper devices. We are going to outline how to use SSH keys as the authentication method to establish communication between Ansible and the Juniper devices.

Getting ready

In order to follow along with this recipe, an Ansible inventory file should be constructed as per the previous recipe. IP reachability between the Ansible control machine and all the devices in the network must be configured.

How to do it...

1. On the Ansible machine, create the private and public SSH keys in our `ch3_junos` working directory, as shown in the following code:

```
$ SSH-keygen -t rsa -b 2048 -f Ansible_SSH_key

Generating public/private rsa key pair.
Enter passphrase (empty for no passphrase):
Enter same passphrase again:
Your identification has been saved in Ansible_SSH_key.
Your public key has been saved in Ansible_SSH_key.pub.
The key fingerprint is:
SHA256:aCqgMYKAWIkv3nVz/q9cYp+2n3doD9jpgw/jeWWcVWI
Ansible@centos7.localdomain
```

2. Capture the public key that was created in the previous step, as follows:

```
$ cat Ansible_SSH_key.pub
 SSH-rsa SSH-rsa
AAAAB3NzaC1yc2EAAAADAQABAAABAQC0/wvdC5ycAanRorlfMYDMAv5OTcYAALlE2bd
boajsQPQNEw1Li3N0J50OJBWXX+FFQuF7JKpM32vNQjQN7BgyaBWQGxv+Nj0ViVP+8X
8Wuif0m6bFxBYSaPbIbGogDjPu4qU90Iv48NGOZpcPLqZthtuN7yZKPshX/0YJtXd2q
uUsVhzVpJnncXZMb4DZQeOin7+JVRRrDz6KP6meIylf35mhG3CV5VqpoMjYTzkDiHwI
rFWVMydd4C77RQu27N2HozUtZgJy9KD8qIJYVdP6skzvp49IdInwhjOA+CugFQuhYhH
SoQxRxpws5RZlvrN7/0h0Ahc3OwHaUWD+P7lz Ansible@centos7.localdomain
```

3. On the Juniper devices, add a new user called `admin` and designate that we will use SSH keys for authentication for this user. Copy the public SSH key that was created on the Ansible machine to the device, as shown in the following code:

```
[edit system login]
Ansible@mxpe01# show
user admin {
  uid 2001;
  class super-user;
  authentication {
    SSH-rsa " SSH-rsa
AAAAB3NzaC1yc2EAAAADAQABAAABAQC0/wvdC5ycAanRorlfMYDMAv5OTcYAALlE2bd
boajsQPQNEw1Li3N0J50OJBWXX+FFQuF7JKpM32vNQjQN7BgyaBWQGxv+Nj0ViVP+8X
8Wuif0m6bFxBYSaPbIbGogDjPu4qU90Iv48NGOZpcPLqZthtuN7yZKPshX/0YJtXd2q
uUsVhzVpJnncXZMb4DZQeOin7+JVRRrDz6KP6meIylf35mhG3CV5VqpoMjYTzkDiHwI
rFWVMydd4C77RQu27N2HozUtZgJy9KD8qIJYVdP6skzvp49IdInwhjOA+CugFQuhYhH
SoQxRxpws5RZlvrN7/0h0Ahc3OwHaUWD+P7lz Ansible@centos7.localdomain";
## SECRET-DATA
  }
}
```

How it works...

We start by creating the public and private SSH keys on the Ansible control machine, using the SSH-keygen command and specifying the following options:

- We specify the encryption algorithm with the -t option, and we set it to rsa.
- We specify the size of the encryption key using the -b option, and we set the size to 2048 bits.
- We specify the location to save the private and public keys using the -f option, and we specify the name for the public and private key that will be generated, which will be Ansible_SSH_key.

Once we run the command, we will see that the following two files (the private and public SSH keys) are generated, as shown here:

```
$ ls -la | grep Ansible_SSH_key
-rw------- 1 Ansible Ansible 1679 Dec 31 23:41 Ansible_SSH_key
-rw-r--r-- 1 Ansible Ansible 409 Dec 31 23:41 Ansible_SSH_key.pub
```

On all the Juniper devices in our inventory, we create the admin user and we specify that we will use SSH keys for authentication. We paste the contents of the public key that we have created on the Ansible control machine under the authentication stanza for this new user. With this configuration, any host who has the corresponding private key can authenticate and log in to the Juniper devices as the admin user.

In order to test and validate that we have successfully logged in to the Junos OS devices from the compute nodes, we can test this using the Ansible command shown in the following code:

```
$ Ansible all -m ping -u admin --private-key Ansible_SSH_key -c network_cli

mxp02 | SUCCESS => {
  "changed": false,
  "ping": "pong"
}
mxpe02 | SUCCESS => {
  "changed": false,
  "ping": "pong"
}
mxpe01 | SUCCESS => {
  "changed": false,
  "ping": "pong"
}
mxp01 | SUCCESS => {
  "changed": false,
```

```
    "ping": "pong"
}
```

We specify the username to connect to the devices using the –u option and we specify the private SSH key using the –private-key option. Finally, we use the –c option in order to specify the connection plugin used to connect to the managed devices, and, in this case, we use the network_cli connection plugin to open an SSH session with the managed Juniper devices.

There's more...

In order to use the SSH keys that we have generated in our playbooks, we can specify the username and the SSH private key file that we will use to authenticate to our Juniper devices as host or group variables in Ansible. In our case, we will set these variables as group variables for the junos group. We create the group_vars directory, and we create the junos.yml file, and we specify the variables as shown in the following code:

```
$ cat group_vars/junos.yml

Ansible_user: admin
 Ansible_SSH_private_key_file: Ansible_SSH_key
```

We test the connection between Ansible and our devices again using the Ansible command; however, this time, without specifying any parameters, as shown in the following code:

```
$ Ansible all –m ping –c network_cli

mxp02 | SUCCESS => {
   "changed": false,
   "ping": "pong"
}
mxpe02 | SUCCESS => {
   "changed": false,
   "ping": "pong"
}
mxpe01 | SUCCESS => {
   "changed": false,
   "ping": "pong"
}
mxp01 | SUCCESS => {
   "changed": false,
   "ping": "pong"
}
```

Enabling NETCONF on Junos OS devices

In this recipe, we will outline how to enable the NETCONF protocol on Junos OS devices. This task is critical since we will use the NETCONF API in all the future recipes to manage the Juniper devices. The NETCONF API provides several advantages compared to the traditional SSH access method, and that is why we will use it in all our interactions with the Junos OS devices.

Getting ready

As a prerequisite for this recipe, an Ansible inventory file must be present, as well as the SSH authentication being deployed and working, as per the previous recipe.

How to do it...

1. Create a new playbook called `pb_jnpr_net_build.yml`, as shown in the following code:

```
$ cat pb_jnpr_net_build.yml

- name: Build Juniper SP Network
  hosts: junos
  tasks:
    - name: "Enable NETCONF"
      junos_netconf:
        netconf_port: 830
        state: present
      vars:
        Ansible_connection: network_cli
      tags: netconf
```

2. Update the `group_vars/junos.yml` file with the connection details, as shown in the following code:

```
$ cat group_vars/junos.yml

Ansible_network_os: junos
Ansible_connection: netconf
```

How it works...

In order to start interacting with the Junos OS devices via NETCONF, we need to enable it first, therefore we need to SSH into the device initially and enable NETCONF. That is why we are using the `network_cli` Ansible connection in order to connect with the Junos OS devices via traditional SSH. In order to use the `network_cli` connection plugin, we need to set `Ansible_network_os` as `junos`.

Since we are going to use the NETCONF API in all interactions with Juniper devices in all coming recipes, we enabled the `network_cli` plugin only for the `junos_netconf` task in this playbook via the `vars` attribute. However, for all future tasks that we will add in this playbook, we will use the `netconf` connection specified in the `Ansible_connection` attribute in the `group_vars/junos.yml` file.

We create a new playbook called `pb_jnpr_net_build.yml`, and in the first task, we use the `junos_netconf` module to enable the NETCONF protocol on the remote Junos OS devices. We state the NETCONF port that will be used (by default, it is `830`), and we outline that this configuration must be present on the remote devices via the `state: present` directive.

Once we run the playbook, we will see that all the Junos OS devices are configured with NETCONF, as shown in the following code:

```
admin@mxpe01# show system services
SSH;
netconf {
  SSH {
    port 830;
  }
}
```

Configuring generic system options on Juniper devices

In this recipe, we will outline how to configure some generic system options such as hostname and **Domain Name System** (**DNS**) servers, and provision users on Juniper devices.

Getting ready

To follow along with this recipe, an Ansible inventory is assumed to be already set up, and NETCONF is enabled on all Juniper devices, as per the previous recipe.

How to do it...

1. Update the `group_vars/all.yml` file with the following parameters to define the various system-level parameters such as `dns` and system users, as shown in the following code:

```
$ cat group_vars/all.yml
tmp_dir: ./tmp
config_dir: ./configs
global:
  dns:
  - 172.20.1.1
  - 172.20.1.15
  root_pwd: $1$ciI4raxU$XfCVzABJKdALim0aWVMq10
  users:
  -   role: super-user
      SSH_key: Ansible_SSH_key.pub
      username: admin
  -   hash: $1$mR940Z9C$ipX9sLKTRDeljQXvWFfJm1
      passwd: 14161C180506262E757A60
      role: super-user
      username: Ansible
```

2. Create a new playbook called `pb_jnpr_basic_config.yml` with the following tasks, to set up `dns`, `hostname` and system users on Juniper devices:

```
$ cat pb_jnpr_basic_config.yml
---
- name: Configure Juniper Devices
  hosts: junos
  tasks:
    - name: "Conifgure Basic System config"
      junos_system:
        hostname: "{{ inventory_hostname }}"
        name_servers: "{{ global.dns }}"
        state: present
    - name: "Configure Users"
      junos_user:
        name: "{{ item.username }}"
```

```
        role: "{{ item.role }}"
        SSHkey: "{{ lookup ('file', item.SSH_key) }}"
        state: present
    with_items: "{{ global.users |
selectattr('SSH_key','defined') | list }}"
```

How it works...

Ansible provides declarative modules to configure various system-level parameters on Juniper devices. The `junos_system` Ansible module enables us to set up the hostname and the DNS servers on the Juniper devices. The `junos_user` module provides us with the ability to set up the basic parameters for the system users on a Juniper device. In this example, we set up all the users who have SSH keys as their authentication method, and we loop over the `users` data structure and select only the users with the `SSH_key` option defined.

Once we run this playbook, we can see that the configuration on the devices is updated, as shown in the following code block:

```
$ Ansible@mxpe01# show system
host-name mxpe01;
}
name-server {
    172.20.1.1;
    172.20.1.15;
}
login {
    user admin {
        uid 2001;
        class super-user;
        authentication {
            SSH-rsa "SSH-rsa
AAAAB3NzaC1yc2EAAAADAQABAAABAQC0/wvdC5ycAanRor1fMYDMAv5OTcYAAL1E2bdboajsQPQ
NEw1Li3N0J5OOJBWXX+FFQuF7JKpM32vNQjQN7BgyaBWQGxv+Nj0ViVP+8X8Wuif0m6bFxBYSaP
bIbGogDjPu4qU90Iv48NGOZpcPLqZthtuN7yZKPshX/0YJtXd2quUsVhzVpJnncXZMb4DZQeOin
7+JVRRrDz6KP6meIylf35mhG3CV5VqpoMjYTzkDiHwIrFWVMydd4C77RQu27N2HozUtZgJy9KD8
qIJYVdP6skzvp49IdInwhjOA+CugFQuhYhHSoQxRxpws5RZ1vrN7/0h0Ahc3OwHaUWD+P71z
Ansible@centos7.localdomain"; ## SECRET-DATA
        }
    }
```

There's more...

The declarative Ansible modules that we have outlined in this section provide a simple way to configure the basic system-level parameters for Juniper devices. However, they might not cover all the parameters that we need to set up on a Juniper device. In order to have more control and flexibility to configure the system-level parameters on a Juniper device, we can use Jinja2 templates along with the Ansible `template` module to generate the specific system-level configuration needed for our deployment. In this section, we will outline this method in order to achieve this goal, and this is the method that we will use in subsequent recipes to generate the configuration for the other devices.

We are going to reuse this method to generate the configuration for our Juniper devices for different sections, such as system, interfaces, OSPF, and MPLS. We are going to create an Ansible role in order to include all the Jinja2 templates and tasks required to generate the final configuration that we will push to our devices. The following procedures outline the steps needed to create the role and to use this role to generate the configuration:

1. Create a new `roles` directory and add a new role called `build_router_config` with the following directory structure:

```
$ tree roles/
 roles/
 └── build_router_config
     ├── tasks
     └── templates
```

2. Under the `tasks` folder, create a `build_config_dir.yml` YAML file to create the required folders to store the configuration that will be generated, as follows:

```
$ cat roles/build_router_config/tasks/build_config_dir.yml

---
- name: Create Config Directory
  file: path={{config_dir}} state=directory
  run_once: yes

- name: Create Temp Directory per Node
  file: path={{tmp_dir}}/{{inventory_hostname}} state=directory

- name: SET FACT >> Build Directory
  set_fact:
  build_dir: "{{tmp_dir}}/{{inventory_hostname}}"
```

3. Under the `templates` folder, create a new folder called `junos`, and within this folder, create a new Jinja2 template called `mgmt.j2`, with the following content:

```
$ cat roles/build_router_config/templates/junos/mgmt.j2

system {
    host-name {{inventory_hostname}};
    no-redirects;
{%  if global.dns is defined %}
    name-server {
{%      for dns_server in global.dns %}
        {{dns_server}};
{%      endfor %}
    }
{%  endif %}
    root-authentication {
        encrypted-password "{{ global.root_pwd}}"; ## SECRET-DATA
    }
    login {
{%      for user in global.users if user.hash is defined %}
        user {{ user.username }} {
            class super-user;
            authentication {
                encrypted-password "{{user.hash}}"; ## SECRET-DATA
            }
        }
{%      endfor %}
{%      for user in global.users if user.SSH_key is defined %}
        user {{ user.username }} {
            class {{ user.role }};
            authentication {
                SSH-rsa "{{lookup('file',user.SSH_key)}}"; ##
SECRET-DATA
            }
        }
{%      endfor %}
    }
}
```

4. Under the `tasks` folder, create a new YAML file called `build_device_config.yml`, with the following task to create the system configuration:

```
$ cat roles/build_router_config/tasks/build_device_config.yml

---
- name: "System Configuration"
```

```
template:
  src: "{{Ansible_network_os}}/mgmt.j2"
  dest: "{{build_dir}}/00_mgmt.cfg"
tags: mgmt
```

5. Create a `main.yml` file under the `tasks` folder, with the following tasks:

```
$ cat roles/build_router_config/tasks/main.yml

---
- name: Build Required Directories
  import_tasks: build_config_dir.yml

- name: Build Device Configuration
  import_tasks: build_device_config.yml

- name: "Remove Old Assembled Config"
  file:
    path: "{{config_dir}}/{{ inventory_hostname }}.cfg"
    state: absent

- name: Build Final Device Configuration
  assemble:
    src: "{{ build_dir }}"
    dest: "{{config_dir}}/{{ inventory_hostname }}.cfg"

- name: Remove Build Directory
  file: path={{ tmp_dir }} state=absent
  run_once: yes
```

6. Update the `pb_jnpr_net_build.yml` playbook with the following task to generate the configuration for all Juniper devices in our inventory:

```
$ cat pb_jnpr_net_build.yml

- name: Build Device Configuration
  import_role:
    name: build_router_config
  vars:
    Ansible_connection: local
  tags: build
```

In this method, we create a role called `build_router_config` and we create a new Jinja2 template called `mgmt.j2`, which includes the template for Junos OS system-level configuration. We use the Ansible `template` module in order to render the Jinja2 template with the Ansible variables defined under the `group_vars/all.yml` file. In order to save the configuration for each device, we create the `configs` folder directory, which stores the final configuration for each device.

Since we will use this approach in order to generate the configuration for each section (MGMT, OSPF, MPLS, and so on), we will segment each section into a separate Jinja2 template, and we will generate each section in a separate file. We use the `assemble` module in order to group all these different sections into a single configuration file, which we will store in the `configs` directory. This is the `final` and `assembled` configuration file for each device. We store the temporary configuration snippets for each section in a temporary folder for each device, and we delete this temporary folder at the end of the playbook run. This is because we assembled the final configuration for the device, and we don't require these configuration snippets anymore.

 In this playbook, we set the `Ansible_connection` to `local` as we don't need to connect to the devices in order to run any of the tasks within our role. We are only generating the configuration on the Ansible control machine, therefore all the tasks need to run locally on the Ansible control machine. Therefore, there is no need to connect to the remotely managed nodes.

Once we run the playbook, we can see that the following configuration files are created inside the `configs` directory:

```
$ tree configs/
 configs/
 ├──── mxp01.cfg
 ├──── mxp02.cfg
 ├──── mxpe01.cfg
 └──── mxpe02.cfg
```

We can see the configuration generated for the `mxpe01` device as an example, as follows:

```
$ cat configs/mxpe01.cfg
system {
    host-name mxpe01;
    no-redirects;
    name-server {
        172.20.1.1;
        172.20.1.15;
```

```
        }
        root-authentication {
            encrypted-password "$1$ciI4raxU$XfCVzABJKdALim0aWVMql0"; ## SECRET-
DATA
        }
        login {
            user Ansible {
                class super-user;
                authentication {
                    encrypted-password "$1$mR940Z9C$ipX9sLKTRDeljQXvWFfJm1"; ##
SECRET-DATA
                }
            }
            user admin {
                class super-user;
                authentication {
                    SSH-rsa "SSH-rsa
AAAAB3NzaC1yc2EAAAADAQABAAABAQC0/wvdC5ycAanRor1fMYDMAv5OTcYAAL1E2bdboajsQPQ
NEw1Li3N0J50OJBWXX+FFQuF7JKpM32vNQjQN7BgyaBWQGxv+Nj0ViVP+8X8Wuif0m6bFxBYSaP
bIbGogDjPu4qU90Iv48NGOZpcPLqZthtuN7yZKPshX/0YJtXd2quUsVhzVpJnncXZMb4DZQeOin
7+JVRRrDz6KP6meIy1f35mhG3CV5VqpoMjYTzkDiHwIrFWVMydd4C77RQu27N2HozUtZgJy9KD8
qIJYVdP6skzvp49IdInwhjOA+CugFQuhYhHSoQxRxpws5RZlvrN7/0h0Ahc3OwHaUWD+P7lz
Ansible@centos7.localdomain"; ## SECRET-DATA
                }
            }
        }
    }
}
```

In subsequent recipes, we will outline how to push the generated configuration into the Juniper devices using another Ansible module.

See also...

For more information regarding the Ansible `template` module and the different parameters supported by this module, please consult the following URL: `https://docs.ansible.com/ansible/latest/modules/template_module.html`.

For more information regarding the Ansible `assemble` module and the different parameters supported by this module, please consult the following URL: `https://docs.ansible.com/ansible/latest/modules/assemble_module.html`.

Configuring interfaces on Juniper devices

In this recipe, we will outline how to manage interfaces on a Juniper device. This allows us to set different parameters for our interfaces, such as the **maximum transition unit** (**MTU**) and the IP addresses on Juniper devices.

Getting ready

To follow along with this recipe, an Ansible inventory is assumed to be already set up, and NETCONF is enabled on all Juniper devices, as per the previous recipe.

How to do it...

1. Update the `group_vars/all.yml` YAML file to include the following data for all the **point-to-point** (**P2P**) and loopback interfaces in our sample network topology:

```
p2p_ip:
  mxp01:
    - {port: ge-0/0/0, ip: 10.1.1.2 , peer: mxpe01, pport:
ge-0/0/0, peer_ip: 10.1.1.3}
    - {port: ge-0/0/1, ip: 10.1.1.4 , peer: mxpe02, pport:
ge-0/0/0, peer_ip: 10.1.1.5}
    - {port: ge-0/0/3, ip: 10.1.1.0 , peer: mxp02, pport: ge-0/0/3,
peer_ip: 10.1.1.1}
  mxp02:
<-- Output Trimmed for brevity ------>
  mxpe01:
<-- Output Trimmed for brevity ------>
  mxpe02:
<-- Output Trimmed for brevity ------>
  xrpe03:
<-- Output Trimmed for brevity ------>
lo_ip:
  mxp01: 10.100.1.254/32
  mxp02: 10.100.1.253/32
  mxpe01: 10.100.1.1/32
mxpe02: 10.100.1.2/32
xrpe03: 10.100.1.3/32
```

2. Update the `pb_jnpr_basic_config.yml` playbook with the following tasks to set up the interfaces on our Juniper devices:

```
- name: "Configure the Physical Interfaces"
  junos_interface:
    name: "{{ item.port }}"
    enabled: true
    description: "peer:{{item.peer}} remote_port:{{item.pport }}"
    mtu: "{{ global.mtu | default(1500) }}"
  with_items: "{{p2p_ip[inventory_hostname]}}"
  tags: intf

- name: "Configure IP Addresses"
  junos_l3_interface:
    name: "{{ item.port }}"
    ipv4: "{{ item.ip }}/{{ global.p2p_prefix }}"
    state: present
  with_items: "{{ p2p_ip[inventory_hostname] }}"
  tags: intf
```

How it works...

We define all the data for all the interfaces in our sample network topology under two main data structures in the `group_vars/all.yml` file. We use the `p2p_ip` dictionary to model all the P2P IP addresses in our sample network, and we use the `lo_ip` dictionary to specify the loopback IP addresses for our nodes.

We use the `junos_interface` Ansible module to enable the interfaces and set the basic parameters for the interfaces, such as MTU and description. We loop over the `p2p_ip` data structure for each device, and we set the correct parameters for each interface on all the devices in our network inventory. We use the `junos_l3_interface` Ansible module to set the correct IPv4 address on all the interfaces in our sample network topology across all the devices.

Once we run the playbook, we can see that the interfaces are configured as required, as shown on the `mxpe01` device:

```
Ansible@mxpe01# show interfaces
ge-0/0/0 {
  description "peer:mxp01 remote_port:ge-0/0/0";
  mtu 1500;
  unit 0 {
    family inet {
      address 10.1.1.3/31;
```

```
        }
      }
    }
  ge-0/0/1 {
    description "peer:mxp02 remote_port:ge-0/0/0";
    mtu 1500;
    unit 0 {
      family inet {
        address 10.1.1.9/31;
      }
    }
  }
}
```

There's more...

In case we need to have more control over the interface configuration, and to set parameters that are not covered by the declarative Ansible modules that we have outlined in this section, we can use Jinja2 templates to achieve this goal. Using the exact same approach that we outlined in the previous recipe for system configuration, we can generate the interface configuration needed for our Juniper devices.

Using the same Ansible role that we have created in the previous recipe, we can extend it to generate the interface configuration for our Juniper devices. We use the following steps in order to accomplish this task:

1. Create a new Jinja2 template file called intf.j2 in the templates folder, with the following data:

```
$ cat roles/build_router_config/templates/junos/intf.j2

interfaces {
{% for intf in p2p_ip[inventory_hostname] | sort(attribute='port')
%}
  {{ intf.port.split('.')[0] }} {
    description "peer:{{intf.peer}} -- peer_port: {{intf.pport}}"
    unit 0 {
      family inet {
        address {{intf.ip}}/{{global.p2p_prefix}};
      }
      family mpls;
    }
  }
{% endif %}
{% endfor %}
lo0 {
```

```
          unit 0 {
            family inet {
              address {{lo_ip[inventory_hostname]}};
            }
          }
        }
```

2. Update the `build_device_config.yml` file under the `tasks` directory with the new task to generate the interface configuration, as follows:

```
$ cat roles/build_router_config/tasks/build_device_config.yml

<-- Output Trimmed for brevity ------>

- name: "Interface Configuration"
  template:
    src: "{{Ansible_network_os}}/intf.j2"
    dest: "{{build_dir}}/01_intf.cfg"
  tags: intf
```

This is the generated interface configuration for the `mxp02` device after running the playbook:

```
interfaces {
    ge-0/0/0 {
        description "peer:mxpe01 -- peer_port: ge-0/0/1"
        unit 0 {
            family inet {
                address 10.1.1.8/31;
            }
            family mpls;
        }
    }
    ge-0/0/1 {
        description "peer:mxpe02 -- peer_port: ge-0/0/1"
        unit 0 {
            family inet {
                address 10.1.1.10/31;
            }
            family mpls;
        }
    }
<--   Output Trimmed for brevity ------>
    lo0 {
        unit 0 {
            family inet {
                address 10.100.1.253/32;
            }
```

```
        }
    }
```

Configuring OSPF on Juniper devices

In this recipe, we will outline how to configure OSPF on Juniper devices as the **interior gateway protocol** (**IGP**) in our sample network topology, along with different OSPF parameters such as OSPF link type and OSPF interface cost.

How to do it...

1. Create a new Jinja2 file, `ospf.j2`, in the `templates/junos` directory, with the following data:

```
$ cat roles/build_router_config/templates/junos/ospf.j2

 protocols {
    ospf {
       area {{global.ospf_area}} {
{%           for intf in
p2p_ip[inventory_hostname]|sort(attribute='port') %}
            interface {{ intf.port }} {
                interface-type p2p;
                metric {{intf.cost | default(100)}};
            }
{%           endfor %}
            interface lo0.0 {
                passive;
            }
        }
    }
}
```

2. In the `junos_build_config.yml` file inside the `tasks` folder, add the following task:

```
$ cat roles/build_router_config/tasks/build_device_config.yml

<-- Output Trimmed for brevity ------>

- name: "OSPF Configuration"
  template:
```

```
src: "{{Ansible_network_os}}/ospf.j2"
dest: "{{config_dir}}/{{ inventory_hostname }}/02_ospf.cfg"
```

How it works...

We use the same interface data that was declared in the p2p_ip data structure in the
all.yml file, in order to provision the OSPF configuration on the network devices in our
sample network. We use a new Jinja2 template defined in the ospf.j2 file under the
templates/junos directory to capture the OSPF configuration parameters (OSPF cost,
OSPF interface type, and so on) that need to be implemented on the Juniper devices.

Under the tasks/Juniper_build_config.yml file, we add a new task that uses
the ospf.j2 Jinja2 template to render the Jinja2 template, and output the OSPF
configuration section for each device outlined in our Ansible inventory.

The following snippet outlines the OSPF configuration generated for the mxpe01 device
after running the playbook with the new task:

```
$ cat configs/mxpe01.cfg

 <--    Output Trimmed for brevity ------>

protocols {
    ospf {
        area 0 {
            interface ge-0/0/0 {
                interface-type p2p;
                metric 100;
            }
            interface ge-0/0/1 {
                interface-type p2p;
                metric 100;
            }
            interface lo0.0 {
                passive;
            }
        }
    }
}
```

Configuring MPLS on Juniper devices

In this recipe, we will outline how to configure MPLS and some of the related protocols such as the **Label Distribution Protocol (LDP)** and the **Resource Reservation Protocol (RSVP)** on Juniper devices. We will outline how to generate the required MPLS configuration using Ansible and Jinja2 templates.

How to do it...

1. Create a new Jinja2 file, `mpls.j2`, under the `templates/junos` directory with the following data:

```
$ cat roles/build_router_config/templates/junos/mpls.j2

 protocols {
     ldp {
{%       for intf in
p2p_ip[inventory_hostname]|sort(attribute='port') %}
         interface {{intf.port}}.{{intf.vlan|default('0')}};
{%       endfor %}
         interface lo0.0;
     }
     rsvp {
{%       for intf in
p2p_ip[inventory_hostname]|sort(attribute='port') %}
         interface {{intf.port}}.{{intf.vlan|default('0')}};
{%       endfor %}
     }
     mpls {
{%       for intf in
p2p_ip[inventory_hostname]|sort(attribute='port') %}
         interface {{intf.port}}.{{intf.vlan|default('0')}};
{%       endfor %}
     }
 }
```

2. In the `build_device_config.yml` file inside the `tasks` folder, add the following task:

```
$ cat roles/build_router_config/tasks/build_device_config.yml

<-- Output Trimmed for brevity ------>

- name: "MPLS Configuration"
  template:
    src: "{{Ansible_network_os}}/mpls.j2"
    dest: "{{config_dir}}/{{ inventory_hostname }}/03_mpls.cfg"
```

How it works...

We use the same methodology as used to configure the interfaces and OSPF, by using a Jinja2 template to generate the needed MPLS configuration for the Juniper devices in our inventory, and the following is a sample of the MPLS configuration for the `mxpe02` router:

```
protocols {
    ldp {
        interface ge-0/0/0.0;
        interface ge-0/0/1.0;
        interface lo0.0;
    }
    rsvp {
        interface ge-0/0/0.0;
        interface ge-0/0/1.0;
    }
    mpls {
        interface ge-0/0/0.0;
        interface ge-0/0/1.0;
    }
}
```

Configuring BGP on Juniper devices

In this recipe, we will outline how to configure BGP on Juniper devices. We will outline how to set up BGP and BGP **Route Reflectors** (**RR**) as part of our sample topology, along with all the required BGP address families to support **virtual private network** (**VPN**) services.

How to do it...

1. Update the `group_vars/all.yml` file with the following BGP information:

```
bgp_topo:
  rr: mxp01
  af:
  - inet
  - inet-vpn
```

2. For each node within our Ansible inventory, we create a file called `bgp.yml` under the `host_vars` directory. This file holds the BGP information and BGP peers for each node. This is the example for the `mxpe01` device:

```
$ cat host_vars/mxpe01/bgp.yml

bgp_asn: 65400

bgp_peers:
  - local_as: 65400
    peer: 10.100.1.254
    remote_as: 65400
```

3. Create a new Jinja2 file, `bgp.j2`, under the `templates/junos` directory, with the following data:

```
$ cat roles/build_router_config/templates/junos/bgp.j2

 protocols {
{%  if bgp_peers is defined %}
    bgp {
        group Core {
            type internal;
            local-address {{ lo_ip[inventory_hostname] |
ipaddr('address')}};
{%          if bgp_topo.rr == inventory_hostname %}
            cluster {{ lo_ip[inventory_hostname].split('/')[0] }};
{%          endif %}
{%          for af in bgp_topo.af %}
{%          if af == 'inet' %}
            family inet {
                unicast;
            }
{%          endif %}
{%          if af == 'inet-vpn' %}
            family inet-vpn {
                unicast;
```

```
                        }
    {%         endif %}
    <--    Output Trimmed for brevity ------>
    {%         endfor %}
    {%         for p in bgp_peers %}
               neighbor {{ p.peer}};
    {%         endfor %}
            }
        }
    {%  endif %}
    }
```

4. In the `build_device_config.yml` file inside the `tasks` folder, add the following highlighted task:

```
$ cat roles/build_router_config/tasks/build_device_config.yml

<-- Output Trimmed for brevity ------>

- name: "BGP Configuration"
  template:
    src: "{{Ansible_network_os}}/bgp.j2"
    dest: "{{config_dir}}/{{ inventory_hostname }}/04_bgp.cfg"
```

How it works...

Using a similar approach to all the previous recipes, we use a Jinja2 template to generate the BGP configuration for the Juniper devices. However, in this section, we declare the BGP parameters in two different places, which are the `group_vars` and `host_vars` directories. In the `group_vars/all.yml` file, we declare the overall parameters for our BGP topology, such as the RR that we will use, and which address families we will configure. For each node in our inventory, we create a directory in the `host_vars` directory, and inside this directory, we create a `bgp.yml` file. This new YAML file holds the BGP peers for each node in our inventory. We use the data defined in these two locations to render the BGP configuration for each device.

This is a sample of the BGP configuration for the `mxp01` router, which is the RR in our topology:

```
protocols {
    bgp {
        group Core {
            type internal;
            local-address 10.100.1.254;
```

```
        cluster 10.100.1.254;
        family inet {
            unicast;
        }
        family inet-vpn {
            unicast;
        }
        neighbor 10.100.1.1;
        neighbor 10.100.1.2;
        neighbor 10.100.1.3;
    }
  }
}
```

Deploying configuration on Juniper devices

In this recipe, we will outline how to push the configuration that we have generated via Jinja2 templates in all the previous sections on Juniper devices using Ansible. This provides us with the capability to push any custom configuration that we create to our Juniper devices.

Getting ready

This recipe requires NETCONF to be enabled on the Juniper devices.

How to do it...

1. In the pb_junos_push_con file, add the following task:

```
$ cat pb_jnpr_net_build.yml

<-- Output Trimmed for brevity ------>

- name: "Deploy Configuration"
  junos_config:
    src: "{{config_dir}}/{{ inventory_hostname }}.cfg"
```

How it works...

In the previous recipe, we generated different sections of the configuration for Juniper devices such as interfaces, OSPF, MPLS, and BGP. We have used the `assemble` module in order to group all these sections per each node in a single configuration file. This file is stored in the `configs` folder for each device.

We use the `junos_config` module in order to push this configuration file that we have generated to each device in our network inventory. We can use the `update` parameter in order to control how the configuration that we want to push will be merged with the existing configuration on the device. It supports the following options:

- `merge`: This causes the configuration from our file to be merged with the configuration on the device (the candidate configuration). This option is the default option that is used.
- `Override/update`: This causes the configuration from our file to override the complete configuration on the managed device.

We can use the `check` mode to run our playbook in dry-run mode. In this case, we will push the configuration to the devices without committing to the configuration. This enables us to check the changes that will be pushed to the devices. This can be accomplished as follows:

```
$ Ansible-playbook pb_jnpr_net_build.yml -l mxpe01 --check -diff
```

We use the `-check` option to run the playbook in check mode (dry-run), and the `-diff` option in order to output the changes that will be pushed to our devices.

There's more...

The `junos_config` module also supports the rollback feature supported by Junos OS, therefore we can add another task to roll back the configuration and control how it is run, as follows:

```
$ cat pb_jnpr_net_build.yml

<-- Output Trimmed for brevity ------>

- name: "Rollback config"
  junos_config:
    rollback: "{{ rollback | default('1') | int }}"
  tags: rollback, never
```

In the preceding playbook, we roll back to the last version of the configuration. However, by changing the number in the `rollback` attribute, we can control the version of the configuration to which we want to roll back. Also, we are using the tags in order to only execute this task when we specify the `rollback` tag during the playbook run, as shown in the following code snippet:

```
$ Ansible-playbook pb_jnpr_net_build.yml --tags rollback -l mxpe01
```

We can specify another rollback point, as follows:

```
$ Ansible-playbook pb_jnpr_net_build.yml --tags rollback -l mxpe01 -e
rollback=2
```

See also...

For more information regarding the `junos_config` module and the different parameters supported by this module, please consult the following URL: `https://docs.ansible.com/ansible/latest/modules/junos_config_module.html`.

Configuring the L3VPN service on Juniper devices

In this recipe, we will outline how to model and configure L3VPNs on Juniper devices using various Ansible modules. This enables us to model our services using **Infrastructure as Code (IaC)** practices, and utilize Ansible to deploy and push the required configuration to have the L3VPN deployed on Juniper devices.

Getting ready

NETCONF must be enabled on the Juniper devices so as to use the Ansible modules in this recipe.

How to do it...

1. Create a new file called `l3vpn.yml` with the following content:

```
---
l3vpns:
  vpna:
    state: present
    rt: "target:{{bgp_asn}}:10"
    rd: "1:10"
    sites:
      - node: mxpe01
        port: ge-0/0/3.10
        ip: 172.10.1.1/24
      - node: mxpe02
        port: ge-0/0/3.10
        ip: 172.10.2.1/24
  vpnb:
    state: present
    rt: "target:{{bgp_asn}}:20"
    rd: "1:20"
    sites:
      - node: mxpe01
        port: ge-0/0/3.20
        ip: 172.20.1.1/24
      - node: mxpe02
        port: ge-0/0/3.20
        ip: 172.20.2.1/24
```

2. Create a new playbook called `pb_junos_l3vpn.yml` with the following tasks to configure the PE-**Customer Edge (CE)** links:

```
---
- name: "Deploy L3VPNs on Juniper Devices"
  hosts: pe
  vars_files:
    - "l3vpn.yml"
  tasks:
    - name: "Set VPN Interfaces"
      set_fact:
        l3vpn_intfs: "{{ l3vpn_intfs|default([]) +
          l3vpns[item.key].sites |
selectattr('node','equalto',inventory_hostname) | list}}"
      with_dict: "{{l3vpns}}"
      delegate_to: localhost

    - name: "Configure Interfaces for L3VPN Sites"
```

```
              junos_config:
                 lines:
                    - set interfaces {{ item.port.split('.')[0]}} vlan-
      tagging
                    - set interfaces {{ item.port}} vlan-id {{
      item.port.split('.')[1] }}
                 loop: "{{ l3vpn_intfs }}"
```

3. Add the following tasks in pb_junos_l3vpn.yml to set up the P2P IP address on the PE-CE links:

```
    - name: "Configure IP address for L3VPN Interfaces"
      junos_l3_interface:
        name: "{{ item.port.split('.')[0]}}"
        ipv4: "{{ item.ip }}"
        unit: "{{ item.port.split('.')[1] }}"
      loop: "{{l3vpn_intfs}}"
      tags: intf_ip
```

4. Add the following task in pb_junos_l3vpn.yml to configure the **virtual routings and forwardings (VRFs)** on the PE nodes:

```
    - name: "Configure L3VPNs"
      junos_vrf:
        name: "{{ item.key }}"
        rd: "{{item.value.rd}}"
        target: "{{ item.value.rt }}"
        interfaces: "{{ l3vpns[item.key].sites |
                        map(attribute='port') | list }}"
        state: "{{ item.value.state }}"
      with_dict: "{{l3vpns}}"
      when: inventory_hostname in (l3vpns[item.key].sites |
    map(attribute='node') | list)
        tags: l3vpn
```

How it works...

We create a new YAML file called l3vpn.yml that describes and models the L3VPN topology and data that we want to implement on all the Juniper devices on our topology. We include this file in the new playbook that we create in order to provision the L3VPNs on our network devices.

In the pb_junos_l3vpn.yml playbook, we use the data from the l3vpn.yml file to capture the data required to provision the L3VPN.

In the first task within our playbook, we create a new variable called `l3vpn_intfs` that captures all the L3VPN interfaces on each PE device, across all the VPNs that we have defined in our `l3vpn.yml` file. We loop over all the L3VPNs in this file, and we create a new list data structure for all the interfaces that belong to a specific node. The following snippet outlines the new data structure `l3vpn_intfs` for `mxpe01`:

```
ok: [mxpe01 -> localhost] => {
    "l3vpn_intfs": [
        {
            "ip": "172.10.1.1/24",
            "node": "mxpe01",
            "port": "ge-0/0/3.10"
        },
        {
            "ip": "172.20.1.1/24",
            "node": "mxpe01",
            "port": "ge-0/0/3.20"
        }
    ]
}
```

Next, in our playbook, we divide the provisioning of our L3VPN service to multiple tasks:

- We use the `junos_config` module to configure all the interfaces that are part of the L3VPNs to be ready to configure **virtual LANs** (**VLANs**) on these interfaces.
- We use the `junos_l3_interface` module to apply the IPv4 addresses on all these interfaces that are part of our L3VPN model.
- We use the `junos_vrf` module to configure the correct routing instances on the nodes, as per our L3VPN data model.

The following outlines the L3VPN configuration that is applied on `mxpe01` after running this playbook:

```
Ansible@mxpe01> show configuration routing-instances
vpna {
    instance-type vrf;
    interface ge-0/0/3.10;
    route-distinguisher 1:10;
    vrf-target target:65400:10;
    vrf-table-label;
}
vpnb {
    instance-type vrf;
    interface ge-0/0/3.20;
    route-distinguisher 1:20;
    vrf-target target:65400:20;
```

```
        vrf-table-label;
    }
```

See also...

For more information regarding the `junos_vrf` module and the different parameters supported by this module to provision L3VPNs on Juniper devices, please consult the following URL: `https://docs.ansible.com/ansible/latest/modules/junos_vrf_module.html#junos-vrf-module`.

Gathering Juniper device facts using Ansible

In this recipe, we will retrieve the basis system facts collected by Ansible for a Juniper device. These basic system facts provide us with a basic health check regarding our Juniper devices, which we can use to validate its operational state.

Getting ready

NETCONF must be enabled on the Juniper devices so as to use the Ansible modules in this recipe.

How to do it...

1. Create a new playbook, `pb_jnpr_facts.yml`, with the following task to collect the facts:

```
$ cat pb_jnpr_facts.yml

---
- name: Collect and Validate Juniper Facts
  hosts: junos
  tasks:
    - name: Collect Juniper Facts
      junos_facts:
```

2. Update the `pb_jnpr_facts.yml` playbook with the following tasks to create a facts report for each node in our inventory:

```
- name: Create Facts Folder
  file: path=device_facts state=directory
  run_once: yes

- name: Create Basic Device Facts Report
  blockinfile:
    path: "device_facts/{{ inventory_hostname }}.txt"
    block: |
      device_name: {{ Ansible_net_hostname }}
      model: {{ Ansible_net_system }} {{ Ansible_net_model }}
      os_version: {{ Ansible_net_version }}
      serial_number: {{ Ansible_net_serialnum }}
    create: yes
```

3. Update the playbook with the following task to validate the operational state for the core interfaces:

```
- name: Validate all Core Interface are Operational
  assert:
    that:
      - Ansible_net_interfaces[item.port]['oper-status'] ==
'up'
    fail_msg: "Interface {{item.port}} is not Operational "
  loop: "{{ p2p_ip[inventory_hostname] }}"
```

How it works...

Ansible provides a fact-gathering module to collect the basic system properties for Juniper devices and returns these facts in a consistent and structured data structure. We can use the facts collected by this module in order to validate the basic properties and operational state of our devices, and we can use this data to build simple reports that capture the state of our devices.

In this recipe, we use the `junos_facts` module to collect the device facts for all our Juniper devices. This module returns the basic facts collected by Ansible for each device in multiple variables, as follows:

```
"Ansible_net_serialnum": "VM5D112EFB39",
"Ansible_net_system": "junos",
"Ansible_net_version": "17.1R1.8",
"Ansible_network_os": "junos",
```

We use this data in order to build a fact report for each device using the `blockinfile` module, and we use this data to validate the operational state of the core interfaces of each device using the `assert` module.

Once we run our playbook, we can see that a facts report for each device is generated, as follows:

```
$ tree device_facts/

device_facts/
├──── mxp01.txt
├──── mxp02.txt
├──── mxpe01.txt
└──── mxpe02.txt


 $ cat device_facts/mxp01.txt

device_name: mxp01
 model: junos vmx
 os_version: 14.1R4.8
 serial_number: VM5701F131C6
```

In the final task, we use the `assert` module in order to validate that all the core interfaces on all the Juniper devices are operational. Ansible stores all the interfaces' operational status for the device under `Ansible_net_interfaces`. We use the data in this data structure to validate that the operational state is up. In the case that all the core interfaces are operational, the task will succeed—otherwise, the task will fail.

See also...

For more information regarding the `junos_facts` module and the different parameters supported by this module, please consult the following URL: `https://docs.ansible.com/ansible/latest/modules/junos_facts_module.html`.

Validating network reachability on Juniper devices

In this recipe, we will outline how to validate network reachability via `ping`, using Ansible on Juniper devices. This will enable us to validate network reachability and traffic forwarding across our sample network topology.

Getting ready

This recipe assumes that the network is already built and configured, as outlined in all the previous recipes.

How to do it...

1. Create a new playbook called `pb_junos_ping.yml` with the following task, to ping all core loopbacks within our sample network:

```
---
- name: "Validate Core Reachability"
  hosts: junos
  tasks:
    - name: "Ping Across All Loopback Interfaces"
      junos_ping:
        dest: "{{ item.value.split('/')[0] }}"
        interface: lo0.0
        size: 512
      with_dict: "{{lo_ip}}"
      vars:
        Ansible_connection: network_cli
      register: ping_rst
      ignore_errors: yes
```

2. Update the `pb_junos_ping.yml` playbook with the following task to create a custom report to capture the ping results:

```
    - name: Create Ping Report
      blockinfile:
        block: |
          Node | Destination | Packet Loss | Delay |
          -----| ------------| ------------| ------|
          {% for node in play_hosts %}
          {% for result in hostvars[node].ping_rst.results %}
          {% if result.rtt is defined %}
          {{ node }} | {{ result.item.value }} | {{
result.packet_loss }} | {{ result.rtt.avg }}
          {% else %}
          {{ node }} | {{ result.item.value }} | {{
result.packet_loss }} | 'N/A'
          {% endif %}
          {% endfor %}
          {% endfor %}
        path: ./ping_report.md
```

```
        create: yes
  run_once: yes
```

How it works...

We use the `junos_ping` module in order to ping from all the nodes in our network inventory to all the loopback interfaces defined in the `lo_ip` data structure, which is defined in the `group_vars/all.yml` file. This module connects to each device and executes ping to all the destinations, and validates that ping packets are reaching their intended destination. This module requires the use of the `network_cli` connection plugin, therefore we supply this parameter as a task variable in order to override the group-level NETCONF connection plugin defined at the group level.

We register the output of the module in order to use this data to generate the ping report. Finally, we set `ignore_errors` to `yes` in order to ignore any failed ping task that we might encounter, and ensure that we will run the subsequent tasks to create the report.

We use the `blockinfile` module in order to create a custom report in Markdown. We use a table layout in order to capture the ping results and display a table that captures these ping results. The following snippet captures the table generated for the `mxpe01` ping test report:

```
$ cat ping_report.md

# BEGIN ANSIBLE MANAGED BLOCK
 Node | Destination | Packet Loss | Delay |
 -----| ------------| ------------| ------|
 mxpe01 | 10.100.1.254/32 | 0% | 3.75
 mxpe01 | 10.100.1.253/32 | 0% | 2.09
 mxpe01 | 10.100.1.1/32 | 0% | 0.27
 mxpe01 | 10.100.1.2/32 | 0% | 4.72
 mxpe01 | 10.100.1.3/32 | 100% | 'N/A'
# END ANSIBLE MANAGED BLOCK
```

Here is the rendered Markdown table for the ping result:

Node	Destination	Packet Loss	Delay
mxpe01	10.100.1.254/32	0%	3.75
mxpe01	10.100.1.253/32	0%	2.09
mxpe01	10.100.1.1/32	0%	0.27
mxpe01	10.100.1.2/32	0%	4.72
mxpe01	10.100.1.3/32	100%	'N/A'

See also...

For more information regarding the `junos_ping` module and the different parameters supported by this module, please consult the following URL: `https://docs.ansible.com/ansible/latest/modules/junos_ping_module.html`.

Retrieving operational data from Juniper devices

In this recipe, we will outline how to execute operational commands on Juniper devices and store these outputs in text files for further processing.

Getting ready

NETCONF must be enabled on the Juniper devices in order to follow along with this recipe.

How to do it...

1. Install the `jxmlease` Python package, as follows:

```
$ pip3 install jxmlease
```

2. Create a new playbook called `pb_get_ospf_peers.yml` and populate it with the following task to extract OSPF peering information:

```
---
- name: "Get OSPF Status"
  hosts: junos
  tasks:
    - name: "Get OSPF Neighbours Data"
      junos_command:
        commands: show ospf neighbor
        display: xml
      register: ospf_output

    - name: "Extract OSPF Neighbour Data"
      set_fact:
        ospf_peers: "{{ ospf_output.output[0]['rpc-reply']\
                        ['ospf-neighbor-information']['ospf-
neighbor'] }}"
```

3. Update the `pb_get_ospf_peers.yml` playbook with the following task to validate that all OSPF peerings across all nodes are in a `Full` state:

```
    - name: "Validate All OSPF Peers are in Full State"
      assert:
        that: item['ospf-neighbor-state'] == 'Full'
        fail_msg: "Peer on Interface {{item['interface-name']}} is
Down"
        success_msg: "Peer on Interface {{item['interface-name']}}
is UP"
      loop: "{{ospf_peers}}"
```

How it works...

One of the advantages of using the NETCONF API to interact with Juniper devices is that we can get a structured output for all the operational commands that we execute on the Juniper devices. The output that the device returns to us over the NETCONF session is in XML, and Ansible uses a Python library called `jxmlease` to decode this XML and transform it to JSON for better representation. That is why our first task was to install the `jxmlease` Python package.

We use the `junos_command` module to send operational commands to a Juniper device, and we specify that we need XML as the output format that gets returned from the node. This XML data structure is transformed to JSON using the `jxmlease` package by Ansible. We save this data using the `register` keyword to a new variable called `ospf_output`. Here is a sample of the JSON data that is returned from this command:

```json
"msg": [
    {
        "rpc-reply": {
            "ospf-neighbor-information": {
                "ospf-neighbor": [
                    {
                        "activity-timer": "34",
                        "interface-name": "ge-0/0/0.0",
                        "neighbor-address": "10.1.1.2",
                        "neighbor-id": "10.100.1.254",
                        "neighbor-priority": "128",
                        "ospf-neighbor-state": "Full"
                    },
                    {
                        "activity-timer": "37",
                        "interface-name": "ge-0/0/1.0",
                        "neighbor-address": "10.1.1.8",
                        "neighbor-id": "10.100.1.253",
                        "neighbor-priority": "128",
                        "ospf-neighbor-state": "Full"
                    }
                ]
            }
        }
    }
]
```

All this data structure is contained in the `ospf_output.output[0]` variable, and we use the `set_fact` module to capture the `ospf-neigbour` data. After that, we use the `assert` module to loop through all the OSPF peers in this data structure and validate that the OSPF neighbor state is equal to `Full`. If all the OSPF peers are in a `Full` state, the task will succeed. However, if the OSPF state is in any other state, the task will fail.

There's more...

If we need to get the operational data from Juniper devices in text format for log collection, we can use the `junos_command` module without the `xml` display option, as shown in this new playbook:

```
$ cat pb_collect_output.yml

---
- name: Collect Network Logs
  hosts: junos
  vars:
    log_folder: "logs"
    op_cmds:
      - show ospf neighbor
  tasks:
    - name: "P1T1: Build Directories to Store Data"
      block:
        - name: "Create folder to store Device config"
          file:
          path: "{{ log_folder }}"
          state: directory
      run_once: yes
      delegate_to: localhost

    - name: "P1T2: Get Running configs from Devices"
      junos_command:
        commands: "{{ item }}"
      loop: "{{ op_cmds }}"
      register: logs_output

    - name: "P1T3: Save Running Config per Device"
      copy:
        content: "{{ item.stdout[0] }}"
        dest: "{{ log_folder }}/{{inventory_hostname}}_{{ item.item |
regex_replace(' ','_') }}.txt"
      loop: "{{ logs_output.results }}"
      delegate_to: localhost
```

This playbook will collect the `show ospf neigbor` command from all the devices, and store them in a new folder called `logs`. Here is the content of the `logs` folder after running the playbook:

```
$ tree logs
 logs
 ├──── mxp01_show_ospf_neighbor.txt
 ├──── mxp02_show_ospf_neighbor.txt
```

```
├──── mxpe01_show_ospf_neighbor.txt
└──── mxpe02_show_ospf_neighbor.txt
```

We can check the content of one of the files to confirm that the required output is captured:

```
$ cat logs/mxpe01_show_ospf_neighbor.txt

Address Interface State ID Pri Dead
 10.1.1.2 ge-0/0/0.0 Full 10.100.1.254 128 35
 10.1.1.8 ge-0/0/1.0 Full 10.100.1.253 128 37
```

Validating the network state using PyEZ operational tables

In this recipe, we will outline how to use Juniper custom Ansible modules to validate the network state. We are going to use the Juniper PyEZ Python library and PyEZ operational tables and views to validate the operational state for Junos OS devices.

Getting ready

NETCONF must be enabled on the Juniper devices in order to follow along with this recipe.

How to do it...

1. Install the `junos-eznc` Python package, as follows:

   ```
   $ pip3 install junos-eznc
   ```

2. Install the `Juniper.junos` Ansible role using `Ansible-galaxy`, as follows:

   ```
   $ Ansible-galaxy install Juniper.junos
   ```

3. Create a new playbook called `pb_jnpr_pyez_table.yml`, and populate it with the following task to extract BGP peering information using PyEZ tables:

   ```
   $ cat pb_jnpr_pyez_table.yml

   ---
   - name: Validate BGP State using PyEZ Tables
   ```

```
hosts: junos
roles:
  - Juniper.junos
tasks:
  - name: Retrieve BGP Neighbor Information Using PyEZ Table
    Juniper_junos_table:
      file: "bgp.yml"
    register: jnpr_pyez_bgp
```

4. Update the playbook with the following task to validate that all BGP peering across all nodes is operational:

```
- name: Validate all BGP Peers are operational
  assert:
    that:
      - item.peer in jnpr_pyez_bgp.resource |
map(attribute='peer_id') | list
        fail_msg: " BGP Peer {{ item.peer }} is Not Operational"
    loop: "{{ bgp_peers }}"
```

How it works...

In addition to the built-in Juniper modules that come pre-installed with Ansible that we have outlined in all our previous recipes, there are additional Ansible modules that are maintained by Juniper and are not part of the Ansible release. These modules are packaged in an Ansible role that is maintained in Ansible Galaxy, and all these modules are based on the Juniper PyEZ Python library that is also developed and maintained by Juniper.

The Juniper PyEZ Python library provides a simple and robust API in order to interact with Juniper devices and simplifies how to manage Juniper devices using Python. The Ansible modules maintained by Juniper are all dependent on the PyEZ Python library, and therefore the first task we need to perform is to ensure that PyEZ (junos-eznc) is installed on our Ansible control machine.

The Ansible modules maintained and developed by Juniper are packaged as an Ansible role, and they provide multiple modules with extra capabilities compared to the built-in Juniper modules that come as part of the Ansible release. We install this role using Ansible Galaxy in order to start to utilize these extra modules. The following snippet outlines the extra modules that are part of this role:

```
$ tree ~/.Ansible/roles/Juniper.junos/library/

/home/Ansible/.Ansible/roles/Juniper.junos/library/
├── Juniper_junos_command.py
```

```
├──── Juniper_junos_config.py
├──── Juniper_junos_facts.py
├──── Juniper_junos_jsnapy.py
├──── Juniper_junos_ping.py
├──── Juniper_junos_pmtud.py
├──── Juniper_junos_rpc.py
├──── Juniper_junos_software.py
├──── Juniper_junos_srx_cluster.py
├──── Juniper_junos_system.py
└──── Juniper_junos_table.py
```

In this recipe, we outline how to use the `Juniper_junos_table` Ansible module, which uses the PyEZ tables and views to execute operational commands on Juniper devices and extract specific information from the Juniper device. It also parses this information into a consistent data structure, which we can utilize in our automation scripts. In our playbook, our first task is to use the `Juniper_junos_table` module using the `bgp.yml` table definition (which is present as part of the `junos-eznc` installation). We do this to get the BGP peers on a device and return the relevant information in a consistent data structure. The following snippet outlines the BGP data returned by the `Juniper_junos_table` for the BGP information on `mxpe01`:

```
ok: [mxpe01] => {
    "jnpr_pyez_bgp": {
        "changed": false,
        "failed": false,
        "msg": "Successfully retrieved 1 items from bgpTable.",
        "resource": [
            {
                "local_address": "10.100.1.1+179",
                "local_as": "65400",
                "local_id": "10.100.1.1",
                "peer_as": "65400",
                "peer_id": "10.100.1.254",
                "route_received": [
                    "0",
                    "2",
                    "1",
                    "1"
                ]
            }
        ],
    }
}
```

The last task in our playbook is using the `assert` module in order to validate that all our BGP peers (defined under the `host_vars`) directory) are present in the returned data structure in the BGP table, which indicates that all the BGP peers are operational.

See also...

For more information regarding the Juniper Ansible modules maintained by Juniper, please consult the following URL: `https://www.juniper.net/documentation/en_US/junos-ansible/topics/reference/general/junos-ansible-modules-overview.html`.

For more information regarding PyEZ tables and views, please consult the following URL: `https://www.Juniper.net/documentation/en_US/junos-pyez/topics/concept/junos-pyez-tables-and-views-overview.html`.

4
Building Data Center Networks with Arista and Ansible

In this chapter, we will outline how to automate Arista switches in a typical data center environment in a leaf-spine architecture. We will explore how to interact with Arista devices using Ansible, and how to deploy **virtual local area networks** (**VLANs**) and **virtual extensible LANs** (**VXLANs**) in a **Border Gateway Protocol/Ethernet virtual private network** (**BGP/EVPN**) setup on the Arista switches using various Ansible modules. We will base our illustration on the following sample network diagram of a basic leaf-spine **data center network** (**DCN**):

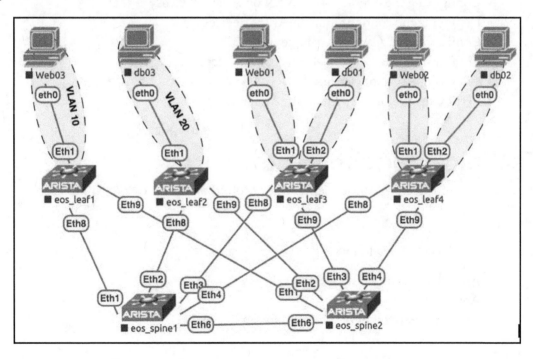

The following table outlines the devices in our sample topology and their respective management **internet protocols** (**IPs**):

Device	Role	Vendor	Management (MGMT) Port	MGMT IP
Spine01	Spine Switch	Arista vEOS 4.20	Management1	172.20.1.35
Spine02	Spine Switch	Arista vEOS 4.20	Management1	172.20.1.36
Leaf01	Leaf Switch	Arista vEOS 4.20	Management1	172.20.1.41
Leaf02	Leaf Switch	Arista vEOS 4.20	Management1	172.20.1.42
Leaf03	Leaf Switch	Arista vEOS 4.20	Management1	172.20.1.43
Leaf04	Leaf Switch	Arista vEOS 4.20	Management1	172.20.1.44

The main recipes covered in this chapter are as follows:

- Building the Ansible network inventory
- Connecting to and authenticating Arista devices from Ansible
- Enabling **extensible operating system** (**EOS**) **API** (**eAPI**) on Arista devices
- Configuring generic system options on Arista devices
- Configuring interfaces on Arista devices
- Configuring the underlay BGP on Arista devices
- Configuring the overlay BGP/EVPN on Arista devices
- Deploying the configuration on Arista devices
- Configuring VLANs on Arista devices
- Configuring VXLAN tunnels on Arista devices
- Gathering Arista device facts
- Retrieving operational data from Arista devices

Technical requirements

The code for all the recipes in this chapter can be found on the following GitHub repo: `https://github.com/PacktPublishing/Network-Automation-Cookbook/tree/master/ch4_arista`.

This chapter is based on the following software releases:

- Ansible machine running CentOS 7
- Ansible 2.9
- Arista **virtualized EOS** (**vEOS**) running EOS 4.20.1F

Check out the following video to see the Code in Action:
`https://bit.ly/3coydTp`

Building the Ansible network inventory

In this recipe, we will outline how to build and structure the Ansible inventory to describe our sample leaf-spine **direct current** (**DC**) network. The Ansible inventory is a pivotal part of Ansible as it outlines and groups devices that should be managed by Ansible.

Getting ready

We need to create a new folder that will host all the files that we will create in this chapter. The new folder should be named `ch4_arista`.

How to do it...

1. Inside the new folder (`ch4_arista`), we create a `hosts` file with the following content:

```
$ cat hosts

[leaf]
 leaf01  ansible_host=172.20.1.41
 leaf02  ansible_host=172.20.1.42
 leaf03  ansible_host=172.20.1.43
 leaf04  ansible_host=172.20.1.44

[spine]
 spine01  ansible_host=172.20.1.35
 spine02  ansible_host=172.20.1.36

[arista:children]
 leaf
 spine
```

2. Create an `ansible.cfg` file, as shown in the following code block:

```
$ cat ansible.cfg

[defaults]
 inventory=hosts
```

```
retry_files_enabled=False
gathering=explicit
host_key_checking=False
```

How it works...

Defining an Ansible inventory is mandatory, in order to describe and classify the devices in our network that should be managed by Ansible. In the Ansible inventory, we also specify the IP addresses through which Ansible will communicate with these managed devices, using the `ansible_host` parameter.

We built the Ansible inventory using the `hosts` file and we defined multiple groups in order to group the different devices in our topology. These groups are as follows:

- We created the `leaf` group, which references all the `leaf` switches in our topology.
- We created the `spine` group, which references all the `spine` switches in our topology.
- We created the `arista` group, which references both the `leaf` and `spine` groups.

Finally, we created the `ansible.cfg` file and configured it to point to our `hosts` file, to be used as the Ansible inventory file. Further, we disabled the `setup` module (by setting `gathering` to `explicit`), which is not needed when running Ansible against network nodes.

Connecting to and authenticating Arista devices from Ansible

In this recipe, we will outline how to connect to Arista devices from Ansible via **Secure Shell (SSH)** in order to start managing the devices from Ansible. We are going to use a username and password to authenticate the Arista devices in our topology.

Getting ready

In order to follow along with this recipe, an Ansible inventory file should be constructed as per the previous recipe. IP reachability between the Ansible control machine and all the devices in the network must also be implemented.

How to do it...

1. Inside the ch4_arista folder, create a group_vars folder.

2. Inside the group_vars folder, create an arista.yml file with the following content:

```
ansible_network_os: eos
ansible_connection: network_cli
ansible_user: ansible
ansible_ssh_pass: ansible123
```

3. On the Arista switches, we configure the username and password and enable SSH, as shown in the following code block:

```
!
username Ansible privilege 15 role network-admin secret sha512
$6$mfU4Ei0AORd6rage$5YObhOI1g0wNBK5onaKDpYJhLZ9138maJKgcOznzFdpM25T
f3rb0PWSojUSM
RQY0Y7.cexCFj5aFLY17tuNU1
!

  !
management ssh
   idle-timeout 300
   authentication mode password
   login timeout 300
!
```

4. On the Arista switches, configure the management interface with the correct IP addresses and place them in the required management **virtual routing and forwarding (VRF)**, as shown here:

```
vrf definition MGMT
 !
 ip routing vrf MGMT
 !
interface Management1
   vrf forwarding MGMT
   ip address $Ansible_host$
   no lldp transmit
   no lldp receive
!
```

How it works...

We specified the username and password that we will configure on all the Arista switches in the `arista.yml` file under the `group_vars` directory. This will apply these parameters to all the Arista switches in our inventory. On the Arista switches, we set up the username and password and enabled SSH, as well as set up the correct IP address (the one used in the `ansible_host` parameter in our inventory) on the management interface. We configured the management VRF and associated the management interface with this VRF.

 We are specifying the SSH password in plaintext in our Ansible variables. This is only for a lab setup; however, for production, we should use the Ansible vault to secure any sensitive information, as outlined in the previous chapters.

At this stage, we are using the `network_cli` connection method so as to use SSH to connect to the Arista switches. We can verify that the Ansible controller can reach and correctly log in to the devices with the following command:

```
$ ansible arista -m ping

  leaf03 | SUCCESS => {
      "changed": false,
      "ping": "pong"
}
leaf04 | SUCCESS => {
      "changed": false,
      "ping": "pong"
}
  <-- Output Omitted for brevity -->
```

Enabling eAPI on Arista devices

In this recipe, we will outline how to enable eAPI on Arista devices. eAPI is a **representational state transfer** (**REST**ful) API on Arista devices, which simplifies the management of such devices and provides a consistent and robust API to manage them. This task is critical since we will use eAPI in all future recipes to manage the Arista device.

Getting ready

As a prerequisite for this recipe, an Ansible inventory file must be present. The SSH authentication should also be deployed and working, as per the previous recipe.

How to do it...

1. Create an `all.yml` file inside the `group_vars` folder, with the following management VRF data:

```
$ cat  group_vars/all.yml

global:
  mgmt_vrf: MGMT
```

2. Create a new playbook called `pb_eos_enable_eapi.yml`, as shown in the following code block:

```
$ cat pb_eos_eanble_eapi.yml
---
- name: "Enable eAPI on Arista Switches"
  hosts: arista
  vars:
    ansible_connection: network_cli
  tasks:
    - name: "Enable eAPI"
      eos_eapi:
        https_port: 443
        https: yes
        state: started
```

3. Update the `pb_eos_enable_eapi.yml` playbook with the following task, to enable eAPI under the management VRF:

```
- name: "Enable eAPI under VRF"
  eos_eapi:
    state: started
    vrf: "{{global.mgmt_vrf}}"
```

4. Update the `arista.yml` file inside the `group_vars` folder with the connection setting to use eAPI as the connection plugin:

```
$ cat group_vars/arista.yml

ansible_network_os: eos
ansible_connection: httpapi
ansible_httpapi_use_ssl: yes
ansible_httpapi_validate_certs: no
```

How it works...

In order to start interacting with the Arista devices via eAPI, we need to enable it first; thus, we need to SSH into the device initially and enable eAPI. That is why, in this recipe, we are using the `network_cli` Ansible connection in order to connect with the Arista devices via traditional SSH. Since we are going to use eAPI in all interactions with Arista devices in all coming recipes, we enabled `network_cli` only under the `vars` parameter on the playbook level, in order to override any group- or host-level setting for the `ansible_connection` setting.

We created a new playbook called `pb_eos_enable_eapi.yml`, and, in the first task, we used the `eos_eapi` module to enable eAPI protocol on the remote Arista devices. We specified that we will use the **Hypertext Transfer Protocol Secure (HTTPS)** and the standard HTTPS port, which is `443`. In the second task, we used the `eos_eapi` module in order to enable eAPI only under a specific VRF, which is the management VRF that we are using to manage our devices.

Finally, in order to start managing the Arista devices using eAPI, we modified our Ansible connection settings, which we defined in the `group_vars/arista.yml` file, and we included the following settings:

- `ansible_connection` was set to `httpapi`.
- `ansible_httpapi_use_ssl` was set to `yes` in order to force the use of HTTPS and not HTTP.
- `ansible_httpapi_validate_certs` was set to `no` in order to disable certificate validations (since we are using the default certificate on the Arista devices, which is not signed by a trusted **certificate authority (CA)**).

Once we run the playbook, we will see that all the Arista devices are configured with eAPI, as shown in the following code block:

```
!
management api http-commands
   no shutdown
   !
   vrf MGMT
      no shutdown
!
```

We can validate that we are using the correct connection setting and that Ansible is able to communicate with the Arista devices using eAPI with the following command:

```
$ ansible all -m ping -l leaf01 -vvvv

<172.20.1.41> attempting to start connection
<172.20.1.41> using connection plugin httpapi
<172.20.1.41> loaded API plugin for network_os eos
<172.20.1.41> ESTABLISH HTTP(S) CONNECTFOR USER: ansible TO
https://172.20.1.41:443
```

See also...

For more information regarding the eos_eapi module and the different parameters supported by this module, please consult the following URL: https://docs.ansible.com/ansible/latest/modules/eos_eapi_module.html.

Configuring generic system options on Arista devices

In this recipe, we will outline how to configure some basic system options such as hostname and **Domain Name System** (**DNS**) servers, and provision users on Arista devices. We will understand how to set up all these system-level parameters using the various Ansible modules, and we will outline the different ways to manage these parameters.

Getting ready

To follow along with this recipe, it is assumed that an Ansible inventory has already been set up and eAPI is enabled on all Arista devices, as per the previous recipe.

How to do it...

1. Update the `group_vars/all.yml` file with the generic system parameters, as shown in the following code block:

```
$ cat  group_vars/all.yml

<-- Output Omitted for brevity -->

global:
 dns:
 - 172.20.1.1
 - 172.20.1.15
 site: DC1
  users:
 -    password: ansible123
      privilege: 15
      role: network-admin
      username: ansible
```

2. Create a new playbook, `pb_arista_basic_config.yml`, and add the following task to set up the DNS and the hostname:

```
$ cat pb_arista_basic_config.yml
---
- name: "Configure Basic Configuration on Arista Fabric"
  hosts: arista
  tasks:
    - name: "Conifgure Basic System config"
      eos_system:
        hostname: " {{global.site|lower}}-{{inventory_hostname}}"
        name_servers: "{{ global.dns }}"
        state: present
```

3. Update the `pb_arista_basic_config.yml` playbook with the following task to create users on the Arista devices:

```
- name: "Configure Users"
  eos_user:
    name: "{{ item.username }}"
    role: "{{ item.role | default('network-admin') }}"
    privilege: "{{ item.privilege | default(15)}}"
    configured_password: "{{ item.password }}"
    state: present
  loop: "{{ global.users }}"
```

How it works...

Ansible provides different declarative modules in order to manage the different resources on the Arista switches. In this recipe, we outlined how to use the `eos_system` and the `eos_user` Ansible modules in order to provision basic system attributes on the Arista devices. We started by defining the data that we will use under the `group_vars/all.yml` file, and we included the DNS and users that we want to provision. We created the `pb_arista_basic_config.yml` playbook, which will include all the tasks needed in order to set up the basic settings on the Arista switches.

The first task in the playbook used the `eos_system` Ansible module, which sets up the DNS and the hostname on all the Arista devices. The second task used the `eos_user` Ansible module to set up the system users on the Arista switches. In this last task, we looped over the `users` data structure that we defined in the `group_vars/all.yml` file in order to provision each user in this `list` data structure.

Once we run the playbook, we can see that the configuration of our Arista switches is updated, as shown in the following code block:

```
!
hostname dc1-leaf01
ip name-server vrf default 172.20.1.1
ip name-server vrf default 172.20.1.15
!
```

There's more...

The declarative Ansible modules that we have outlined in this section provide a simple way to configure the basic system-level parameters for Arista devices; however, they might not cover all the parameters that we need to set up on an Arista switch. In order to have more control and flexibility to configure the system-level parameters, we can use Jinja2 templates along with the `template` Ansible module to generate the specific system-level configuration needed for our deployment. In this section, we will outline this method in order to achieve this goal. This will be the method that we will use in subsequent recipes to generate the configuration for other configuration sections, which don't have a built-in Ansible module that can satisfy all our requirements.

We are going to reuse this method to generate the configuration for our Arista devices for different sections such as system, interfaces, and BGP. We are going to create an Ansible role in order to include all the Jinja2 templates and tasks required to generate the final configuration that we will push to our devices. The following procedure outlines the steps needed to create the role, and the playbook required to generate the configuration:

We are going to use the same role structure and tasks that we used in Chapter 3, *Automating Juniper Devices in the Service Providers Using Ansible,* to generate the Juniper devices' configuration. The only difference will be in the Jinja2 templates that we will use to generate the specific configuration for Arista devices.

1. Create a new `roles` directory and add a new role called `dc_fabirc_config`, with the following directory structure:

```
$ tree roles/
roles/
└── dc_fabric_config
    ├── tasks
    └── templates
```

2. In the `tasks` folder, create a `build_config_dir.yml` file to create the required folders to store the configuration that will be generated, as follows:

```
$ cat roles/dc_fabric_config/tasks/build_config_dir.yml

---
- name: Create Config Directory
  file: path={{config_dir}}    state=directory
  run_once: yes
- name: Create Temp Directory per Node
  file: path={{tmp_dir}}/{{inventory_hostname}}    state=directory
- name: SET FACT >> Build Directory
  set_fact:
    build_dir: "{{tmp_dir}}/{{inventory_hostname}}"
```

3. In the `templates` folder, create a new folder called `eos`, and within this folder, create a new Jinja2 template called `mgmt.j2`, as shown in the following code block:

```
$ cat roles/dc_fabric_config/templates/eos/mgmt.j2

!
hostname {{global.site|lower}}-{{inventory_hostname}}
```

```
!
!
spanning-tree mode none
!
aaa authorization exec default local
!
{% for user in global.users%}
username {{user.name}} privilege {{user.privilege}} role
{{user.role|default('network-admin')}} secret {{user.password}}
{% endfor%}
!
{% for dns_server in global.dns%}
ip name-server vrf default {{ dns_server }}
{% endfor %}
!
```

4. In the `tasks` folder, create a new YAML file called `build_device_config.yml`
   to create a system configuration, as shown in the following code block:

```
$ cat roles/dc_fabric_config/tasks/build_device_config.yml

---
- name: "System Configuration"
  template:
    src: "{{ansible_network_os}}/mgmt.j2"
    dest: "{{build_dir}}/00_mgmt.cfg"
  tags: mgmt
```

5. Create a `main.yml` file in the `tasks` folder, with the following tasks:

```
$ cat roles/build_router_config/tasks/main.yml

---
- name: Build Required Directories
  import_tasks: build_config_dir.yml
- name: Build Device Configuration
  import_tasks: build_device_config.yml

 - name: "Remove Old Assembled Config"
   file:
     path: "{{config_dir}}/{{ inventory_hostname }}.cfg"
     state: absent
- name: Build Final Device Configuration
  assemble:
    src: "{{ build_dir }}"
    dest: "{{config_dir}}/{{ inventory_hostname }}.cfg"
- name: Remove Build Directory
```

```
          file: path={{ tmp_dir }}  state=absent
          run_once: yes
```

6. Create a new playbook called `pb_arista_dc_fabric.yml` to generate the
   configuration for all `arista` devices in our inventory:

```
$ cat pb_arista_dc_fabric.yml

---
- name: "Build Arista DC Fabric"
  hosts: arista
  tasks:
    - name: Generate DC Fabric Configuration
      import_role:
        name: dc_fabric_config
      delegate_to: localhost
```

Using this method, we created a role called `dc_fabric_config` and we created a new
Jinja2 template called `mgmt.j2`, which includes the template for `arista` system-level
configuration. We used the `template` Ansible module in order to render the Jinja2
template with the Ansible variables defined under the `group_vars/all.yml` file. In order
to save the configuration for each device, we created the `configs` folder directory, which
stores the final configuration for each device.

Since we are utilizing the Jinja2 approach in order to generate the configuration for each
section (MGMT, interfaces, BGP, and so on), we will segment each section into a separate
Jinja2 template and we will generate each section in a separate file. We use the `assemble`
module in order to group all these different sections into a single configuration file, which
we will store in the `configs` directory, and this is the final and assembled configuration
file for each device. We store the temporarily assembled sections in a temporary folder for
each device, and we delete this temporary folder at the end of the playbook run.

In this playbook, we use the `delegate_to` localhost in the `import_role`
task. Since in all the tasks within this role we don't need to connect to the
remote device, all these tasks should be run on the Ansible control
machine so as to store the file locally on the Ansible machine. Thus, we
use the `delegate_to` localhost in order to run all the tasks on the Ansible
control machine.

Once we run the `pb_junos_net_build.yml` playbook, we can see that the following configuration files are created inside the `configs` directory and, at this stage, it has only the management section of the configuration:

```
$ tree configs/
configs/
├──── leaf01.cfg
├──── leaf02.cfg
├──── leaf03.cfg
├──── leaf04.cfg
├──── spine01.cfg
└──── spine02.cfg
```

We can check the configuration generated for one of the devices (`leaf01`, for example), as shown in the following code block:

```
!
hostname dc1-leaf01
!
snmp-server enable traps
!
spanning-tree mode none
!
aaa authorization exec default local
!
username ansible privilege 15 role network-admin secret ansible123
!
ip name-server vrf default 172.20.1.1
ip name-server vrf default 172.20.1.15
!
```

At this stage, we have generated the system configuration for all the `arista` switches in our inventory; however, we still haven't pushed this configuration to the devices. In later recipes, we will outline how to push the configuration to the `arista` devices.

Configuring interfaces on Arista devices

In this recipe, we will outline how to configure different interface parameters on Arista devices, such as the interface description and IP address information. We will outline how to use the various Ansible modules to interact with the interfaces on Arista devices, and how to set up the interfaces on all the Arista devices in our sample network topology.

Getting ready

We are assuming the network inventory is already in place and that eAPI is already enabled on Arista switches, as per the previous recipes.

How to do it...

1. Add the following content to the `group_vars/all.yml` file, which describes the interfaces on our sample DC fabric network:

```
p2p_ip:
  leaf01:
    - {port: Ethernet8, ip: 172.31.1.1 , peer: spine01, pport:
Ethernet1, peer_ip: 172.31.1.0}
    - {port: Ethernet9, ip: 172.31.1.11 , peer: spine02, pport:
Ethernet1, peer_ip: 172.31.1.10}
  leaf02:
  < -- Output Omitted for brevity -->
  leaf03:
  < -- Output Omitted for brevity -->
  leaf04:
  < -- Output Omitted for brevity -->
  spine01:
  < -- Output Omitted for brevity -->
  spine02:
  < -- Output Omitted for brevity -->

lo_ip:
  leaf01: 10.100.1.1/32
  leaf02: 10.100.1.2/32
  leaf03: 10.100.1.3/32
  leaf04: 10.100.1.4/32
  spine01: 10.100.1.254/32
  spine02: 10.100.1.253/32
```

2. Update the `pb_arista_basic_config.yml` playbook with the following task to enable the interfaces and set the description on all the fabric interfaces:

```
- name: "Configure the Physical Interfaces"
  eos_interface:
    name: "{{ item.port }}"
    enabled: true
    description: "{{global.site}} | Rpeer:{{item.peer}} |
Rport:{{item.pport}}"
    with_items: "{{p2p_ip[inventory_hostname]}}"
```

3. Update the `pb_arista_basic_config.yml` playbook with the following task to set up the IPv4 address on all the **point-to-point (P2P)** fabric links:

```
- name: "Configure IP Addresses"
  eos_l3_interface:
    name: "{{ item.port }}"
    ipv4: "{{ item.ip }}/{{ global.p2p_prefix }}"
    state: present
  with_items: "{{ p2p_ip[inventory_hostname] }}"
```

How it works...

We defined all the data for all the interfaces in our sample network topology in two main data structures in the `group_vars/all.yml` file. We used the `p2p_ip` dictionary to model all the P2P IP addresses in our sample network, and we used the `lo_ip` dictionary to specify the loopback IP addresses for our nodes.

We used the `eos_interface` Ansible module to enable the interfaces and set the basic parameters for the interfaces, such as interface description. We looped over the `p2p_ip` data structure for each device, and we set the correct parameters for each interface on all the devices in our network inventory. We used the `eos_l3_interface` Ansible module to set the correct IPv4 address on all the interfaces in our sample network topology across all the devices.

There's more...

In case we need to have more control over the interface configuration and to set parameters that are not covered by the declarative Ansible modules that we have outlined in this section, we can use Jinja2 templates to achieve this goal. Using the exact same approach that we outlined in the previous recipe for system configuration, we can generate the interface configuration needed for our Juniper devices.

Using the same Ansible role that we have created in the previous recipe, we can extend it to generate the interface configuration for our Arista devices. We use the following steps in order to accomplish this task:

1. Create a new Jinja2 template file, `intf.js`, in the `templates` folder, with the following data:

```
$ cat roles/dc_fabric_config/templates/eos/intf.j2

{% set node_intfs = p2p_ip[inventory_hostname] %}
```

```
{% for p in node_intfs| sort(attribute='port') %}
!
interface {{p.port}}
  description "{{global.site}} | Rpeer: {{p.peer}} | Rport:
{{p.pport}}"
  no switchport
  ip address {{p.ip}}/{{global.p2p_prefix}}
{% endfor %}
!
!
interface Loopback0
  ip address {{lo_ip[inventory_hostname]}}
!
```

2. Update the `build_device_config.yml` file in the `tasks` directory with the new task to generate the interface configuration:

```
$ cat roles/dc_fabric_config/tasks/build_device_config.yml

<-- Output Trimmed for brevity ------>

- name: "Interface Configuration"
  template:
    src: "{{ansible_network_os}}/intf.j2"
    dest: "{{build_dir}}/01_intf.cfg"
  tags: intf
```

3. Once we run our `pb_arista_dc_fabric.yml` playbook, we will generate the configuration for our devices, with the `interface` section updated for `leaf01`, as an example:

```
$ cat configs/leaf01.cfg

< -- Output Omitted for brevity -->

!
interface Ethernet8
  description "DC1 | Rpeer: spine01 | Rport: Ethernet1"
  no switchport
  ip address 172.31.1.1/31
!
interface Ethernet9
  description "DC1 | Rpeer: spine02 | Rport: Ethernet1"
  no switchport
  ip address 172.31.1.11/31
!
!
interface Loopback0
```

```
    ip address 10.100.1.1/32
  !
```

See also...

For more information regarding the `eos_interface` module and the different parameters supported by this module, please consult the following URL: `https://docs.ansible.com/ansible/latest/modules/eos_interface_module.html`.

For more information regarding the `eos_l3_interface` module and the different parameters supported by this module, please, consult the following URL: `https://docs.ansible.com/ansible/latest/modules/eos_l3_interface_module.html`.

Configuring the underlay BGP on Arista devices

In this recipe, we will outline how to configure eBGP as the underlay routing protocol for our sample leaf/spine DC fabric. We are going to build the eBGP peering setup, using the P2P IP address between the leaf switches and spine switches. The BGP **autonomous system number (ASN)** assignment is as shown in the following table:

Node	BGP ASN
Spine01	65100
Spine02	65100
Leaf01	65001
Leaf02	65002
Leaf03	65003
Leaf04	65004

Getting ready

In this recipe, we are assuming that the interface and IP address information is already configured, as per the previous recipe.

How to do it...

1. Create a `host_vars` directory and create a folder for each device in our inventory. In each folder, create a new YAML file, `underlay_bgp.yml`, with the BGP peering details. Here is an example for the `leaf01` device in our inventory:

```
## Leaf01 BGP Data ###
bgp_asn: 65001
bgp_peers:
  - peer: spine01
    peer_ip: 172.31.1.0
    remote_as: 65100
  - peer: spine02
    peer_ip: 172.31.1.10
    remote_as: 65100
```

2. Create a new Jinja2 file, `underlay_bgp.j2`, in the `templates/eos` directory, with the following data. This template is for the `prefix-list` that we will use to control BGP advertisement in our DC fabric:

```
$ cat roles/dc_fabric_config/templates/eos/underlay_bgp.j2

{% set bgp_grp = 'LEAF' if 'spine' in inventory_hostname else
'SPINE' %}
!
route-map loopback permit 10
  match ip address prefix-list loopback
!
{% if 'spine' in inventory_hostname %}
!
ip prefix-list loopback
{% for node,ip in lo_ip.items() | sort %}
{% if 'leaf' in node or inventory_hostname in node %}
  seq {{loop.index + 10 }} permit {{ip}}
{% endif %}
{% endfor %}
!
{% else %}
!
ip prefix-list loopback
  seq 10 permit {{lo_ip[inventory_hostname]}}
!
{% endif %}
```

3. Update the `underlay_bgp.j2` Jinja2 file in the `templates/eos` directory with the BGP template, as shown in the following code block:

```
$ cat roles/dc_fabric_config/templates/eos/underlay_bgp.j2

!
router bgp {{bgp_asn}}
  router-id {{lo_ip[inventory_hostname].split('/')[0]}}
  maximum-paths 2
  bgp bestpath tie-break router-id
  neighbor {{ bgp_grp }} peer-group
  neighbor {{ bgp_grp }} description "Peer Group for All
{{bgp_grp}} Nodes"
  neighbor {{ bgp_grp }} graceful-restart-helper
  neighbor {{ bgp_grp }} send-community standard extended
  neighbor {{ bgp_grp }} maximum-routes 100000 warning-only
{% for p in bgp_peers %}
  neighbor {{ p.peer_ip}} peer-group {{ bgp_grp }}
  neighbor {{ p.peer_ip}} remote-as {{p.remote_as}}
{% endfor %}
  redistribute connected route-map loopback
  !
    address-family ipv4
    neighbor {{ bgp_grp }} activate
    neighbor {{ bgp_grp }} route-map loopback out
!
```

4. In the `build_config.yml` file inside the `tasks` folder, add the following task to render the underlay BGP configuration:

```
$ cat roles/dc_fabric_config/tasks/build_device_config.yml

< -- Output Omitted for brevity -->

- name: "Underlay BGP Configuration"
  template:
    src: "{{ansible_network_os}}/underlay_bgp.j2"
    dest: "{{config_dir}}/{{ inventory_hostname }}/03_bgp.cfg"
```

How it works...

As per our design, we are going to run eBGP between the leaf and spine nodes, and each leaf switch in our topology will have its own BGP ASN. The optimal method to describe this setup is to include all this data on a per-host basis, using the `host_vars` folder. We created a folder for each node to include all the relevant host data under this folder. We created a YAML file to hold the BGP information for each device, thus we can easily add a new file if we need to add more host-specific data for another protocol:

```
$ tree host_vars
 host_vars
 ├────── leaf01
 │     └────── underlay_bgp.yml
 ├────── leaf02
 │     └────── underlay_bgp.yml
 ├────── leaf03
 │     └────── underlay_bgp.yml
 ├────── leaf04
 │     └────── underlay_bgp.yml
 ├────── spine01
 │     └────── underlay_bgp.yml
 └────── spine02
       └────── underlay_bgp.yml
```

In the `tasks/build_device_config.yml` file, we added a new task that uses the `underlay_bgp.j2` Jinja2 template to render the Jinja2 template and output the underlay BGP configuration section for each device outlined in our Ansible inventory.

For each device, we generated a `prefix-list` to match all the prefixes that will advertise to its eBGP peers, as per the following criteria:

- For spine switches, we advertise all the leaf loopback IP addresses along with the spine loopback interface.
- For the leaf switches, we advertise only the loopback IP address.

The following snippet outlines the BGP configuration generated for the `leaf01` device after running the playbook with the new task:

```
$ cat configs/leaf01/04_bgp.cfg

!
route-map loopback permit 10
  match ip address prefix-list loopback
!
ip prefix-list loopback
  seq 10 permit 10.100.1.1/32
```

```
!
router bgp 65001
  router-id 10.100.1.1
  maximum-paths 2
  bgp bestpath tie-break router-id
  neighbor SPINE peer-group
  neighbor SPINE description "Peer Group for All SPINE Nodes"
  neighbor SPINE graceful-restart-helper
  neighbor SPINE send-community standard extended
  neighbor SPINE maximum-routes 100000 warning-only
  neighbor 172.31.1.0 peer-group SPINE
  neighbor 172.31.1.0 remote-as 65100
  neighbor 172.31.1.10 peer-group SPINE
  neighbor 172.31.1.10 remote-as 65100
  redistribute connected route-map loopback
  !
  address-family ipv4
    neighbor SPINE activate
    neighbor SPINE route-map loopback out
!
```

Configuring the overlay BGP EVPN on Arista devices

In this recipe, we will outline how to configure the overlay BGP EVPN as the control plane for VXLAN tunnels across our leaf-spine DC fabric in our sample topology, using Ansible.

Getting ready

This recipe assumes the P2P IP addresses and loopback interfaces have been configured as per previous recipes. Also, the underlay BGP configuration should already be generated as per the previous recipe.

How to do it...

1. Create a new Jinja2 file, `overlay_bgp.j2`, in the `templates/eos` directory, with the following data:

```
$ cat roles/dc_fabric_config/templates/eos/overlay_bgp.j2

{% set bgp_evpn_grp = 'LEAF_EVPN' if 'spine' in inventory_hostname
else 'SPINE_EVPN' %}

service routing protocols model multi-agent
!
router bgp {{bgp_asn}}

  neighbor {{ bgp_evpn_grp }} peer-group
  neighbor {{ bgp_evpn_grp }} description "Peer Group for All
{{bgp_evpn_grp}} EVPN Nodes"
  neighbor {{ bgp_evpn_grp }} graceful-restart-helper
  neighbor {{ bgp_evpn_grp }} send-community extended
  neighbor {{ bgp_evpn_grp }} maximum-routes 100000 warning-only
  neighbor {{ bgp_evpn_grp }} ebgp-multihop 2
  neighbor {{ bgp_evpn_grp }} update-source Loopback0
{% for p in bgp_peers %}
  neighbor {{ lo_ip[p.peer].split('/')[0]}} peer-group {{
bgp_evpn_grp }}
  neighbor {{ lo_ip[p.peer].split('/')[0]}} remote-as
{{p.remote_as}}
{% endfor %}
  !
  address-family evpn
    neighbor {{ bgp_evpn_grp }} activate
  !
  address-family ipv4
    no neighbor {{ bgp_evpn_grp }} activate
!
```

2. In the `build_config.yml` file inside the `tasks` folder, add the following highlighted task:

```
$ cat tasks/build_config.yml

< -- Output Omitted for brevity -->

- name: "Overlay BGP EVPN Configuration"
  template:
    src: "{{ansible_network_os}}/overlay_bgp.j2"
    dest: "{{config_dir}}/{{ inventory_hostname }}/04_evpn.cfg"
```

How it works...

In this recipe, we used a similar methodology to how we configured the underlay eBGP. We built a Jinja2 template to generate the needed BGP EVPN configuration for the Arista devices in our inventory. The following code block shows a sample of the BGP EVPN configuration for the `leaf01` switch:

```
service routing protocols model multi-agent
!
router bgp 65001

  neighbor SPINE_EVPN peer-group
  neighbor SPINE_EVPN description "Peer Group for All SPINE_EVPN EVPN
Nodes"
  neighbor SPINE_EVPN graceful-restart-helper
  neighbor SPINE_EVPN send-community extended
  neighbor SPINE_EVPN maximum-routes 100000 warning-only
  neighbor SPINE_EVPN ebgp-multihop 2
  neighbor SPINE_EVPN update-source Loopback0
  neighbor 10.100.1.254 peer-group SPINE_EVPN
  neighbor 10.100.1.254 remote-as 65100
  neighbor 10.100.1.253 peer-group SPINE_EVPN
  neighbor 10.100.1.253 remote-as 65100
  !
  address-family evpn
    neighbor SPINE_EVPN activate
  !
  address-family ipv4
    no neighbor SPINE_EVPN activate
!
```

Deploying the configuration on Arista devices

In this recipe, we will outline how to push the configuration to the Arista devices. We will use the configuration that we have generated in the previous recipes to provision the devices in our topology. We will learn how to interact with the Arista configuration using the suitable Ansible module, in order to correctly provision the devices as per the intended network design.

Getting ready

This recipe requires eAPI to be enabled on the Arista devices.

How to do it...

In the `pb_arista_dc_fabric.yml` file, add the following task to deploy the configuration to the Arista switches:

```
- name: "Deploy Configuration"
  eos_config:
    src: "{{config_dir}}/{{ inventory_hostname }}.cfg"
    replace: config
    save_when: changed
  tags: deploy
```

How it works...

In the previous recipes, we generated different sections of the configuration for the Arista switches, such as interfaces, and underlay/overlay BGP. We have used the `assemble` Ansible module in order to combine the different sections of the configuration into a single configuration file that holds all the device configurations. In this recipe, we used the `eos_config` module in order to push the configuration file to the Arista switch.

In the `eos_config` module, we used the `src` parameter in order to specify the location of the configuration file that we want to load into our devices. We used the `replace` directive with the `config` option in order to replace all the configuration on the target device with the new configuration that we specified in the `src` option. Thus, the configuration on the devices is completely managed and controlled by Ansible. This also means that if there is any configuration that was implemented outside of our Ansible playbook, the configuration will be deleted once we run the playbook and push the new configuration to the devices.

Finally, we used the `save_when` parameter and set it to `changed` in order to copy the running configuration to the `startup-config` and save the configuration. We only perform this action in case the task changed the configuration on the device.

See also...

For more information regarding the `eos_config` module and the different parameters supported by this module, please consult the following URL: `https://docs.ansible.com/ansible/latest/modules/eos_config_module.html`.

Configuring VLANs on Arista devices

In this recipe, we will outline how to configure VLANs on Arista switches. The VLANs that we will build across our DC fabric are shown in the following table:

Node	Interface	Interface Type	VLANs
Leaf01	Ethernet1	Access	10
Leaf02	Ethernet1	Access	20
Leaf03	Ethernet1	Access	10
Leaf03	Ethernet2	Access	20
Leaf04	Ethernet1	Access	10
Leaf04	Ethernet2	Access	20

Getting ready

This recipe is assuming that underlay and overlay BGP configuration is already generated, as per the previous recipes.

How to do it...

1. Create a new YAML file called `vlan_design.yml` that will hold our VLAN design for our DC fabric, as shown in the following code block:

```
$ cat vlan_design.yml
vlan_data:
  leaf01:
    - id: 10
      description: DB
      ports:
        - Ethernet1
  leaf02:
    - id: 20
      description: web
      ports:
```

```
        - Ethernet1
< -- Output Omitted for brevity -->
```

2. Create a new role, `provision_vlans`, in the `roles` folder, with the following structure:

```
$ tree roles/provision_vlans/
 roles/provision_vlans/
 ├──── tasks
 │   └──── main.yml
 ├──── templates
 └──── vars
     └──── main.yml
```

3. In the `tasks/main.yml` file, include the following task to configure the VLANs on our DC fabric:

```
$ cat roles/provision_vlans/tasks/main.yml

---
- name: Deploy VLANs on DC Fabric
  eos_vlan:
    name: "VLAN_{{vlan.id}}_{{ vlan.description }}"
    vlan_id: "{{ vlan.id }}"
    state: present
    interfaces: "{{ vlan.ports }}"
  loop: "{{ vlan_data[inventory_hostname] }}"
  loop_control:
    loop_var: vlan
  tags: vlans
```

4. Create a new playbook, `pb_deploy_vlans.yml`, that uses the role to order to provision VLANs on our DC fabric, as shown in the following code block:

```
$ cat pb_deploy_vlans.yml

---
- name: Provision VLANs on DC Fabric
  hosts: arista
  vars_files: vlan_design.yml
  tasks:
    - name: Deploy Vlans on DC Fabric
      import_role:
        name: provision_vlans
      when: inventory_hostname in vlan_data.keys()
```

How it works...

In order to provision the VLANs on our DC fabric, we modeled and defined our VLAN membership in a YAML file called `vlan_design.yml`. This file models all the VLANs across all the switches in our fabric in the `vlan_data` dictionary. Each key in this dictionary is the device, and the values are a list of dictionaries, each corresponding to a single VLAN definition.

We created a specific role, `provision_vlans`, to provision VLANs on our fabric, and the initial task in this role used the `eos_vlan` Ansible module to provision the VLANs. We looped over the `vlan_data` specific to each node and provisioned these VLANs.

We created a `pb_deploy_vlans.yml` playbook that uses this role to deploy the VLANs. We read the `vlan_design.yml` file using the `vars_files` parameter, and we imported the `provision_vlans` role using `import_roles`. We used the `when` directive in order to only call this role on the devices defined in our VLAN `design` file.

Once we run our playbook, we can see that the VLANs are deployed across our fabric as outlined here for `leaf03`, as an example:

```
dc1-leaf03#sh vlan
 VLAN Name Status Ports
 ----- ------------------------------- ---------- -------------------------
 1 default active Et3, Et4, Et5, Et6, Et7
 10 VLAN_10_DB active Et1
 20 VLAN_20_web active Et2
```

See also...

For more information regarding the `eos_vlan` module and the different parameters supported by this module, please consult the following URL: `https://docs.ansible.com/ansible/latest/modules/eos_vlan_module.html`.

Configuring VXLANs tunnels on Arista devices

In this recipe, we will outline how to configure VXLAN tunnels using BGP EVPN across our leaf-spine fabric. In an IP fabric similar to our sample topology, we need to have VXLAN tunnels in order to transport the L2 VLANs across our fabric. The following table outlines the VLAN to the **virtual network identifier** (**VNI**) mapping that we will use across our fabric:

VLAN	VNI
10	1010
20	1020

Getting ready

This recipe is assuming that BGP EVPN is already deployed across our fabric and that all the VLANs are provisioned.

How to do it...

1. Update the `vars/main.yml` folder in the `provision_vlans` role with the following variable. This will define the directory to store the VXLAN configuration:

   ```
   $ cat roles/provision_vlans/vars/main.yml
   ---
   config_dir: ./vxlan_configs
   ```

2. In our `provision_vlans` role, create a `templates` folder. Then, in it, create an `eos` folder. After that, create a Jinja2 `vxlan.j2` file with the following content:

   ```
   $ cat roles/provision_vlans/templates/eos/vxlan.j2

   {% set vlans = vlan_data[inventory_hostname] %}
   {% set all_vlans = vlans | map(attribute='id') | list %}
   !
   interface Vxlan1
      vxlan source-interface Loopback0
   {% for vlan in all_vlans %}
     vxlan vlan {{ vlan }} vni 10{{vlan}}
   ```

```
  {% endfor %}
  !
  router bgp {{bgp_asn}}
  !
  {% for vlan in all_vlans %}
    vlan {{ vlan }}
      rd {{lo_ip[inventory_hostname].split('/')[0]}}:10{{vlan}}
      route-target both 10{{vlan}}:10{{vlan}}
      redistribute learned
  {% endfor %}
    !
```

3. Update the `tasks/main.yml` file in the `provision_vlans` role with the following tasks to generate the VXLAN configuration:

```
- name: Create VXLAN Configs Folder
  file: path={{config_dir}} state=directory
  run_once: yes
  delegate_to: localhost
  tags: vxlan

- name: "Create VXLAN Configuration"
  template:
    src: "{{ansible_network_os}}/vxlan.j2"
    dest: "{{config_dir}}/{{ inventory_hostname }}.cfg"
  delegate_to: localhost
  tags: vxlan
```

4. Update the `tasks/main.yml` file with the following tasks to deploy the VXLAN configuration on our DC fabric switches:

```
- name: "Deploy Configuration"
  eos_config:
    src: "{{config_dir}}/{{ inventory_hostname }}.cfg"
    save_when: changed
  tags: vxlan
```

How it works...

In the previous recipe, we outlined how to provision VLANs across our DC fabric. However, in an IP fabric, we need to have tunneling in order to transport the L2 VLANs across the DC fabric. In this recipe, we outlined how to build VXLAN tunnels using BGP EVPN in order to transport the L2 VLANs and to finish the VLAN provisioning task across our DC fabric.

Since the VXLAN tunnels are tightly coupled with the respective VLANs, we included the setup of the VXLAN tunnels within our `provision_vlans` role. We used the Jinja2 templates and the `template` Ansible module in order to generate the VXLAN and BGP configuration needed on each switch to deploy our VXLAN tunnels. We created a new folder to house the VXLAN configuration that we will generate for each switch. We utilized the `template` Ansible module to render the VLAN data defined in our `vlan_design.yml` file with the Jinja2 template to generate the VXLAN configuration for each switch.

Once we run our updated playbook, we can see that the new folder is created and the configuration for all our switches is generated:

```
$ tree vxlan_configs/
vxlan_configs/
├── leaf01.cfg
├── leaf02.cfg
├── leaf03.cfg
└── leaf04.cfg
```

The following code block shows a sample configuration for the VXLAN configuration, generated for the `leaf01` switch:

```
$ cat vxlan_configs/leaf01.cfg

interface Vxlan1
  vxlan source-interface Loopback0
  vxlan udp-port 4789
  vxlan vlan 10 vni 1010
!
router bgp 65001
!
  vlan 10
    rd 10.100.1.1:1010
    route-target both 1010:1010
    redistribute learned
    !
```

Gathering Arista device facts

In this recipe, we will outline how to retrieve the basis system facts collected by Ansible for an Arista device running the Arista EOS software. These basic system facts provide us with a basic health check regarding our Arista devices, which we can use to validate its operational state.

Getting ready

eAPI must be enabled on the Arista devices so you can use the Ansible modules in this recipe.

How to do it...

1. Create a new playbook, `pb_arista_facts.yml`, with the following task to collect the facts:

   ```
   $ cat pb_jnpr_facts.yml

   ---
   - name: Collect and Validate Arista DC Fabric Facts
     hosts: arista
     tasks:
       - name: Collect Arista Device Facts
         eos_facts:
   ```

2. Update the `pb_arista_facts.yml` playbook with the following tasks to validate the operational state of all our fabric interfaces:

   ```
   - name: Validate all DC Fabric Interface are Operational
     assert:
       that:
         - ansible_net_interfaces[item.port].lineprotocol == 'up'
       fail_msg: "Interface {{item.port}} is not Operational "
     loop: "{{ p2p_ip[inventory_hostname] }}"
   ```

3. Update the playbook with the following task to validate the correct IP address assignment for all our fabric interfaces:

   ```
   - name: Validate all DC Fabric Interface are has Correct IP
     assert:
       that:
         - ansible_net_interfaces[item.port].ipv4.address == item.ip
       fail_msg: "Interface {{item.port}} has Wrong IP Address"
     loop: "{{ p2p_ip[inventory_hostname] }}"
   ```

How it works...

Ansible provides a fact-gathering module to collect the basic system properties for Arista devices and returns these facts in a consistent and structured data structure. We can use the facts collected by this module in order to validate the basic properties and operational state of our devices.

In this recipe, we used the `eos_facts` module to collect the device facts for all our Arista devices. This module returned the basic facts collected by Ansible for each device in multiple variables. The main variable that we are interested in is the `ansible_net_interfaces` variable, which holds all the operational state of all the interfaces on the device. The following snippet outlines a sample of the data stored in this variable:

```
"ansible_net_interfaces": {
  "Ethernet8": {
    "bandwidth": 0,
    "description": "DC1 | Rpeer: spine01 | Rport: Ethernet1",
    "duplex": "duplexFull",
    "ipv4": {
      "address": "172.31.1.1",
      "masklen": 31
    },
    "lineprotocol": "up",
    "macaddress": "50:00:00:03:37:66",
    "mtu": 1500,
    "operstatus": "connected",
    "type": "routed"
  }
}
```

We used the data retrieved by Ansible and stored in the `ansible_net_interfaces` variable in order to validate that all the fabric interfaces are operational and that they have the correct IP address assigned as per our design. We used the `assert` module in order to perform this validation, and we looped over the `p2p_ip` data structure for each device in order to validate the state for only our fabric interfaces.

See also...

For more information regarding the `eos_facts` module and the different parameters supported by this module, please consult the following URL: `https://docs.ansible.com/ansible/latest/modules/eos_facts_module.html`.

Retrieving operational data from Arista devices

In this recipe, we will outline how to execute operational commands on Arista devices, and use the output to validate the state of the devices.

Getting ready

eAPI must be enabled on the Arista devices in order to follow along with this recipe.

How to do it...

1. Create a new playbook called `pb_get_vlans.yml` and populate it to execute the `show vlan` command on all leaf switches and store the output in a variable:

```
---
- name: " Play 1: Retrieve All VLANs from Arista Switches"
  hosts: leaf
  vars_files: vlan_design.yml
  tasks:
    - name: "Get All VLANs"
      eos_command:
        commands: show vlan | json
      register: show_vlan
```

2. Update the `pb_get_vlans.yml` playbook and populate it with the following task to compare and validate that correct VLANs are configured on the devices:

```
    - name: "Validate VLANs are Present"
      assert:
        that: (item.vlan | string) in
show_vlan.stdout[0].vlans.keys()
        fail_msg: "VLAN:{{ item.vlan }} is NOT configured "
        success_msg: "VLAN:{{ item.vlan }} is configured "
      loop: "{{ access_interfaces[inventory_hostname] }}"
      delegate_to: localhost
```

How it works...

We executed operational commands on the Arista switches using the `eos_command` Ansible module and, in order to return structured output, we used the `json` keyword in the command to return the JSON output of the operational command (if supported). In this example, we sent the `show vlan` command to get the list of VLANs configured on the devices, and we collected the output in the `show_vlan` variable. The following snippet outlines the output we get from the devices, which is stored in this variable:

```
ok: [leaf01] => {
  "show_vlan": {
    < -- Output Omitted for brevity -->
    "stdout": [
    {
      "vlans": {
        "1": {
          "dynamic": false,
          "interfaces": {
            < -- Output Omitted for brevity -->
          },
          "name": "default",
          "status": "active"
        },
        "10": {
          "dynamic": false,
          "interfaces": {
            "Ethernet1": {
              "privatePromoted": false
            },
            "Vxlan1": {
              "privatePromoted": false
            }
          },
          "name": "VLAN_10",
          "status": "active"
        }
      }
    }
  ]
```

We used the `assert` module to validate that the VLANs defined within our design (in the `vlans_design.yml` file) were all configured and operational for each of the switches. We compared the VLANs defined in this file with the output that we retrieved from the devices using the `eos_command` module (which is stored in the `show_vlan` variable) in order to ensure that each VLAN was active on the switches.

 We are using the `string` Jinja2 filter in our `assert` statement since the VLANs are defined as integers in our `vlan_design.yml` file. However, the VLANs stored in the `show_vlan` variable are strings. Thus, in order for the `assert` statement to succeed, we need to make sure that the type is similar.

See also...

For more information regarding the `eos_command` module and the different parameters supported by this module, please consult the following URL: `https://docs.ansible.com/ansible/latest/modules/eos_command_module.html`

5
Automating Application Delivery with F5 LTM and Ansible

In this chapter, we will outline how to automate F5 BIG-IP platforms running as **load balancers** (**LBs**) or **Local Traffic Manager** (**LTM**) appliances. We will explore how to interact with F5 LTM nodes using Ansible and how to onboard these devices and accelerate application deployment hosted by these devices, using various Ansible modules. We will base our illustration on the following sample network diagram. The diagram shows single F5 LTM nodes connected to **direct current** (**DC**) switches:

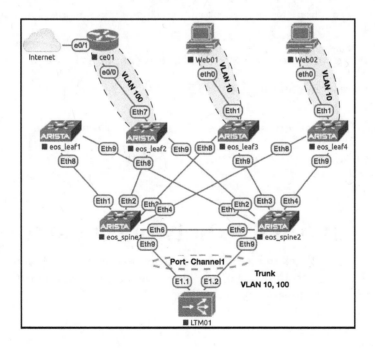

The main recipes covered in this chapter are as follows:

- Building an Ansible network inventory
- Connecting and authenticating to BIG-IP devices
- Configuring generic system options on BIG-IP devices
- Configuring interfaces and trunks on BIG-IP devices
- Configuring **virtual local area networks** (**VLANs**) and **self-internet protocols** (**self-IPs**) on BIG-IP devices
- Configuring static routes on BIG-IP devices
- Deploying nodes on BIG-IP devices
- Configuring a load balancing pool on BIG-IP devices
- Configuring virtual servers on BIG-IP devices
- Retrieving operational data from BIG-IP nodes

Technical requirements

All the code used in the recipes in this chapter can be found on the following GitHub repository: `https://github.com/PacktPublishing/Network-Automation-Cookbook/tree/master/ch5_f5`.

The following are the software releases on which this chapter is based:

- Ansible machine running CentOS 7
- Ansible 2.9
- F5 BIG-IP device running BIG-IP 13.1.1, Build 0.0.4 final

Check out the following video to see the Code in Action:
`https://bit.ly/2RE5tOL`

Building an Ansible network inventory

In this recipe, we will outline how to build and structure our Ansible inventory to describe our sample F5 BIG-IP nodes. Building an Ansible inventory is a mandatory step in telling Ansible how to connect to the managed devices.

Getting ready

We will create a new folder that will host all the files that we will create in this chapter. The new folder is named ch5_f5.

How to do it...

1. Inside the new folder, ch5_f5, we create a hosts file with the following content:

```
$ cat hosts
[ltm]
ltm01 Ansible_host=172.20.1.34
```

2. Create an Ansible.cfg file, as shown in the following code:

```
$ cat Ansible.cfg
[defaults]
inventory=hosts
retry_files_enabled=False
gathering=explicit
host_key_checking=False
```

How it works...

Since we have a single LTM node in our network topology, this simplifies our Ansible inventory file. In our hosts file, we create a single group (called ltm) and we specify a single node in it, which is called ltm01. We specify the management IP addresses for the nodes, using the Ansible_host parameter.

The management port on the BIG-IP device must have this IP address configured, and IP connectivity between the Ansible control machine and the BIG-IP node is established over this management port.

Finally, we create the Ansible.cfg file and configure it to point to our hosts file, to be used as an Ansible inventory file. We disable the setup module, which is not needed when running Ansible against network nodes.

Connecting and authenticating to BIG-IP devices

In this recipe, we will outline how to connect to BIG-IP nodes from Ansible via the **Representational State Transfer** (**REST**) API exposed by BIG-IP device, in order to start managing the devices from Ansible. We are going to use usernames and passwords to authenticate to the BIG-IP node in our topology.

Getting ready

In order to follow along with this recipe, an Ansible inventory file should be constructed as per the previous recipe. IP reachability must be established between the Ansible control machine and all the devices in the network.

How to do it...

1. Inside the `ch5_f5` folder, create a `group_vars` folder.
2. Create a new `group_vars/all.yml` file with the following connection parameters settings:

```
conn_parameters:
    user: admin
    password: admin
    server: "{{ Ansible_host }}"
    server_port: 443
    validate_certs: no
admin_passwd: NewP@sswd
users:
    - name: Ansible
      passwd: Ansible123
      role: all:admin
      state: present
```

3. Create a new playbook with the name `pb_f5_onboard.yml`, with the following task to create new system users:

```
- name: Onboarding a New LTM
  hosts: ltm01
  connection: local
  tasks:
    - name: "P1T1: Create new Users"
      bigip_user:
        username_credential: "{{ item.name }}"
        password_credential: "{{ item.passwd }}"
        partition_access: "{{ item.role }}"
        state: "{{ item.state | default('present')}}"
        provider: "{{ conn_parameters }}"
      loop: "{{ users }}"
```

4. Update the `pb_f5_onboard.yml` playbook with the following task to update the admin user account:

```
- name: "P1T1: Update admin Password"
  bigip_user:
  username_credential: admin
  password_credential: "{{ admin_passwd }}"
  state: present
  provider: "{{ conn_parameters }}"
```

How it works...

Ansible uses the REST API on the F5 LTM nodes in order to manage the BIG-IP nodes. Ansible establishes an HTTPS connection to the BIG-IP node and uses it as the transport mechanism to invoke the REST API on the BIG-IP node. In order to establish the HTTPS connection with the BIG-IP system, we need to provide some parameters in order for Ansible to initiate and establish a connection with the BIG-IP node. These parameters include the following:

- Username/password to authenticate with the BIG-IP REST API
- IP address and port, over which we can reach the REST API endpoint on the BIG-IP node
- Whether we validate the certificate for the BIG-IP node negotiated over the HTTPS session

We include all these parameters in a dictionary called `conn_parameters`, which we include in the `group_vars/all.yml` file, so as to be applied on any BIG-IP node.

By default, a new LTM device comes with the `admin/admin` default username and password for the **graphical user interface** (**GUI**) and REST API access. We use these credentials as the user and password variables inside the `conn_parameters` dictionary, and we specify the `Ansible_host` variable as the IP address over which the REST API can be established over port `443`. Finally, we disable certificate validation, since the certificate on the BIG-IP node is self-signed.

We create a new variable called `users`, which holds all the new users that we want to configure on our LTM, along with their role/privilege. In this case, we want to provide administrative privileges for the Ansible user across all the partitions on the LTM node.

We create a new playbook for onboarding a new LTM node. In the first task, we create the new users using the `bigip_user` module, and we provide the parameters to establish the HTTPS connection, using the `provider` attribute. We loop over all the users in our `users` variable to provision them.

The second task also uses the `bigip_user` module in order to update the default `admin` profile on the LTM and to change this default password to a new password specified in the `admin_passwd` variable.

On the playbook level, we are setting the connection to `local`. This is because we are going to establish the HTTPS connection from the Ansible control machine, and we want to prevent Ansible from using **Secure Shell** (**SSH**) to connect to the LTM node.

The following screenshot shows the new Ansible user created on the BIG-IP node:

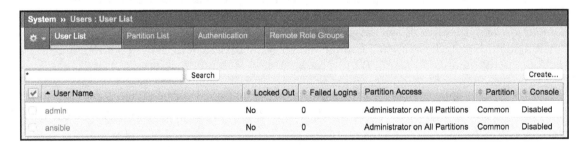

The following screenshot shows the details of the Ansible user created using the playbook:

 We are using a plaintext password for simplicity; however, a plaintext password should never be used. Ansible Vault should be used to secure the password.

There's more...

After adding the new Ansible user, we update the conn_parameters dictionary with the new user that we have created. We can start managing the LTM nodes with this user, as shown here:

```
$ cat group_vars/all.yml
conn_parameters:
  user: Ansible
  password: Ansible123
  server: "{{ Ansible_host }}"
  server_port: 443
  validate_certs: no
< -- Output Omitted for brevity -->
```

Configuring generic system options on BIG-IP devices

In this recipe, we will outline how to configure some basic system options such as hostname, **Domain Name System** (**DNS**), and the **Network Time Protocol** (**NTP**) on BIG-IP nodes. We will understand how to set up all these system-level parameters using the various Ansible modules available.

Getting ready

To follow along with this recipe, an Ansible inventory is assumed to be already set up. IP connectivity between Ansible and the BIG-IP nodes is already established, with the correct user credentials.

How to do it...

1. Update the `group_vars/all.yml` file with the following system-level parameters:

```
$ cat group_vars/all.yml
< -- Output Omitted for brevity -->
domain: lab.net
nms_servers:
  - 172.20.1.250
```

2. Create a new folder called `tasks` and create an `f5_system.yml` file with the following content:

```
$ cat tasks/f5_system.yml
---
- name: "Setup BIG-IP Hostname"
  bigip_hostname:
    hostname: "{{ inventory_hostname }}.{{ domain }}"
    provider: "{{ conn_parameters }}"
- name: "Setup BIG-IP DNS Servers"
  bigip_device_dns:
    ip_version: '4'
    name_servers: "{{ nms_servers }}"
    provider: "{{ conn_parameters }}"
- name: "Setup BIG-IP NTP Servers"
  bigip_device_ntp:
```

```
        ntp_servers: "{{ nms_servers }}"
        provider: "{{ conn_parameters }}"
```

3. In the `pb_f5_onboard.yml` file, add the following highlighted tasks:

```
$ cat pb_f5_onboard.yml
< -- Output Omitted for brevity -->
- name: "P1T3: Configure System Parameters"
  import_tasks: "tasks/f5_system.yml"
  tags: system
```

How it works...

In order to configure the various system parameters on BIG-IP nodes, we use a separate module for each task. We group all these tasks in a single file called `f5_system.yml` under the `tasks` folder, and inside this file, we use three separate tasks/modules, as follows:

- `bigip_hostname` to set up the hostname
- `bigip_device_dns` to set up the DNS server that the BIG-IP node will use
- `bigip_device_ntp` to set up the NTP servers on the BIG-IP node

All these modules take the `conn_parameters` dictionary to correctly set up how to communicate with the REST API of the BIG-IP node. In our sample topology, we use a single server as the DNS and NTP. We describe it using the `nms_servers` variable in the `group_vars/all.yml` file, to apply to all our nodes in our Ansible inventory.

In order to configure the hostname, we need to supply a **fully qualified domain name (FQDN)** for the device. So, we configure our domain again under the `group_vars/all.yml` file and use it in conjunction with the device name to set up its hostname.

After running this playbook, we can see that the configuration is applied to the BIG-IP node. The following screenshot shows that the **Host Name** is correctly provisioned:

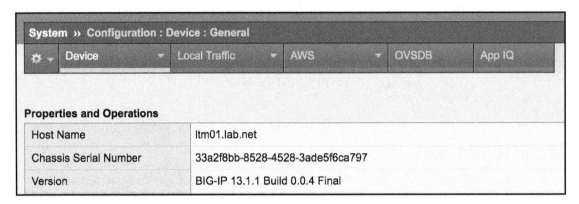

The **NTP** configuration is deployed correctly, as per the following screenshot:

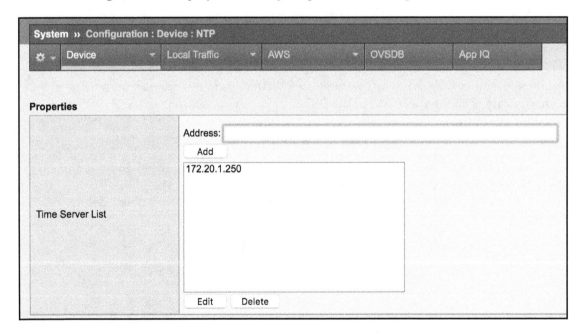

The **DNS** is configured correctly, as per the following screenshot:

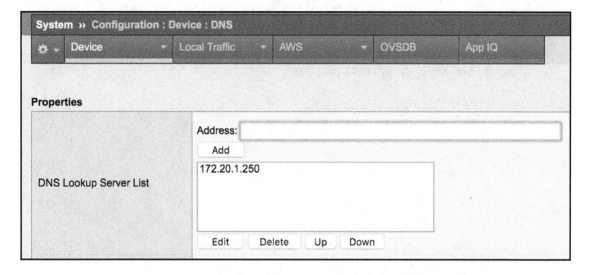

Configuring interfaces and trunks on BIG-IP devices

In this recipe, we will outline how to set up trunks on BIG-IP devices. Trunk ports on BIG-IP nodes are used to provide increased redundancy for the device, by combining multiple interfaces into a single logical interface. It is very similar to port channels in traditional network vendors.

Getting ready

To follow along with this recipe, an Ansible inventory is assumed to be already set up. IP connectivity between Ansible and the BIG-IP nodes is already established, with the correct user credentials.

How to do it...

1. Create a `host_vars` folder and create a `ltm01.yml` file with the following content:

```
$ cat host_vars/ltm01.yml
----
phy_interfaces:
  - 1.1
  - 1.2
trunks:
  - name: po1
    members: "{{ phy_interfaces }}"
```

2. Under the `tasks` folder, add a new file called `f5_interfaces.yml` with the following content:

```
$ cat tasks/f5_interfaces.yml
---
- name: Create a Port channel on BIG-IP
  bigip_trunk:
    name: "{{ item.name}}"
    interfaces: "{{ item.members }}"
    link_selection_policy: maximum-bandwidth
    frame_distribution_hash: destination-mac
    lacp_enabled: no
    provider: "{{ conn_parameters }}"
    state: present
  loop: "{{ trunks }}"
```

3. Update the `pb_f5_onboard.yml` playbook with the following new task:

```
$ cat pb_f5_onboard.yml
< -- Output omitted for brevity -->
- name: "P1T4: Configure Interfaces"
  import_tasks: "tasks/f5_interfaces.yml"
  tags: intfs
```

How it works...

We define the host-specific data for the LTM device under the `host_vars` folder, in a file called `ltm01.yml`. In this file, we define the physical interface on the LTM node under the `phy_interfaces` variable. We define another variable called `trunks` in order to define the trunks available on the device. In the `trunks` variable, we reference the `phy_interfaces` variable in order to limit data duplication.

In the `f5_interfaces.yml` task file, we add a new task using the `bigip_trunk` module to provision the required trunks on the BIG-IP node. We loop over the `trunks` data structure to provision all the required trunk ports. In this task, we supply different parameters that adjust the trunk properties (such as disable the **Link Aggregation Control Protocol (LACP)**) and set up the correct method to distribute the frames across the trunk ports.

After running the playbook, we can see that the required trunk **Interfaces** are provisioned, as shown in the following screenshot:

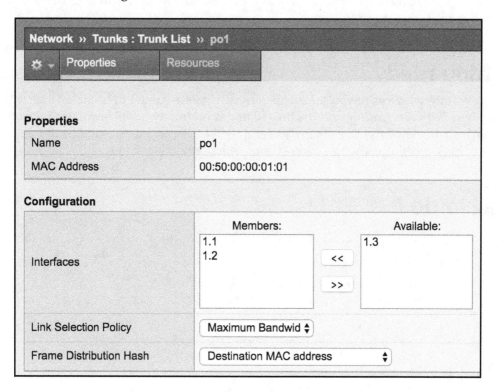

See also...

For more information regarding the `bigip_trunk` Ansible module, and the different options regarding how to deploy trunk ports on the BIG-IP nodes, please refer to the following URL: `https://docs.Ansible.com/Ansible/latest/modules/bigip_trunk_module.html`.

Configuring VLANs and self-IPs on BIG-IP devices

In this recipe, we will outline how to configure VLANs on BIG-IP nodes. VLANs on the BIG-IP nodes are fundamental for traffic separation for the different applications hosted by the BIG-IP LTM nodes. They are fundamental to designating external (internet-facing) and internal (server-facing) domains. We will also outline how to assign an IP address on the VLAN interfaces that we provision.

Getting ready

To follow along with this recipe, an Ansible inventory is assumed to be already set up. IP connectivity between Ansible and the BIG-IP nodes is already established, with the correct user credentials. As all the VLANs in this setup will be deployed on trunk ports, we need to have the trunk ports already provisioned, as per the previous recipe.

How to do it...

1. Update the `host_vars/ltm01.yml` file under the `host_vars` folder with the following VLAN data:

```
$ cat host_vars/ltm01.yml
< -- Output Omitted for brevity -->
vlans:
  - vlan: 100
    description: Extrnal VLAN (Internet)
    ip: 10.1.100.254/24
    tagged_intf: po1
  - vlan: 10
    description: Server VLAN10 (Internal)
    ip: 10.1.10.254/24
```

```
        tagged_intf: po1
```

2. Update the `f5_interfaces.yml` file under the `tasks` folder with the task to provision VLANs, as follows:

```
$ cat tasks/f5_interfaces.yml
< -- Output Omitted for brevity -->
- name: Create VLANs on BIG-IP
  bigip_vlan:
    tagged_interfaces: "{{ item.tagged_intf }}"
    name: "VL{{item.vlan}}"
    description: "{{ item.description }}"
    tag: "{{item.vlan}}"
    provider: "{{ conn_parameters }}"
    state: present
  loop: "{{ vlans }}"
```

3. Update the `f5_interfaces.yml` file under the `tasks` folder with the task to provision the IP addresses on the respective VLANs, as follows:

```
$ cat tasks/f5_interfaces.yml
< -- Output Omitted for brevity -->
- name: Provision IP addresses on BIG-IP
  bigip_selfip:
    address: "{{ item.ip | ipv4('address') }}"
    name: "VL{{ item.vlan }}_IP"
    netmask: "{{ item.ip | ipv4('netmask') }}"
    vlan: "VL{{ item.vlan }}"
    provider: "{{ conn_parameters }}"
    state: present
  loop: "{{ vlans }}"
```

How it works...

We add the `vlans` data structure in `host_vars/ltm01.yml` to declare all the VLANs that we need to provision on the LTM node, along with the IP addresses associated with this VLAN.

We update the `f5_interfaces.yml` file with a task using the `bigip_vlan` module to provision the VLANs on the BIG-IP node, and we loop over the `vlans` data structure to extract all the required parameters to set up the needed VLANs. Next, we add another task using the `bigip_selfip` Ansible module to deploy the IP addresses on the VLANs.

After running the playbook again, we can see the VLANs and self-IPs on the BIG-IP node, as shown in the following screenshot:

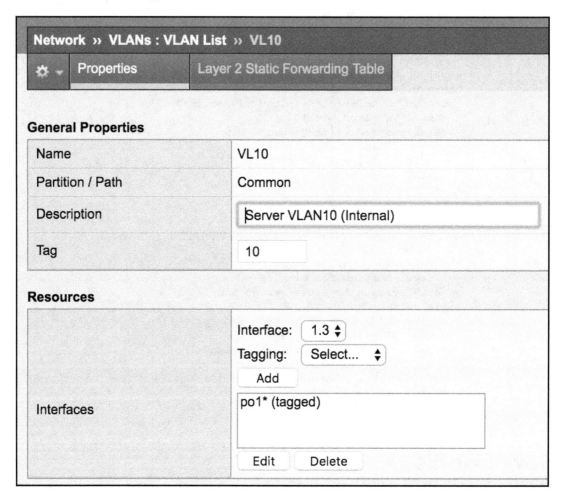

The correct IP address is configured correctly on the VLAN interface, as per the following screenshot:

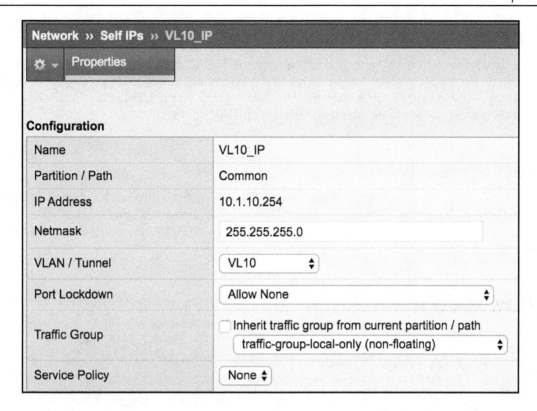

See also...

For more options regarding how to deploy VLANs and self-IPs on the BIG-IP nodes, please refer to the following URLs:

```
bigip-vlan
https://docs.ansible.com/ansible/latest/modules/bigip_vlan_module.html
```

```
bigip-selfip
https://docs.Ansible.com/Ansible/latest/modules/bigip_selfip_module.html#bigip-
selfip-module
```

Configuring static routes on BIG-IP devices

After deploying the VLANs and IP addresses on the BIG-IP device, we need to configure routing on the BIG-IP nodes in order to reach the external destination. We use static routes in our topology in order to provision the required routing on the LTM node. In this recipe, we will outline how to configure static routes on BIG-IP devices.

Getting ready

To follow along with this recipe, an Ansible inventory is assumed to be already set up, and IP connectivity between Ansible and the BIG-IP nodes is already established, with the correct user credentials. Furthermore, we need to deploy the VLANs and IP addresses in the BIG-IP node, as per the previous recipe.

How to do it...

1. Update the `host_vars/ltm01.yml` file with the following routing data:

```
$ cat host_vars/ltm01.yml
< -- Output Omitted for brevity -->
routes:
  - dst: 0.0.0.0/0
    gw: 10.1.100.1
    name: default_route
```

2. Update the `pb_f5_onboard.yml` file with the following task:

```
$ cat pb_f5_onboard.yml
< -- Output Omitted for brevity -->
- name: "P1T5: Setup External Routing"
  bigip_static_route:
    destination: "{{ item.dst.split('/')[0] }}"
    netmask: "{{item.dst | ipv4('prefix')}}"
    gateway_address: "{{ item.gw }}"
    name: "{{ item.name }}"
    provider: "{{ conn_parameters }}"
  loop: "{{ routes }}"
  tags: routing
```

How it works...

We add the `routes` data structure under the `host_vars/ltm01.yml` file to declare all the static routes that need to be provisioned on the LTM node.

We update the `pb_f5_onboard.yml` playbook with a task to provision the static routes using the `bigip_static_route` module, and we loop over the `routes` data structure to provision all the needed routes on the device.

After running the playbook again, we can see the correct static routes, as shown in the following screenshot:

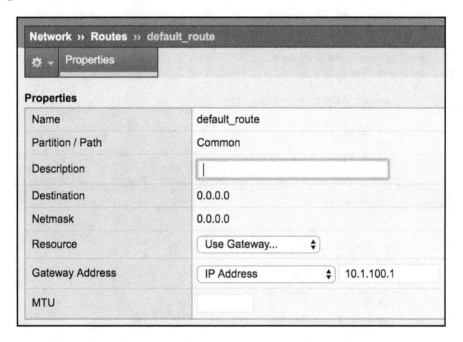

Deploying nodes on BIG-IP devices

Using BIG-IP LTM to deploy an application requires load balancing of the application traffic across multiple servers. This requires us to define the servers/instances that are hosting the application. In BIG-IP, these instances are called nodes and they identify each server with a unique IP address. In this recipe, we are going to start deploying a new application (web server) on the BIG-IP device, and we will provision the nodes that are carrying this service using Ansible.

Getting ready

The basic setup for the BIG-IP should be already completed as per the previous recipes, and the correct VLANs to reach these nodes (physical servers) must be deployed.

How to do it...

1. Create a new YAML file called `web_app.yml` with the following content:

```
---
vip: 10.1.100.100
vip_port: 443
endpoint: dev.internet.net
pool_name: dev_web_app
pool_members:
  - ip: 10.1.10.10
    name: "dev01.internal.net"
    port: 443
  - ip: 10.1.10.11
    name: "dev01. internal.net"
    port: 443
```

2. Create a new Ansible playbook called `pb_f5_deploy_app.yml` with the following content:

```
---
- name: Deploying a New App on BIG-IP
  hosts: ltm01
  connection: local
  vars_file: web_app.yml
  tasks:
    - name: "Create Nodes on BIG-IP"
      bigip_node:
        address: "{{ item.ip }}"
        name: "{{ item.name }}"
        provider: "{{ conn_parameters }}"
        state: present
      loop: "{{ pool_members }}"
```

How it works...

We define all the parameters for our new web application that should be hosted on the BIG-IP LTM device in a YAML file called `web_app.yaml`. In this file, we include a `pool_members` parameter to outline the web servers that will house the application. We use this parameter to create the nodes on the BIG-IP LTM.

We create a new playbook for application deployment, called `pb_f5_deploy_app.yml`. We include the `web_app.yml` file so as to have access to all the parameters defined for this app. We create a new task using the `bigip_node` module to provision a new node on the BIG-IP appliance, and we loop through the `pool_members` parameter derived from the `web_app.yml` file to provision all the required nodes on the BIG-IP appliance. In order to connect to the BIG-IP node, we use the same previous provider attribute with the `conn_parameters` parameter defined in the `group_vars/all.yml` file to establish the connection with the BIG-IP.

Running this playbook, we create all the required nodes, as shown in the following screenshot:

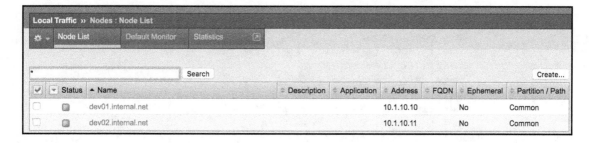

Configuring a load balancing pool on BIG-IP devices

After creating a node on the BIG-IP, we need to create a load balancing pool for the application that we are deploying and assign pool members from the nodes that we have created into this pool. In this recipe, we will outline how to provision load balancing pools on the BIG-IP nodes, and how to assign members to the load balancing pool.

Getting ready

This recipe assumes that all the previous recipes have been implemented and that the nodes on the BIG-IP are already provisioned, as per the previous recipe.

How to do it...

1. Update the `pb_f5_deploy_app.yml` playbook with the following task to create a new pool:

```
- name: Create New LB Pool
  bigip_pool:
    name: "POOL_{{ website }}_{{ vip_port }}"
    lb_method: round-robin
    state: present
    provider: "{{ conn_parameters }}"
```

2. Update the `pb_f5_deploy_app.yml` playbook with the following task to assign pool members to the newly created pool:

```
- name: Add Members to the Pool
  bigip_pool_member:
    pool: "POOL_{{ website }}_{{ vip_port }}"
    host: "{{ item.ip }}"
    name: "{{ item.name }}"
    port: "{{ item.port }}"
    description: "Web Server for {{ website }}"
    provider: "{{ conn_parameters }}"
  loop: "{{ pool_members }}"
```

How it works...

In this recipe, we create a load balancing pool on the BIG-IP system using the `bigip_pool` module, and we specify the load balancing technique that should be used on this pool. In this example, we are using the `round-robin` technique. We create the pool name using the different parameters extracted from the `web_app.yml` file (mainly the website and `vip_port`).

Next, we assign the pool members to this newly created pool using the `bigip_pool_member` module and loop through all the `pool_members` defined in the `web_app.yml` file.

We can see that all these procedures create a consistent method for defining the pool names, as well as assigning the required pool members to the correct pool member. All the information is retrieved from a single definition file that describes and outlines how the service should be deployed.

Running these two tasks, we will see that the pool is correctly created with the correct pool members, as shown in the following screenshot:

The following screenshot shows the current members:

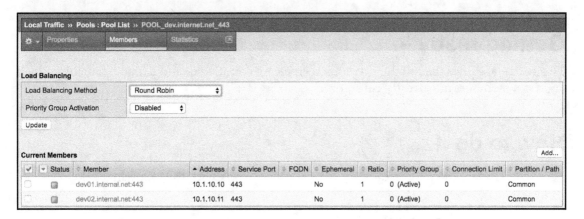

See also...

In this recipe, we outlined the basic use for the Ansible modules to provision load balancing pools on the BIG-IP nodes. However, there are more options available for these modules, such as specifying the load balancing ratio for each member, as well as attaching monitors for the overall pool. Please consult the following URLs for more options:

- `bigip_pool`: https://docs.Ansible.com/Ansible/latest/modules/bigip_pool_module.htmlb
- `bigip_pool_member`: https://docs.Ansible.com/Ansible/latest/modules/bigip_pool_member_module.html

Configuring virtual servers on BIG-IP devices

The last part in deploying an application on the BIG-IP LTM for load balancing is configuring the virtual server on the BIG-IP LTM node, and creating a **virtual IP** (**VIP**) on the BIG-IP node for this virtual server. In this recipe, we outline how to deploy the virtual server using Ansible.

Getting ready

This recipe assumes that all the previous recipes are completed, and a load balancing pool and pool members are already configured.

How to do it...

1. Update the `pb_f5_deploy_app.yml` playbook with the following task:

```
- name: Create Virtual Server
  bigip_virtual_server:
    name: "{{ website }}_{{ vip_port }}_VS"
    destination: "{{ vip }}"
    port: "{{ vip_port}}"
    pool: "POOL_{{ website }}_{{ vip_port }}"
    description: "VIP for {{ website }}"
    profiles:
      - http
      - name: clientssl
```

```
        context: client-side
    - name: serverssl
        context: server-side
        state: present
        provider: "{{ conn_parameters }}"
```

How it works...

We use the `bigip_virtual_server` module to provision the required virtual server on the BIG-IP appliance, by specifying the parameters defined in the `web_app.yml` file. We also define and provision the profiles that need to be applied to the newly created virtual server. These profiles are the HTTP and SSL profiles. These profiles are already created by default on the BIG-IP node, and in a case where we need to create custom profiles, we need to create these in a separate task, using the appropriate Ansible module.

Running this last task, we can see that the **Virtual Server** is created, as illustrated in the following screenshot:

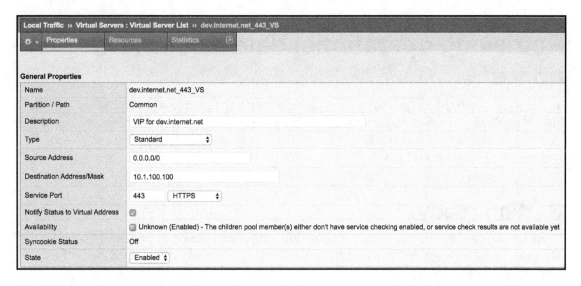

In this last task, we have created a functional service VIP on the LTM node, in order to start processing HTTP requests for our new website and to load balance the traffic across all the instances in the load balancing group.

See also...

In this recipe, we discussed the basic use of the Ansible module to provision virtual servers on the BIG-IP nodes. However, there are more options available in order to tweak the configuration for the virtual server that needs to be deployed.

There are more Ansible modules that let you create profiles you can use to attach to the virtual server, and the following are some links for these modules:

- `bigip_virtual_server`: https://docs.Ansible.com/Ansible/latest/ modules/bigip_virtual_server_module.html
- `bigip_profile_http`: https://docs.Ansible.com/Ansible/latest/modules/ bigip_profile_http_module.html
- `bigip_profile_client_ssl`: https://docs.Ansible.com/Ansible/latest/ modules/bigip_profile_client_ssl_module.html
- `bigip_profile_server_ssl`: https://docs.Ansible.com/Ansible/latest/ modules/bigip_profile_server_ssl_module.html

Retrieving operational data from BIG-IP nodes

In this recipe, we outline how to retrieve operational data for different components on the BIG-IP appliance in terms of the network state of the BIG-IP nodes, such as interfaces and VLANs, as well as data relating to the components responsible for application delivery, such as virtual servers and pools.

Getting ready

To follow along with this recipe, an Ansible inventory is assumed to be already set up, and IP connectivity between Ansible and the BIG-IP nodes is already established, with the correct user credentials.

How to do it...

1. Create a new Ansible playbook, `pb_f5_validate.yml`, with the following content:

```yaml
---
- name: Validating BIG-IP Health
  hosts: ltm01
  connection: local
  tasks:
    - name: Collect Device Facts from BIG-IP
      bigip_device_facts:
        gather_subset:
          - interfaces
        provider: "{{ conn_parameters }}"
      register: bigip_facts
```

2. Update the playbook with a new task to filter the interface facts, as follows:

```yaml
    - name: Set Device Links
      set_fact:
        net_intfs: "{{ net_intfs | default([]) +
          bigip_facts.interfaces |
selectattr('name','equalto',item|string) | list }}"
      loop: "{{ phy_interfaces }}"
```

3. Update the `pb_f5_validate.yml` playbook with a new task to validate the interface status, as follows:

```yaml
    - name: Validate All Interface are operational
      assert:
        that:
          - item.enabled == 'yes'
            fail_msg: " Interface {{ item.name }} is Down"
      loop: "{{net_intfs}}"
```

How it works...

The REST API supported on the BIG-IP node uses different methods to retrieve operational data from the device, and it outputs all this data in JSON format. The following snippet outlines the interface status gathered from the BIG-IP nodes using the `bigip_device_facts` module:

```
"bigip_facts": {
< -- Output Omitted for brevity -->
  "interfaces": [
    {
      "active_media_type": "10000T-FD",
      "bundle": "not-supported",
      "bundle_speed": "not-supported",
      "enabled": "yes",
      "flow_control": "tx-rx",
      "full_path": "1.1",
      "if_index": 48,
      "lldp_admin": "txonly",
      "mac_address": "00:50:00:00:01:01",
      "media_sfp": "auto",
      "mtu": 1500,
      "name": "1.1",
< -- Output Omitted for brevity -->
    }
```

We retrieve the operational facts from the BIG-IP nodes using `bigip_device_facts`, and we restrict only the data retrieved from the node using `gather_subset`. We include the `interfaces` option only to get the interface data. We save all the retrieved output to the `bigip_facts` variable.

We create a new fact for the device, called `net_intfs`. The only use of this new fact is to filter the interface facts retrieved from the previous task to the interface that we have defined for our device in the `phy_interfaces` parameter (which is defined under the `host_vars` folder). This new parameter will include only the interface facts for the interfaces that we declared in our design.

We use the `assert` module to validate that all the interfaces that we defined for our application are enabled and operational from the retrieved data, and we loop over the `net_intfs` variable (which is a list) to loop over all the interfaces and confirm that they are enabled.

There's more...

If we need to get the operational data for the application that we have deployed on the LTM node, we create a new playbook to validate the application deployment as shown in the following code, using the `bigip_device_facts` module. We limit the data retrieved to only the virtual servers. We validate the data using the `assert` statement, as we did in the previous playbook. The following code shows the playbook contents for application deployment validation.

1. We create a new playbook, `pb_f5_app_validate.yml`, with the following task to collect `virtual-servers` facts:

```
---
- name: Validating BIG-IP App Health
  hosts: ltm01
  connection: local
  vars_files: web_app.yml
  tasks:
    - name: Collect Virtual-Servers Facts from BIG-IP
      bigip_device_facts:
        gather_subset:
          - virtual-servers
        provider: "{{ conn_parameters }}"
      register: bigip_app_facts
```

2. We update the playbook with the following tasks to filter the `virtual-servers` facts:

```
    - name: Create Virtual Server Name Fact
      set_fact:
        vs_name: "{{ website }}_{{ vip_port }}_VS"
    - name: Create App Virtual Servers
      set_fact:
        app_vs: "{{ app_vs | default([]) +
          bigip_app_facts.virtual_servers |
selectattr('name','equalto',vs_name) | list }}"
```

3. We update the playbook with the following task to validate the state of the virtual server for our application:

```
- name: Validate Virtual Address Status
  assert:
    that:
      - item.enabled == 'yes'
      - item.destination_address == vip
      - item.destination_port == vip_port
    fail_msg: " {{ item.name }} is No Setup Correctly"
  loop: "{{app_vs}}"
```

These validation playbooks can be extended to validate multiple parameters on the virtual servers. Also, we can validate other components such as LTM load balancing pools, to build a more comprehensive validation for the application deployed.

See also...

For more information regarding the Ansible `bigip_device_facts` module and all the information that we can retrieve from the BIG-IP node, please visit the following website: `https://docs.Ansible.com/Ansible/latest/modules/bigip_device_facts_module.html`.

6
Administering a Multi-Vendor Network with NAPALM and Ansible

Network Automation and Programmability Abstraction Layer with Multivendor support (NAPALM), as the name implies, is a multi-vendor Python library intended to interact with different vendor equipment, and it provides a consistent method to interact with all these devices, irrespective of the vendor equipment used.

In previous chapters, we have seen how to interact with different network devices using Ansible. However, for each vendor OS, we had to use a different Ansible module to support that specific OS. Furthermore, we saw that the data returned from each vendor OS is completely different. Although writing a playbook for multi-vendor devices is still possible, it requires the use of multiple different modules, and we need to work with the different data structures returned by these devices. This is the main issue that NAPALM tries to address. NAPALM attempts to provide an abstracted and consistent API to interact with multiple vendor OSes, while the data returned by NAPALM from these different vendor OSes is normalized and consistent.

NAPALM interacts with each device according to the most common API supported by this node, and the API that is widely adopted by the community. The following diagram outlines how NAPALM interacts with the most common network devices, as well as the libraries used in NAPALM to interact with the APIs on these devices:

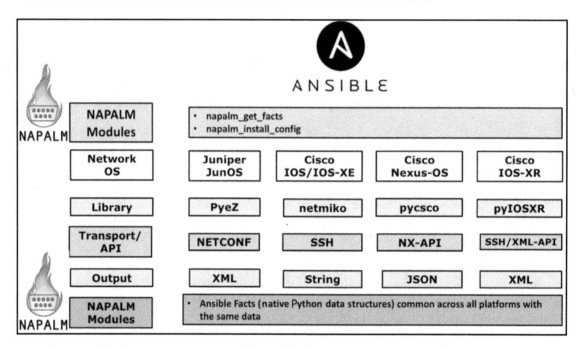

Since NAPALM tries to provide a consistent method to interact with network equipment, it supports a specific set of vendor devices. NAPALM also supports the most common tasks that are carried out on these devices, such as device configuration, retrieving the operational state for interfaces, **Border Gate Protocol** (**BGP**) and **Link Layer Discovery Protocol** (**LLDP**), and many others. For more information regarding the supported devices, as well as the supported methods when interacting with these devices, please check the following link: https://napalm.readthedocs.io/en/latest/support/index.html.

In this chapter, we will outline how to automate a multi-vendor network using NAPALM and Ansible. We will outline how to manage the configuration of these different vendor OSes, as well as how to retrieve the operational state from these devices. We will base our illustration on the following sample network diagram of a basic service provider network:

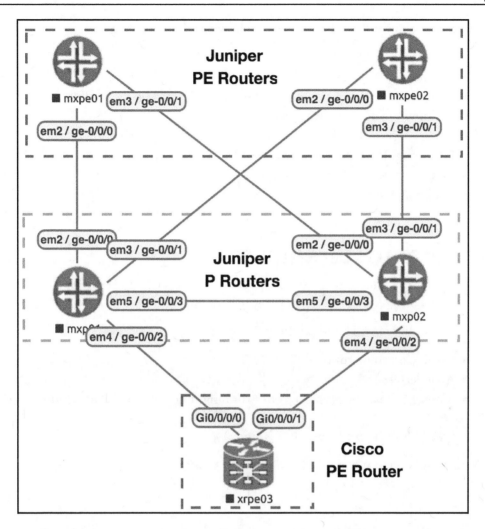

The following table outlines the devices in our sample topology and their respective management **Internet Protocols** (**IPs**):

Device	Role	Vendor	Management (MGMT) Port	MGMT IP
mxp01	P Router	Juniper vMX 14.1	fxp0	172.20.1.2
mxp02	P Router	Juniper vMX 14.1	fxp0	172.20.1.3
mxpe01	PE Router	Juniper vMX 14.1	fxp0	172.20.1.4
mxpe01	PE Router	Juniper vMX 17.1	fxp0	172.20.1.5
xrpe03	PE Router	Cisco XRv 6.1.2	Mgmt0/0/CPU0/0	172.20.1.6

The main recipes covered in this chapter are shown in the following list:

- Installing NAPALM and integrating with Ansible
- Building an Ansible network inventory
- Connecting and authenticating to network devices using Ansible
- Building the device configuration
- Deploying configuration on network devices using NAPALM
- Collecting device facts with NAPALM
- Validating network reachability using NAPALM
- Validating and auditing networks with NAPALM

Technical requirements

The code files for this chapter can be found here: `https://github.com/PacktPublishing/`
`Network-Automation-Cookbook/tree/master/ch6_napalm`.

The following software will be required in this chapter:

- Ansible machine running CentOS 7
- Ansible 2.9
- Juniper **Virtual MX (vMX)** router running Junos OS 14.1R8 and Junos OS 17.1R1 release
- Cisco XRv router running IOS XR 6.1.2

Check out the following video to see the Code in Action:
`https://bit.ly/2Veox8j`

Installing NAPALM and integrating with Ansible

In this recipe, we outline how to install NAPALM and integrate it to work with Ansible. This task is mandatory since NAPALM Ansible modules are not part of the core modules that are shipped with Ansible by default. So, in order to start working with these modules, we need to install NAPALM and all of its Ansible modules. Then, we need to inform Ansible of where to find it and start working with the specific modules developed by the NAPALM team for Ansible.

Getting ready

Ansible and Python 3 need to be installed on the machine, along with the `python3-pip` package, which we will use to install NAPALM.

How to do it...

1. Install the `napalm-ansible` Python package, as shown in the following code snippet:

   ```
   $ pip3 install napalm-ansible
   ```

2. Run the `napalm-ansible` command, as shown in the following code block:

   ```
   $ napalm-ansible
   ```

3. To ensure Ansible can use the NAPALM modules you will have to add the following configurtion to your Ansible configuration file (`ansible.cfg`):

   ```
   [defaults]
    library = /usr/local/lib/python3.6/site-packages/napalm_ansible/modules
    action_plugins = /usr/local/lib/python3.6/site-packages/napalm_ansible/plugins/action
   ```

   For more details on Ansible's configuration file, visit `https://docs.ansible.com/ansible/latest/intro_configuration.html`.

4. Create a new folder called `ch6_napalm` and create the `ansible.cfg` file, updating it as shown in the following code block:

   ```
   $ cat ansible.cfg
   [defaults]
   inventory=hosts
   retry_files_enabled=False
   gathering=explicit
   host_key_checking=False
   library = /usr/local/lib/python3.6/site-packages/napalm_ansible/modules
   action_plugins = /usr/local/lib/python3.6/site-packages/napalm_ansible/plugins/action
   ```

How it works...

Since the NAPALM package and corresponding NAPALM Ansible modules are not part of the core modules shipped and installed by default with Ansible, we need to install it on the system in order to start working with the NAPALM Ansible modules. The NAPALM team has shipped a specific Python package to install NAPALM along with all the Ansible modules and all the dependencies, in order to start working with NAPALM from inside Ansible. This package is `napalm-ansible`. We will use the `pip3` program to install this package since we are using Python 3.

In order to tell Ansible where the Ansible module is installed, we need to enter the path for these modules into Ansible. The NAPALM team also provides simple instruction on how to find the path where the NAPALM modules are installed, and how to integrate it with Ansible via the `napalm-ansible` program. We execute the `napalm-ansible` command, which outputs the required configuration that we need to include in the `ansible.cfg` file so that Ansible can find the NAPALM modules that we will be using.

We update the `ansible.cfg` file with the output that we obtained from the `napalm-ansible` command. We then update the library and action plugin options, which tell Ansible to include these folders in its path when it is searching for modules or action plugins. In the `ansible.cfg` file, we include the normal configuration that we used before in the previous chapters.

Building an Ansible network inventory

In this recipe, we will outline how to build and structure our Ansible inventory to describe our sample service provider network setup outlined in this chapter. Building an Ansible inventory is a mandatory step, in order to tell Ansible how to connect to the managed devices. In the case of NAPALM, we need to sort the different nodes in our network into the correct vendor types supported by NAPALM.

How to do it...

1. Inside the new folder (`ch6_napalm`), we create a `hosts` file with the following content:

```
$ cat hosts
[pe]
 mxpe01 ansible_host=172.20.1.3
```

```
mxpe02 ansible_host=172.20.1.4
xrpe03 ansible_host=172.20.1.5

[p]
mxp01 ansible_host=172.20.1.2
mxp02 ansible_host=172.20.1.6

[junos]
mxpe01
mxpe02
mxp01
mxp02

[iosxr]
xrpe03
[sp_core:children]
pe
p
```

How it works...

We built the Ansible inventory using the hosts file, and we defined multiple groups in order to segment our infrastructure, as follows:

- We created the PE group, which references all the **Multiprotocol Label Switching (MPLS) Provider Edge (PE)** nodes in our topology.
- We created the P group, which references all the MPLS **Provider (P)** nodes in our topology.
- We created the junos group to reference all the Juniper devices in our topology.
- We created the iosxr group to reference all the nodes running IOS-XR.

Segmenting and defining groups per vendor or per OS is a best practice when working with NAPALM since we use these groups to specify the required parameters needed by NAPALM to identify the vendor of the remotely managed node, and how to establish network connectivity with this remote node. In the next recipe, we will outline how we will employ these groups (junos and iosxr), and which parameters we will include in order for NAPALM to establish a connection to the remotely managed nodes.

Connecting and authenticating to network devices using Ansible

In this recipe, we will outline how to connect to both Juniper and IOS-XR nodes using Ansible, in order to start interacting with the devices.

Getting ready

In order to follow along with this recipe, an Ansible inventory file should be constructed as per the previous recipe. Also, IP reachability between the Ansible control machine and all the devices in the network must be configured.

How to do it...

1. On the Juniper devices, configure the username and password, as shown in the following code block:

```
system {
  login {
    user ansible {
      class super-user;
      authentication {
        encrypted-password "$1$mR940Z9C$ipX9sLKTRDeljQXvWFfJm1"; ##
ansible123
      }
    }
  }
}
```

2. On the Cisco IOS-XR devices, configure the username and password, as shown in the following code block:

```
!
  username ansible
  group root-system
  password 7 14161C180506262E757A60 # ansible123
!
```

3. Enable the **Network Configuration Protocol** (**NETCONF**) on the Juniper devices, as follows:

```
system {
  services {
    netconf {
      ssh {
        port 830;
      }
    }
  }
}
```

4. On the IOS-XR devices, we need to enable **Secure Shell** (**SSH**), as well as enable `xml-agent`, as follows:

```
!
xml agent tty
iteration off
!
xml agent
!
ssh server v2
ssh server vrf default
```

5. On the Ansible machine, create the `group_vars` directory in the `ch6_napalm` folder, and create the `junos.yml` and `iosxr.yml` files, as shown in the following code block:

```
$ cat group_vars/iosxr.yml
---
  ansible_network_os: junos
  ansible_connection: netconf

  $ cat group_vars/junos.yml
---
  ansible_network_os: iosxr
  ansible_connection: network_cli
```

6. Under the `group_vars` folder, create the `all.yml` file with the following login details:

```
$ cat group_vars/all.yml
ansible_user: ansible
  ansible_ssh_pass: ansible123
```

How it works...

NAPALM uses a specific transport API for each vendor equipment supported by NAPALM. It uses this API in order to connect to the device, so in our sample topology, we need NETCONF to be enabled on the Juniper devices. For Cisco IOS-XR devices, we need to enable SSH, as well as enabling the XML agent on the IOS-XR devices.

The username/password used on the Ansible control machine to authenticate with the devices must be configured on the remote nodes. We perform all these steps on the devices in order to make them ready for NAPALM to communicate with them.

Using the legacy `xml agent` on the IOS-XR devices in production is not recommended and needs to be evaluated as per the Cisco documentation. For further details, refer to `https://www.cisco.com/c/en/us/td/docs/routers/asr9000/software/asr9k_r5-3/sysman/command/reference/b-sysman-cr53xasr/b-sysman-cr53xasr_chapter_01010.html`.

On the Ansible machine, we set the `ansible_connection` parameter per each vendor (`netconf` for `juniper` and `network_cli` for `iosxr`), and we specify the `ansible_network_os` parameter to designate the vendor OS. All these parameters are defined under the `group_vars` hierarchy in `junos.yml` and `iosxr.yml`, corresponding to the groups that we defined in our inventory for grouping the devices on vendor OS basics. Finally, we specify the username and password via `ansible_user` and `ansible_ssh_pass` in the `all.yml` file, since we are using the same user to authenticate to both Juniper and Cisco devices.

To test and validate that, we can communicate with the devices from the Ansible control machine using the Ansible `ping` module, as shown in the following code block:

```
$ ansible all -m ping
mxpe01 | SUCCESS => {
  "changed": false,
  "ping": "pong"
}
mxpe02 | SUCCESS => {
  "changed": false,
  "ping": "pong"
}
mxp02 | SUCCESS => {
  "changed": false,
  "ping": "pong"
}
mxp01 | SUCCESS => {
  "changed": false,
```

```
    "ping": "pong"
  }
xrpe03 | SUCCESS => {
    "changed": false,
    "ping": "pong"
  }
```

Building the device configuration

NAPALM doesn't provide declarative modules to configure the various system parameters on the managed devices, such as interfaces' BGP, **Quality of Service (QoS)**, and so on. However, it provides a common API to push text-based configuration to all the devices, so it requires the configuration for the devices to be present in text format in order to push the required configuration. In this recipe, we will create the configuration for all our devices. This is the configuration that we will push to our devices using NAPALM, in the next recipe.

Getting ready

As a prerequisite for this recipe, an Ansible inventory file must be present.

How to do it...

1. Create a `roles` folder, and inside this folder, create a new role called `build_router_config`, as follows:

   ```
   $ mkdir roles && mkdir roles/build_router_config
   ```

2. Use the exact same contents (Jinja2 templates and tasks) for the `build_router_config` role that we developed for Juniper devices in Chapter 3, *Automating Juniper Devices in the Service Providers Using Ansible,* to generate the configuration for the devices. The directory layout should be as shown in the following code block:

   ```
   $ tree roles/build_router_config/

   roles/build_router_config/
   ├── tasks
   │   ├── build_config_dir.yml
   │   ├── build_device_config.yml
   ```

```
|   └──── main.yml
└──── templates
└──── junos
├──── bgp.j2
├──── intf.j2
├──── mgmt.j2
├──── mpls.j2
└──── ospf.j2
```

3. Create a new folder called `iosxr` under the `templates` folder and populate it with the Jinja2 templates for the different IOS-XR configuration sections, as shown in the following code block:

```
$ tree roles/build_router_config/templates/iosxr/

roles/build_router_config/templates/iosxr/
├──── bgp.j2
├──── intf.j2
├──── mgmt.j2
├──── mpls.j2
└──── ospf.j2
```

4. Update the `group_vars/all.yml` file with the required data to describe our network topology, as shown in the following code block:

```
$ cat group_vars/all.yml
tmp_dir: ./tmp
config_dir: ./configs
p2p_ip:
< -- Output Omitted for brevity -->
  xrpe03:
    - {port: GigabitEthernet0/0/0/0, ip: 10.1.1.7 , peer: mxp01,
pport: ge-0/0/2, peer_ip: 10.1.1.6}
    - {port: GigabitEthernet0/0/0/1, ip: 10.1.1.13 , peer: mxp02,
pport: ge-0/0/2, peer_ip: 10.1.1.12}

lo_ip:
  mxp01: 10.100.1.254/32
  mxp02: 10.100.1.253/32
  mxpe01: 10.100.1.1/32
  mxpe02: 10.100.1.2/32
  xrpe03: 10.100.1.3/32
```

5. Create a specific directory for each host in the `host_vars` directory, and in each directory, create the `bgp.yml` file with the following BGP peering content:

```
$ cat host_vars/xrpe03/bgp.yml
bgp_asn: 65400
bgp_peers:
  - local_as: 65400
    peer: 10.100.1.254
    remote_as: 65400
```

6. Create a new playbook called `pb_napalm_net_build.yml` that utilizes the `build_router_config` role in order to generate the device configuration, as shown in the following code block:

```
$ cat pb_napalm_net_build.yml
---
- name: " Generate and Deploy Configuration on All Devices"
  hosts: sp_core
  tasks:
    - name: Build Device Configuration
      import_role:
        name: build_router_config
      delegate_to: localhost
      tags: build
```

How it works...

In this recipe, our main goal is to create the device configuration that we will deploy on the devices in our sample topology. We are using the same Ansible role that we used to generate the configuration for Juniper devices in Chapter 3, *Automating Juniper Devices in the Service Providers Using Ansible*. The only addition to this role is that we are adding the required Jinja2 templates for IOS XR.

Here is a quick explanation of the steps, as a quick review:

- Modeling the network via Ansible variables

We describe the different aspects of our network topology, such as **Peer-to-Peer (P2P)** interface, loopback interfaces, and **Open Shortest Path First (OSPF)** parameters under different data structures in the `group_vars/all.yml` file. For any host-specific data, we use the `host_vars` directory to populate all variables/parameters that are specific to a specific node, and, in our case, we use this approach for BGP data to outline `bgp_peers` variable for each node. This provides us with all the required data to populate the Jinja2 templates needed to generate the final configuration for each device in our sample network.

- Building the Jinja2 templates

We place all our Jinja2 templates in the `templates` folder inside our role, and we segment our Jinja2 templates per the vendor OS, each in a separate folder. Next, we create a Jinja2 template for each section of the configuration. The following code snippet outlines the directory structure for the templates folder:

```
templates/
├── iosxr
│   ├── bgp.j2
│   ├── intf.j2
│   ├── mgmt.j2
│   ├── mpls.j2
│   └── ospf.j2
└── junos
    ├── bgp.j2
    ├── intf.j2
    ├── ospf.j2
    ├── mgmt.j2
    └── mpls.j2
```

For a detailed explanation of the different Jinja2 templates used in this recipe and how they use the defined Ansible variables to generate the final configuration, please refer to `Chapter 3` of this book, *Automating Juniper Devices in the Service Providers Using Ansible*, since we are using the exact same network topology and the same data structures for both JunOS and IOS-XR devices.

Running this playbook will generate the configuration for all the devices in our Ansible inventory in the `configs` folder, as shown in the following code block:

```
$ tree configs/
configs/
├── mxp01.cfg
├── mxp02.cfg
├── mxpe01.cfg
├── mxpe02.cfg
└── xrpe03.cfg
```

Deploying configuration on network devices using NAPALM

In this recipe, we will outline how to push configurations on different vendor devices using Ansible and NAPALM. NAPALM provides a single Ansible module for configuration management, and this module allows us to use a single common method to push any configuration on any vendor equipment supported by NAPALM, greatly simplifying Ansible playbooks.

Getting ready

To follow along with this recipe, you will need to have an Ansible inventory already set up, with network reachability between the Ansible controller and the network devices established. The configuration that we will be pushing to the devices is the one we generated in the previous recipe.

How to do it...

1. Update the `pb_napalm_net_build.yml` playbook file, and add the tasks shown in the following code block:

```
$ cat pb_napalm_net_build.yml

---
- name: " Play 1: Deploy Config on All JunOS Devices"
  hosts: sp_core
  tasks:
```

```
< -- Output Omitted for brevity -->

    - name: "P1T5: Deploy Configuration"
      napalm_install_config:
        hostname: "{{ ansible_host }}"
        username: "{{ ansible_user }}"
        password: "{{ ansible_ssh_pass }}"
        dev_os: "{{ ansible_network_os }}"
        config_file: "{{config_dir}}/{{ inventory_hostname }}.cfg"
        commit_changes: "{{commit | default('no')}}"
        replace_config: yes
      tags: deploy, never
```

How it works...

As previously outlined, NAPALM provides a single Ansible module to push configurations to the network devices. It requires the configuration to be present in a text file. When it connects to the network device, it pushes the configuration to the respective device.

Since we are using a single configuration module that can be used across all the vendor OS devices supported by NAPALM, and since NAPALM uses a different connection API to manage the device, we need to tell the module the vendor OS for the device. We also need to provide the other parameters, such as username/password, to log in and authenticate with the device.

The `napalm_install_config` module requires the following mandatory parameters in order to correctly log in to the managed device and push the configuration to it:

- `hostname`: This is the IP address through which we can reach the device. We supply the value of `ansible_host` for this parameter.
- `username/password`: This is the username and password to connect to the device. We need to supply the `ansible_user` and `ansible_ssh_pass` attributes.
- `dev_os`: This parameter provides the vendor OS name that NAPALM requires in order to choose the correct API and the correct library to communicate with the device. For this option, we provide the `ansible_network_os` parameter.
- The `napalm_install_config` module uses the following parameters to manage the configuration on remote devices:
  - `config_file`: This provides the path of the configuration file containing the device configuration that needs to be pushed to the managed device.

- `commit_changes`: This tells the device whether or not to commit the configuration. NAPALM provides a consistent method for configuration commits, even for devices that don't support it by default (for instance, Cisco IOS devices).
- `replace_config`: This parameter controls how to merge between the existing configuration on the device and the configuration in the `config_file` parameter. In our case, since we are generating the whole device configuration and all the configuration sections are managed under Ansible, we replace the entire configuration with the configuration that we generate. This will cause any configuration on the device not present in our configuration file to be removed.

As per the configuration outlined in this recipe, when we run the playbook using the `deploy` tag, NAPALM will connect to the device and push the configuration. However, it will not commit the configuration on the remote device, since we have specified the default value for `commit_changes` to be no. In case we need to push and commit the configuration on the remote device, we can set the value for the `commit` parameter to `yes` when running the playbook, as shown in the following code snippet:

```
$ ansible-playbook pb_napalm_net_build.yml --tags deploy --e commit=yes
```

There's more...

The `napalm_install_config` module provides extra options to control how to manage the configuration on the remote devices, such as the configuration diff. With this option, we can collect the differences between the running configuration on the device and the configuration that we will push via NAPALM. This option can be enabled as follows:

- Create a folder called `config_diff` to store the configuration diff captured by NAPALM, as shown in the following code block:

```
$ cat group_vars/all.yml

< -- Output Omitted for brevity -->
config_diff_dir: ./config_diff

$ cat tasks/build_config_dir.yml

- name: "Create Config Diff Directory"
  file: path={{config_diff_dir}} state=directory
  run_once: yes
```

- Update the `pb_napalm_net_build.yml` playbook, as shown in the following code block:

```
$ cat pb_napalm_net_build.yml

---
- name: "Generate and Deploy Configuration on All Devices"
  hosts: sp_core
  tasks:

< -- Output Omitted for brevity -->

    - name: "Deploy Configuration"
      napalm_install_config:
      hostname: "{{ ansible_host }}"
      username: "{{ ansible_user }}"
      password: "{{ ansible_ssh_pass }}"
      dev_os: "{{ ansible_network_os }}"
      config_file: "{{config_dir}}/{{ inventory_hostname }}.cfg"
      diff_file: "{{ config_diff_dir}}/{{ inventory_hostname
}}_diff.txt"
      commit_changes: "{{commit | default('no')}}"
      replace_config: yes
    tags: deploy, never
```

Next, we create a new folder to house all the configuration diff files that we will generate for each device, and add the `diff_file` parameter to the `napalm_install_config` module. This will collect the configuration diff for each device and save it to the `config_diff` directory for each device.

When we run the playbook again with a modified configuration on the devices, we can see that the `config_diff` files for each device are generated, as shown in the following code block:

```
$ tree config_diff/
config_diff/
├──── mxp01_diff.txt
├──── mxpe01_diff.txt
├──── mxpe02_diff.txt
└──── xrpe03_diff.txt
```

Collecting device facts with NAPALM

In this recipe, we will outline how to collect the operational state from network devices using the NAPALM fact-gathering Ansible module. This can be used to validate the network state across multi-vendor equipment since NAPALM Ansible's fact-gathering module returns a consistent data structure across all vendor OSes supported by NAPALM.

Getting ready

To follow along with this recipe, it is assumed that an Ansible inventory is already in place and network reachability between the Ansible controller and the network is already established. Finally, the network is configured as per the previous recipe.

How to do it...

1. Create an Ansible playbook named `pb_napalm_get_facts.yml` with the following content:

```
$ cat cat pb_napalm_get_facts.yml

---
- name: " Collect Network Facts using NAPALM"
  hosts: sp_core
  tasks:
    - name: "P1T1: Collect NAPALM Facts"
      napalm_get_facts:
        hostname: "{{ ansible_host }}"
        username: "{{ ansible_user }}"
        password: "{{ ansible_ssh_pass }}"
        dev_os: "{{ ansible_network_os }}"
        filter:
          - bgp_neighbors
```

2. Update the playbook with the following tasks to validate the data returned by the NAPALM facts module:

```
$ cat pb_napalm_get_facts.yml

< -- Output Omitted for brevity -->

- name: Validate All BGP Routers ID is correct
  assert:
```

```
              that: napalm_bgp_neighbors.global.router_id ==
          lo_ip[inventory_hostname].split('/')[0]
            when: napalm_bgp_neighbors

          - name: Validate Correct Number of BGP Peers
            assert:
              that: bgp_peers | length ==
          napalm_bgp_neighbors.global.peers.keys() | length
              when: bgp_peers is defined

          - name: Validate All BGP Sessions Are UP
            assert:
              that: napalm_bgp_neighbors.global.peers[item.peer].is_up ==
          true
            loop: "{{ bgp_peers }}"
            when: bgp_peers is defined
```

How it works...

We use the `napalm_get_facts` Ansible module to retrieve the operational state from the network devices. We supply the same parameters (`hostname`, `username/password`, and `dev_os`) that we used with `napalm_install_config` to be able to connect to the devices and collect the required operational state from these devices.

In order to control which information we retrieve using NAPALM, we use the `filter` parameter and supply the required information that we need to retrieve. In this example, we are limiting the data retrieved to `bgp_neighbors`.

The `napalm_get_facts` module returns the data retrieved from the nodes as Ansible facts. This data can be retrieved from the `napalm_bgp_neighbors` variable, which stores all the NAPALM BGP facts retrieved from the device.

The following snippet outlines the output from `napalm_bgp_neighbors`, retrieved from a Junos OS device:

```
ok: [mxpe02] => {
  "napalm_bgp_neighbors": {
    "global": {
      "peers": {
        "10.100.1.254": {
          "address_family": {
            "ipv4": {
              "accepted_prefixes": 0,
              "received_prefixes": 0,
              "sent_prefixes": 0
```

```
            },
 < -- Output Omitted for brevity -->
            },
            "description": "",
            "is_enabled": true,
            "is_up": true,
            "local_as": 65400,
            "remote_as": 65400,
            "remote_id": "10.100.1.254",
            "uptime": 247307
        }
      },
      "router_id": "10.100.1.2"
    }
  }
}
```

The following snippet outlines the output from `napalm_bgp_neighbors`, retrieved from an IOS-XR device:

```
ok: [xrpe03] => {
  "napalm_bgp_neighbors": {
    "global": {
      "peers": {
        "10.100.1.254": {
          "address_family": {

 < -- Output Omitted for brevity -->
            },
            "description": "",
            "is_enabled": false,
            "is_up": true,
            "local_as": 65400,
            "remote_as": 65400,
            "remote_id": "10.100.1.254",
            "uptime": 247330
        }
      },
      "router_id": "10.100.1.3"
    }
  }
}
```

As we can see, the data returned from NAPALM for the BGP information from different network vendors is consistent between different network vendors. This simplifies parsing this data and allows us to run much simpler playbooks to validate the network state.

We use the data returned by NAPALM to compare and validate the operational state of the network against our network design, which we defined using Ansible variables such as `bgp_peers`. We use the `assert` module to validate multiple BGP information, such as the following:

- Correct number of BGP peers
- BGP router ID
- All BGP sessions are operational

We use the `when` statement in the different `assert` modules in scenarios in which we have a router in our topology that doesn't run BGP (`mxp02` is an example). Consequently, we skip these checks on these nodes.

See also...

The `napalm_get_fact` module can retrieve a huge range of information from the network devices based on the vendor equipment supported and the level of facts supported by this vendor. For example, it supports the retrieval of interfaces, IP addresses, and LLDP peers for almost all the known networking vendors.

For the complete documentation for the `napalm_get_facts` module, please check the following URL:
`https://napalm.readthedocs.io/en/latest/integrations/ansible/modules/napalm_get_facts/index.html`.

For complete facts/getters supported by NAPALM and their support matrix against vendor equipment, please consult the following URL:
`https://napalm.readthedocs.io/en/latest/support/`.

Validating network reachability using NAPALM

In this recipe, we will outline how to utilize NAPALM and its Ansible modules to validate network reachability across the network. This validation performs pings from the managed devices to the destination that we specify, in order to make sure that the forwarding path across the network is working as expected.

Getting ready

To follow along with this recipe, it is assumed that an Ansible inventory is already in place and network reachability between the Ansible controller and the network is established. The network in this recipe is assumed to be configured as per the relevant previous recipe.

How to do it...

1. Create a new playbook called `pb_napalm_ping.yml` with the following content:

```
$ cat pb_napalm_ping.yml

---
- name: " Validation Traffic Forwarding with NAPALM"
  hosts: junos:&pe
  vars:
    rr: 10.100.1.254
    max_delay: 5 # This is 5 msec
  tasks:
    - name: "P1T1: Ping Remote Destination using NAPALM"
      napalm_ping:
        hostname: "{{ ansible_host }}"
        username: "{{ ansible_user }}"
        password: "{{ ansible_ssh_pass }}"
        dev_os: "{{ ansible_network_os }}"
        destination: "{{ rr }}"
        count: 2
      register: rr_ping
```

2. Update the playbook with the validation tasks shown in the following code block:

```
$ cat pb_napalm_ping.yml

< -- Output Omitted for brevity -->
- name: Validate Packet Loss is Zero and No Delay
  assert:
    that:
      - rr_ping.ping_results.keys() | list | first == 'success'
      - rr_ping.ping_results['success'].packet_loss == 0
      - rr_ping.ping_results['success'].rtt_avg < max_delay
```

How it works...

NAPALM provides another Ansible module, `napalm_ping`, which connects to the remote managed device and executes pings from the remote managed device toward a destination that we specify. Using this module, we are able to validate the forwarding path between the managed devices and the specified destination.

This `napalm_ping` module does not currently support Cisco IOS-XR devices, which is why we only select all PE devices that are in the Junos OS group. In our playbook, we use the `junos:&pe` pattern in order to do this.

In our example, we create a new playbook and we specify the destination that we want to ping, along with the maximum delay for our ping packets within the playbook itself, using the `vars` parameter. Then, we use the `napalm_ping` module to connect to the MPLS PE devices (only Junos OS ones) in our topology to execute `ping` from all these PE nodes toward the destination that we specified (in our case, this is the loopback for our **route reflector (RR)** router). We store all this data in a variable called `rr_ping`.

The following snippet shows the output returned from `napalm_ping`:

```
"ping_results": {
  "success": {
    "packet_loss": 0,
    "probes_sent": 2,
    "results": [
      {
        "ip_address": "10.100.1.254",
        "rtt": 2.808
      },
      {
        "ip_address": "10.100.1.254",
        "rtt": 1.91
      }
    ],
    "rtt_avg": 2.359,
    "rtt_max": 2.808,
    "rtt_min": 1.91,
    "rtt_stddev": 0.449
  }
}
```

Finally, we use the `assert` module to validate and compare the results returned by NAPALM against our requirements (ping is successful, no packet loss, and delay less than `max_delay`).

Validating and auditing networks with NAPALM

In this recipe, we will outline how we can validate the operational state of the network by defining the intended state of the network and letting NAPALM validate that the actual/operational state of the network matches our intended state. This is useful in network auditing and compliance reports for our network infrastructure.

Getting ready

To follow along with this recipe, it is assumed that an Ansible inventory is already in place and network reachability between the Ansible controller and the network is established. Finally, the network is configured as per the previously outlined recipe.

How to do it...

1. Create a new folder called `napalm_validate` and create a YAML file for each device. We will validate its state, as shown in the following code block:

```
$ cat napalm_validate/mxpe01.yml

---
- get_interfaces_ip:
    ge-0/0/0.0:
      ipv4:
        10.1.1.3:
          prefix_length: 31
- get_bgp_neighbors:
    global:
      router_id: 10.100.1.1
```

2. Create a new `pb_napalm_validation.yml` playbook with the following content:

```
$ cat pb_napalm_validation.yml

---
- name: " Validating Network State via NAPALM"
  hosts: pe
  tasks:
    - name: "P1T1: Validation with NAPALM"
```

```
              napalm_validate:
                hostname: "{{ ansible_host }}"
                username: "{{ ansible_user }}"
                password: "{{ ansible_ssh_pass }}"
                dev_os: "{{ ansible_network_os }}"
                validation_file: "napalm_validate/{{
    inventory_hostname}}.yml"
                ignore_errors: true
                register: net_validate
```

3. Update the playbook to create a folder that will store the compliance reports for each device, as shown in the following code block:

```
$ cat pb_napalm_validation.yml

< -- Output Omitted for brevity -->

- name: Create Compliance Report Folder
  file: path=compliance_folder state=directory

- name: Clean Last Compliance Report
  file: path=compliance_folder/{{inventory_hostname}}.txt
state=absent

- name: Create Compliance Report
  copy:
    content: "{{ net_validate.compliance_report | to_nice_yaml }}"
    dest: "compliance_folder/{{ inventory_hostname }}.txt"
```

How it works...

NAPALM provides another module for network validation, which is the `napalm_validate` module. This module is mainly used to perform auditing and generate compliance reports for the network infrastructure. The main idea is to declare the intended state of the network and define it in a YAML document. This YAML file has a specific format, following the same structure with which the different NAPALM facts are generated. In this YAML file, we specify the NAPALM facts that we want to retrieve from the network, along with the network's expected output.

We supply these validation files to the `napalm_validate` module, and NAPALM will connect to the devices, retrieve the facts specified in these validation files, and compare the output retrieved from the network against the network state declared in these validation files.

Next, NAPALM generates a `compliance_report` object, which has the result of the comparison and whether the network complies with these validation files or not. We also set the `ignore_errors` parameter in order to continue with the other tasks in this playbook in case the device doesn't comply, so we can capture this compliance problem in the compliance report that we will generate.

Finally, we save the output in a separate folder called `compliance_folder` for each node, copy the contents of the `compliance_report` parameter, and format it using the `to_nice_yaml` filter.

The code for a correct compliance report generated for a `mxpe01` device is shown in the following snippet:

```
complies: true
get_bgp_neighbors:
  complies: true
  extra: []
  missing: []
  present:
    global:
      complies: true
      nested: true
get_interfaces_ip:
  complies: true
  extra: []
  missing: []
  present:
    ge-0/0/0.0:
      complies: true
      nested: true
skipped: []
```

See also...

For further information on validating deployments and the other options available for `napalm_validate`, please check the following URLs:

- https://napalm.readthedocs.io/en/latest/integrations/ansible/modules/napalm_validate/index.html
- https://napalm.readthedocs.io/en/latest/validate/index.html

7
Deploying and Operating AWS Networking Resources with Ansible

The cloud is one technology that is transforming multiple industries. It is having a significant impact on the overall infrastructure of IT, how applications are deployed, and how they are architected to be adopted for the cloud.

AWS is one of the main cloud providers. It provides multiple networking resources and services to build scalable and highly available networking designs to house applications on the AWS cloud.

One of the main pillars of cloud adoption is automation and how quickly we can deploy workloads. Each cloud provider has its own automation capabilities. In the case of AWS, this is a service called CloudFormation, which enables us to describe the AWS infrastructure using **Infrastructure as Code (IaC)** and to deploy the infrastructure on the AWS cloud. However, Ansible's advantage, when compared to CloudFormation, is its ability to describe/deploy resources across all cloud providers, including AWS. This allows us to have a consistent tool to deploy our workload in a multi-cloud environment.

Ansible provides multiple modules to interact with the AWS cloud to provision and control the different resources within.

In this chapter, we will focus on the deployment of the basic network services offered by AWS, which allow us to build a scalable network design in AWS. We will use the following sample AWS network design in our illustration and outline how to build this network using Ansible:

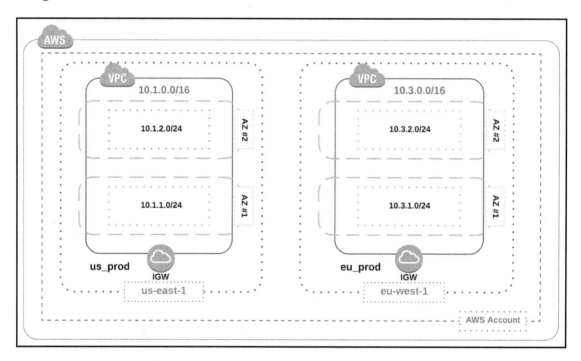

The main recipes covered in this chapter are as follows:

- Installing the AWS SDK
- Building an Ansible inventory
- Authenticating to your AWS account
- Deploying VPCs using Ansible
- Deploying subnets using Ansible
- Deploying IGWs using Ansible
- Controlling routing within a VPC using Ansible
- Deploying network ACLs using Ansible
- Deployment validation using Ansible

- Decommissioning AWS resources using Ansible

Technical requirements

The GitHub code used in this chapter can be found here:
`https://github.com/PacktPublishing/Network-Automation-Cookbook/tree/master/ch7_`
`aws`

The following are the software releases that this chapter is based on:

- An Ansible machine running CentOS 7
- Ansible 2.9
- Python 3.6.8

Check out the following video to see the Code in Action:
`https://bit.ly/3ckoAFe`

Installing the AWS SDK

In this recipe, we will outline how to install the Python libraries required by Ansible to start interacting with the AWS orchestration system. This step is mandatory as these Python libraries must be installed on the Ansible control machine in order for all of the Ansible AWS modules to work.

Getting ready

You need to have sudo access on the machine in order to install the required Python libraries. Furthermore, you need to have the `python-pip` package installed since we will be using **pip** to install the required Python libraries.

How to do it...

1. We can test any Ansible AWS module to check whether the required Python library is installed:

```
$ ansible localhost -m aws_az_facts

localhost | FAILED! => {
```

```
        "changed": false,
        "msg": "boto3 required for this module"
    }
```

2. Install the `boto` and `boto3` packages, as follows:

```
$ sudo pip3 install boto3 boto
```

How it works...

The Python SDK libraries that interact with the AWS orchestration system API are `boto` and `boto3`. These python packages must be present on the Ansible control machine since, with Ansible, all the AWS modules rely on one of these python packages to operate. We can check whether this package is already installed on the system using the preceding first step to run any AWS module (`aws_az_facts`, for example) using the `ansible` command. If the `boto3` library is not present, we will get an error message informing us that `boto3` is not installed.

We can install the `boto` and `boto3` packages using the Python pip program using the `pip3` command, which will install the packages and all the dependencies needed to install and run the package correctly. At this stage, we have all that we need to run all the Ansible AWS modules.

Building an Ansible inventory

In this recipe, we will outline how to build an Ansible inventory to describe the infrastructure network setup that we will build across the AWS public cloud. This is a mandatory step in order to define all of our VPCs across all the regions where we will deploy our infrastructure.

How to do it...

1. Create a new `ch7_aws` folder and create a `hosts` file inside it, as shown here:

```
$ cat hosts

[us]
 us_prod_vpc

[eu]
```

```
      eu_prod_vpc

  [prod_vpcs]
   us_prod_vpc
   eu_prod_vpc
```

2. Create the `ansible.cfg` file inside `ch7_aws` with the contents shown here:

```
$ cat ansible.cfg

[defaults]
 inventory=hosts
 vault_password_file=~/.ansible_vault_passwd
 gathering=explicit
 transport=local
 retry_files_enabled=False
 action_warnings=False
```

How it works...

We created the host's Ansible inventory file and we now need to declare our VPCs as nodes in our inventory, similarly to how we define a network node. The only exception is that a VPC doesn't have a management IP address, so we don't specify the `ansible_host` argument for those VPCs.

We need to create the following groups in our inventory file:

- A US group, which groups all the VPCs in the United States
- An EU group, which groups all the VPCs in Europe
- `prod_vpcs`, which groups all of our production VPCs

We also need to define the `ansible.cfg` file with all the configuration options that we used in all the previous recipes. We need to specify the vault password file that includes the encryption password that we will use to encrypt all of our sensitive information.

Authenticating to your AWS account

In this recipe, we will outline how to create the credentials required to programmatically authenticate to our AWS account and how to secure these credentials using Ansible Vault. This is a mandatory step in order to be able to run any Ansible modules in all the following recipes.

Getting ready

The Ansible controller must have internet access and the Ansible inventory must be set up as outlined in the previous recipe. Also, the user performing these steps must have the required access privileges on the AWS account to be able to create new users.

How to do it...

1. Create a new user using **IAM** with **Programmatic access**, as follows:

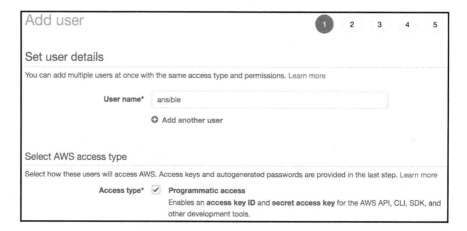

2. Assign the correct IAM policy to this new user, which allows them to create all the networking resources that it should manage (or a full access policy, for simplicity):

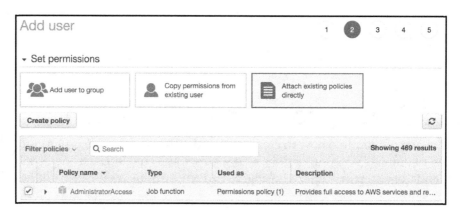

3. Finish creating the user and, on the last page, the **Add user** wizard will display the access key ID and the secret access key in a `.csv` file to download. These parameters will be used to authenticate to the AWS API for this account:

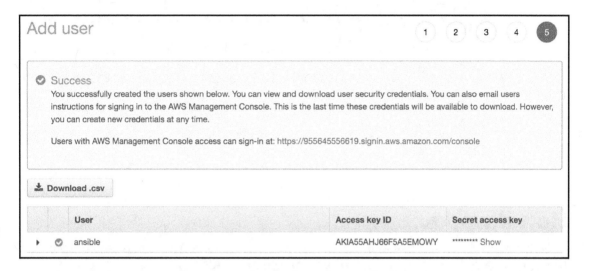

4. Encrypt the access key ID and secret access key using Ansible Vault, as follows:

```
$ ansible-vault encrypt_string <ACCESS_KEY_ID> --name
aws_access_key

$ ansible-vault encrypt_string <SECRET_ACCESS_KEY> --name
aws_secret_key_id
```

5. Create `group_vars` inside `ch7_aws` and create the `all.yml` file inside `group_vars`. Populate the `all.yml` file with the passwords encrypted using the `ansible-vault` in the previous step:

```
ansible_connection: local

aws_access_key: !vault |
  $ANSIBLE_VAULT;1.1;AES256
37623631653336633662666138353639653365323637323665353731386661343164393664333434
34303065626235323661376638356361386163633835660a656235363130303035383965663464
39326130613433643861653933623230323937353764663338613265376465636437363566632303435
66313265316666461310a3534613964313037653938306364323634303234383736353833132336462
```

```
373561636436626236336439653864656565636135336139386662323430633962
6
1

aws_secret_key_id: !vault |
  $ANSIBLE_VAULT;1.1;AES256
383531656664373932623030356465316661396239636430666230663466333939
4633438626539
626662393734303637626637346362326631646261313966660a33666435356462353
1393332613433
343363633939626666333636303936313761356566666238623739666439353866
5363733376133
623632646232656632306536336433646463696362313636336326666632396133613386
3376166343135
373738393164306433373535643730623333232656136393564613132333306531663
8383739326238
    3530386534303033363646362666434623465313635353534633265
```

How it works...

The first step is to ensure that a user account has programmatic access to the AWS console through the API. In order for a user to authenticate to the AWS API, the user must be assigned two passwords, which are generated by AWS during user creation or when the user requests to change their password. These two passwords are the access key ID and the secret access key. These two passwords are only visible and available upon creation and AWS provides them in a CSV file that you can download. Furthermore, we need to ensure that this user has the correct IAM permission to create the necessary resources (the VPC, subnets, routing tables, and so on). So, in our example, this new user is assigned the administrator policy, which gives them full access to the AWS account to create any resources (such as EC2 instances, VPCs, subnets, and so on). The steps that we have outlined to create a new user are optional if a user already has programmatic access and the required IAM privileges; we have just demonstrated this for completeness.

Since we have the secrets generated by AWS for this account in the CSV file in plain text, we can take these passwords and encrypt them using Ansible Vault and store them in the `group_vars/all.yml` file so that we can use these credentials when we are creating all the resources for our VPCs. We store these secrets into the `aws_access_key` and `aws_secret_key_id` parameters after they have been encrypted by the `ansible-vault encrypt_string` command. Ansible Vault uses the Vault password file that we have declared in the `ansible.cfg` file and this file has the encryption password that we will use to encrypt all of these passwords.

In the next recipe, we will outline how to use these encrypted variables that we have created to authenticate to the AWS console when creating VPCs.

Deploying VPCs using Ansible

In this recipe, we will outline how to deploy AWS VPCs using Ansible. AWS VPCs are the foundational networking construct in AWS and they can be thought of as a virtual data center within the cloud that the administrator creates within their AWS account. In order to start building any other infrastructure-related services within AWS, a VPC must first be created. We will outline how to describe all the required VPCs and how to automate their creation using Ansible.

Getting ready

To connect to the AWS API, the AWS control machine must be connected to the internet. The AWS account must also be prepared, as outlined in the previous recipe, with the required AWS credentials.

How to do it...

1. Create the `us.yml` and `eu.yml` files under the `group_vars` directory and populate these files with the AWS region name definitions, as follows:

   ```
   $ cat group_vars/eu.yml
     aws_region: eu-west-1

   $ cat group_vars/eu.yml
     aws_region: us-east-1
   ```

2. Create the `eu_prod_vpc.yml` and `us_prod_vpc.yml` files under the `host_vars` directory and populate them with the VPC parameters, as follows:

   ```
   $ cat host_vars/eu_prod_vpc.yml

   vpc_name: EU_Prod_Public_VPC
   vpc_cidr: 10.3.0.0/16
   vpc_tags:
     role: prod
     region: eu EU
   ```

```
$ cat host_vars/us_prod_vpc.yml
vpc_name: US_Prod_Public_VPC
vpc_cidr: 10.1.0.0/16
vpc_tags:
  role: prod
  region: US
```

3. Create a new playbook, `pb_aws_net_build.yml`, and populate it, as follows:

```
$ cat pb_aws_net_build.yml

- name: Create all AWS Networks
  hosts: prod_vpcs
    environment:
    AWS_ACCESS_KEY: "{{ aws_access_key }}"
    AWS_SECRET_KEY: "{{ aws_secret_key_id }}"
  tasks:
    - name: Create New VPC
      ec2_vpc_net:
        cidr_block: "{{ vpc_cidr }}"
        region: "{{ aws_region }}"
        name: "{{ vpc_name }}"
        state: "{{ vpc_state | default('present') }}"
        tags: "{{ vpc_tags }}"
      register: create_vpc
```

How it works...

AWS has a global presence and it segregates each part of its infrastructure in each part of the world into Regions. An AWS Region is a collection of AWS facilities in a part of the world and each Region in AWS is considered to be an isolated fault domain with its own orchestration and management systems. So, when we are creating a VPC, we need to specify which region we will deploy this VPC into, so we need to describe this information in our Ansible variables. In our case, we specify the AWS Region for all of our VPCs in the US as us-east-1 and all of our VPCs in the EU as eu-west-1. This is achieved by defining the aws_region variable under the eu.yml and us.yml files and under the group_vars directory.

This logic of the AWS Region is critical for most of the services in AWS that are region-specific, and all of the networking constructs that we will build are all region-specific. For almost all the AWS Ansible modules, we need to specify the AWS Region in order to initiate the correct API call to the correct API endpoint in the designated region. This is because the API endpoint for each region has a different FQDN. For more information regarding AWS endpoints for all of the services in AWS in all of the regions, use the following link:

https://docs.aws.amazon.com/general/latest/gr/rande.html

We need to declare the variables for each VPC under the host_vars directory and create a YAML file for each of our VPCs. We need to specify the VPC name, prefix, and the tags that should be assigned to the VPC. Finally, we need to create the Ansible playbook to build our infrastructure and use a new option within the playbook, which is the environment. This option creates temporary environment variables (AWS_ACCESS_KEY and AWS_SECRET_KEY) during the playbook's execution. These environment variables have their values set to the same values as the aws_access_key and aws_secret_key_id variables that we defined in the group_vars/all.yml file. This makes the values contained within these environment variables present during the playbook execution so that the AWS modules within each task can use this information to authenticate all the API calls.

We can create the VPCs on the AWS cloud using the ec2_vpc_net Ansible module and we can specify the AWS Region where this VPC will be deployed using the region attribute. We need to define its IP prefix, name, and any associated tags. All this information is derived from the variables that we have defined in the host_vars file for this VPC.

As the module creates the VPC, it returns all of the information for the VPC that was created, and we can save this information in a new variable called create_vpc.

The following is a snippet of the data returned by the VPC creation task:

```
"create_vpc": {
  "vpc": {
    "cidr_block": "10.1.0.0/16",

< -- Output Omitted for brevity -->

    "dhcp_options_id": "dopt-b983c8c2",
    "id": "vpc-0d179be0eb66847f3",
    "instance_tenancy": "default",
    "is_default": false,
    "owner_id": "955645556619",
    "state": "available",
    "tags": {
      "Name": "US_Prod_Public_VPC",
```

```
        "region": "US",
        "role": "prod"
    }
  }
}
```

The following screenshot outlines the VPC created on AWS from the console:

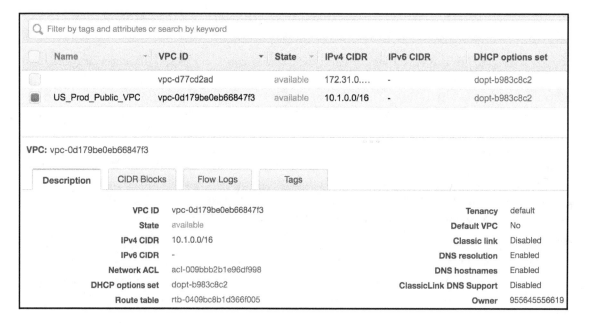

See also

For more information regarding the `ec2_vpc_net` module and the other parameters available within this module, use the following URL:

`https://docs.ansible.com/ansible/latest/modules/ec2_vpc_net_module.html`

Deploying subnets using Ansible

In this recipe, we will outline how to deploy subnets within our AWS VPCs using Ansible. Subnets are a fundamental networking construct within AWS in order to provide more resiliency for applications deployed on the AWS cloud. This extra resiliency is achieved by the fact that subnets can be mapped to different availability zones. Using this logic, we can provide high availability for our deployment by spreading our resources into different availability zones.

Getting ready

The Ansible control machine must have internet reachability and the VPCs must already be provisioned as per the previous recipe.

How to do it...

1. Update the `host_vars/eu_prod_vpc.yml` file with the subnet's data, as shown here. The same is done for `host_vars/us_prod_vpc.yml` to include all of the subnet's data:

```
$ cat host_vars/eu_prod_vpc.yml

< -- Output Omitted for brevity -->

vpc_subnets:
  eu-prod-public-a:
    cidr: 10.3.1.0/24
    az: "{{ aws_region }}a"
    tags: "{{ vpc_tags }}"
    public: true

  eu-prod-public-b:
    cidr: 10.3.2.0/24
    az: "{{ aws_region}}b"
    tags: "{{ vpc_tags }}"
    public: true
```

2. Update the `pb_aws_net_build.yml` playbook and populate it with the new task to build the subnets:

```
- name: "set fact: VPC ID"
  set_fact:
    vpc_id: "{{ create_vpc.vpc.id }}"

- name: create VPC subnets
  ec2_vpc_subnet:
    region: "{{ aws_region }}"
    vpc_id: "{{ vpc_id }}"
    cidr: "{{ item.value.cidr }}"
    az: "{{ item.value.az }}"
    tags: "{{{item.value.tags | combine({ 'Name': item.key })}}}"
  with_dict: "{{ vpc_subnets }}"
  register: create_vpc_subnets
```

How it works...

The availability zone is the construct that provides resiliency for the physical infrastructure within an AWS Region. In order to use availability zones efficiently, we need to map our infrastructure within a VPC to be allocated to different availability zones within a region. This is accomplished using AWS subnets.

In our sample deployment, we use two subnets spread across two availability zones in order to provide high availability for our network setup. We declare the subnets that we will deploy within each VPC using the `vpc_subnets` variable. These variables include the CIDR that we will use within each subnet (which must be a subset of the VPC CIDR), the availability zone that we want this subnet to be attached to, and, finally, the tags that we want to assign to this subnet. We build the availability zone's name using the AWS Region plus a suffix (a, b, c, and so on). This is the naming convention that AWS uses to name the availability zones within a region.

In order to create subnets in AWS, we need to associate a subnet with its parent VPC. In order to do this, we need to specify the `vpc-id` parameter during the API call to create the subnet. This `vpc-id` is a unique identifier that AWS assigns to a VPC during its creation. We get this value from the VPC creation task that was executed to create the VPC and we saved the output of this task to the `vpc_create` variable. We can use this variable to retrieve the ID of the VPC and assign it to the `vpc-id` variable using the `set_fact` module.

Finally, we can build the subnets using the `ec2_vpc_subnet` module to create the necessary subnets within each VPC and loop over the `vpc_subnets` data structure in order to build all the required subnets.

The following screenshot shows the subnets that are correctly provisioned on the AWS cloud in our `US_Prod` VPC:

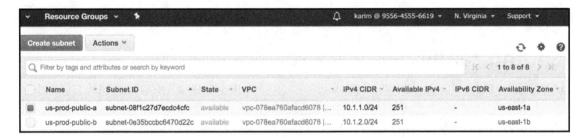

The following are the tags assigned to this subnet:

Key	Value
Name	us-prod-public-a
region	US
role	prod

See also

For more information regarding the `ec2_vpc_subnet` module and the other parameters available within this module, use the following URL:

https://docs.ansible.com/ansible/latest/modules/ec2_vpc_subnet_module.html#ec2-vpc-subnet-module

Deploying IGWs using Ansible

In this recipe, we will outline how to deploy **Internet Gateways** (**IGWs**) to our AWS VPCs using Ansible. IGWs are our exit points from our VPC to the internet in order to reach a public external destination. Since we are building a public-facing service, we need to have internet reachability from our VPC. This is accomplished by the IGW construct in the AWS cloud.

Getting ready

The Ansible control machine must have internet reachability and the VPCs must already be provisioned, as per the previous recipe.

How to do it...

1. Update the `eu_prod_vpc.yml` file with the IGW data, as shown here, and do the same for `us_prod_vpc.yml`:

```
$ cat host_vars/eu_prod_vpc.yml

< -- Output Omitted for brevity -->

igw_name: eu_prod_igw

$ cat host_vars/eu_prod_vpc.yml

< -- Output Omitted for brevity -->

igw_name: us_prod_igw
```

2. Update the `pb_aws_net_build.yml` playbook and populate it with the new task to build the IGW nodes:

```
- name: Create IGW
  ec2_vpc_igw:
    region: "{{ aws_region }}"
    vpc_id: "{{ vpc_id }}"
    state: present
    tags: "{{ vpc_tags | combine({'Name': igw_name}) }}"
  register: vpc_igw_create

- name: Extract VPC IGW ID
```

```
set_fact:
  igw_id: "{{ vpc_igw_create.gateway_id }}"
```

How it works...

The IGW network construct is our exit point from our VPC to reach public destinations across the internet. The IGW is attached to the VPC and it provides internet connectivity to any resource located within the VPC (such as EC2 or RDS instances). In order to create an IGW, we need to specify the VPC that this IGW will be attached to. So, we need the ID for the VPC.

As we discussed in the previous recipe, we get the VPC ID when we create the VPC and we can save this variable using a separate task. We can use the value of this variable during the IGW's creation. We can use the `ec2_vpc_igw` module to create the IGW and specify the region that we want this IGW deployed into. We can also specify the VPC ID that the IGW will be attached to. Finally, we can specify the tags that we will allocate to the IGW node. The IGW tags are optional, but they are critical when using automated deployment since they allow us to reference the objects that we have created. We will outline the use of tags when we discuss deployment validation and fact collection in the following recipes.

When we deploy a new IGW, the `ec2_vpc_igw` module returns the IGW parameters that were provisioned inside AWS. One particular parameter that is important is `igw-id`. This parameter uniquely identifies the IGW node that was provisioned and we must use it when we reference the IGW in any operation related to this IGW node.

The following is a snippet of the IGW parameters returned by `ec2_vpc_igw`, which we captured in the `vpc_igw_create` variable for the IGW node in `us_prod_vpc`:

```
ok: [us_prod_vpc] => {
  "vpc_igw_create": {
    "changed": true,
    "failed": false,
    "gateway_id": "igw-05d3e4c664486790b",
    "tags": {
      "Name": "us_prod_igw",
      "region": "US",
      "role": "prod"
    },
    "vpc_id": "vpc-0abc32281330c9bc6"
  }
}
```

In the previous task, we captured the `gateway-id` variable returned by `ec2_vpc_igw` and stored it in a new variable, called `igw_id`, which we will use in subsequent tasks when referencing the IGW node.

The following screenshot outlines the IGW node that was provisioned and attached to the VPC:

See also

For more information regarding the `ec2_igw_vpc` module and the other parameters available within this module, use the following URL:

`https://docs.ansible.com/ansible/latest/modules/ec2_vpc_igw_module.html#ec2-vpc-igw-module`

Controlling routing within a VPC using Ansible

In this recipe, we will outline how to adjust the routing inside an AWS VPC in order to control the traffic forwarding within the subnets inside a VPC. Controlling the routing within a VPC allows us to customize the VPC design and how the traffic is forwarded within the VPC, as well as how to exit the VPC to external destinations.

Getting ready

The Ansible control machine must have internet reachability and the VPCs must already be provisioned as per the previous recipe.

How to do it...

1. Update the `eu_prod_vpc.yml` file with the routing table data, as shown here, and do the same for `us_prod_vpc.yml`:

    ```
    $ cat host_vars/eu_prod_vpc.yml

    < -- Output Omitted for brevity -->

    route_table:
      tags:
        Name: eu_public_rt
      igw:
        - dest: 0.0.0.0/0
          gateway_id: "{{ igw_id }}"
      public:
        - eu-prod-public-a
        - eu-prod-public-b
    ```

2. Update the `pb_aws_net_build.yml` playbook and populate it with the following tasks to attach the route table to the VPC that we have created:

    ```
    - name: Get Default VPC Route Table
      ec2_vpc_route_table_facts:
        region: "{{ aws_region }}"
        filters:
          vpc-id: "{{ vpc_id }}"
      register: vpc_route_table_facts
      tags: rt

    - name: Extract Route Table IDs
      set_fact:
        rt_id: "{{vpc_route_table_facts.route_tables[0].id }}"
      tags: rt
    ```

3. Update the playbook and populate it with the following tasks to update the route table with the required routes:

```
- name: Update Default VPC Route Table
  ec2_vpc_route_table :
    region: "{{ aws_region }}"
    vpc_id: "{{ vpc_id }}"
    route_table_id: "{{ rt_id }}"
    routes: "{{ route_table.igw }}"
    subnets: "{{ route_table.public }}"
    lookup: id
    state: present
    tags: "{{ vpc_tags | combine(route_table.tags) }}"
```

How it works...

Up until this point, we have managed to set up the VPC, the subnets, and the IGW. However, although the IGW node is connected to the internet and it is attached to the VPC, none of the traffic within the VPC will use the IGW node since the routing table associated with the VPC is still not updated and there is no route to point the IGW.

The following is a snippet of the default routing table for `us_prod_vpc` before changing the route table:

AWS VPCs have a default route table that is assigned to the VPC and to all the subnets that don't have a specific route table associated with them. So, by default, all the subnets within the VPC are associated with the VPC's default route table.

The following is a screenshot that shows that the subnets created within `us_prod_vpc` are associated with the default route table:

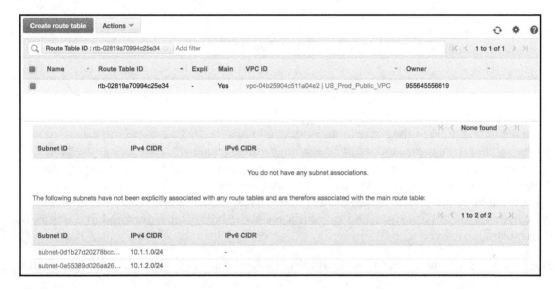

In the VPC definition that we have declared for each of our VPCs, we included a new data structure called `route_table`, which includes all the information we need to adjust the routing table for our VPC and associate all the subnets with it.

The first task that we will execute in this recipe is getting the ID for the default route table that is associated with the VPC that we have created. We will use the `ec2_vpc_route_table_facts` module to get the facts for the route table and supply the VPC ID to uniquely identify the VPC. We can store the ID for the default route table in the new variable: `rt_id`.

The following snippet outlines the route table facts that we retrieved from the `ec2_vpnc_facts` module:

```
ok: [us_prod_vpc] => {
  "vpc_route_table_facts": {
    "route_tables": [
      {
```

```
< -- Output Omitted for brevity --> ],
        "id": "rtb-0b6669ba5fd9eb9c8",
        "routes": [
            {
                "destination_cidr_block": "10.1.0.0/16",
                "gateway_id": "local",

< -- Output Omitted for brevity -->

            }
        ],
        "tags": {},
        "vpc_id": "vpc-005b1dcb981791d86"
    }
  ]
 }
}
```

Once we have the ID of the route table associated with the VPC, we can use the
`ec2_vpc_route_table` module to adjust the routing table for the default route table
associated with the VPC. We must supply the VPC and route table IDs to uniquely identify
the exact route table that we want to modify. We can specify the routes that we want to
inject in the routing table and the subnets that we want to associate with this route table.
We can inject the default route and point it toward the IGW that we created in the previous
recipe using `igw-id`.

The following screenshot outlines the routing table for our VPC after adjusting the routing:

The following screenshot outlines how the two subnets that we have in the VPC are now associated with this default route table:

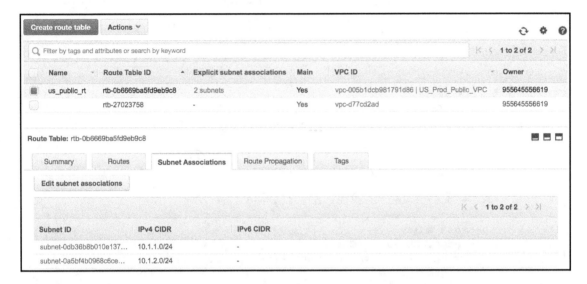

See also

For more information regarding the multiple modules to interact with the routing table of the AWS VPC and the associated modules, use the following links:

- https://docs.ansible.com/ansible/latest/modules/ec2_vpc_route_table_module.html#ec2-vpc-route-table-module
- https://docs.ansible.com/ansible/latest/modules/ec2_vpc_route_table_facts_module.html#ec2-vpc-route-table-facts-module

Deploying network ACLs using Ansible

In this recipe, we will outline how to deploy **network ACLs** (**NACLs**) on AWS. NACLs are one of the security solutions available in AWS to secure computer resources deployed in the AWS cloud. In this recipe, we will outline how to describe and automate the deployment of NACLs in AWS.

Getting ready

The Ansible control machine must have internet reachability to reach the AWS API endpoints, and the VPCs and subnets must already be provisioned, as per the previous recipe.

How to do it...

1. Update the `eu_prod_vpc.yml` file with the NACL definition data, as shown here, and do the same for `us_prod_vpc.yml`:

```
$ cat host_vars/eu_prod_vpc.yml

< -- Output Omitted for brevity -->

network_acls:
  - name: EU_Prod_ACLs
    subnets: "{{ vpc_subnets.keys() | list }}"
    ingress_rules:
      - [100,'tcp','allow','0.0.0.0/0',null,null,80,80]
      - [200,'tcp','allow','0.0.0.0/0',null,null,443,443]
```

2. Update the `pb_aws_net_build.yml` playbook and populate it with the following task to create the NACLs:

```
- name: Create Network ACLs
  ec2_vpc_nacl:
    region: "{{ aws_region }}"
    vpc_id: "{{ vpc_id }}"
    name: "{{ item.name }}"
    subnets: "{{ item.subnets }}"
    ingress: "{{ item.ingress_rules }}"
    tags: "{{ vpc_tags | combine({'Name':item.name}) }}"
  loop: "{{ network_acls }}"
```

How it works...

AWS NACLs are stateless ACLs that have the ability to allow or deny IP traffic based on L3 and L4 IP address information. They are enforced on the subnet level and are associated with subnets in order to protect all the resources provisioned on a subnet. They can block traffic in the ingress (traffic entering the subnet) or egress (traffic exiting the subnet) direction. The rules within an NACL are processed based on the rule number, so the first matching rule will be applied to the traffic flow.

All subnets have a default NACL attached and AWS sets up the following rules for the default NACL:

- On ingress, all traffic is permitted. The following screenshot outlines the rules applied to the default NACL:

Rule #	Type	Protocol	Port Range	Source	Allow / Deny
100	ALL Traffic	ALL	ALL	0.0.0.0/0	ALLOW
*	ALL Traffic	ALL	ALL	0.0.0.0/0	DENY

- On egress, all traffic is permitted. The following screenshot outlines the rules applied to the default NACL:

Rule #	Type	Protocol	Port Range	Destination	Allow / Deny
100	ALL Traffic	ALL	ALL	0.0.0.0/0	ALLOW
*	ALL Traffic	ALL	ALL	0.0.0.0/0	DENY

In our sample setup, we will apply an NACL on all of our subnets that enforces the following security policy:

- All TCP traffic to ports 80 and 443 must be allowed.
- Any other traffic should be dropped.

 By default, there is a DENY rule at the end of any NACL that drops all traffic.

We define the `network_acls` data structure that holds the NACL definitions and all the required fields to set up the required NACLs on all of our subnets in both the EU and US regions. In this data structure, we need to define the following parameters:

- `Name`: This is the name of the NACL and it serves as an identifier.
- `Subnets`: This defines the subnets that should be associated with this NACL. We use the data in our `vpc_subnets` definition to construct this list.
- `Ingress_rules`: This defines all the rules that should be applied as part of this NACL in the ingress direction.
- `Engress_rules`: This defines all the rules that should be applied as part of this NACL in the egress direction.

We can create a new task within our playbook using `ec2_net_nacl` to provision the NACL and attach it to all of our subnets.

The following screenshot outlines the new NACL deployed in the `EU_prod` VPC:

The following screenshot outlines the subnets associated with our NACL in the `EU_prod` VPC:

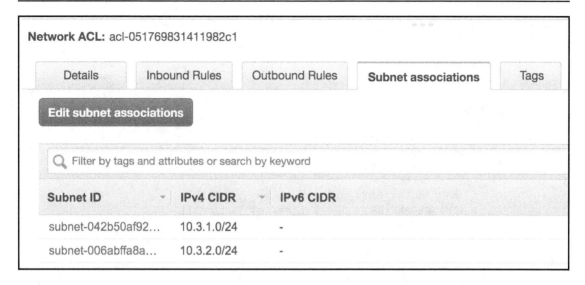

See also

For more information regarding the `ec2_net_nacl` Ansible module and the different parameters supported by this module, consult the following URL:

```
https://docs.ansible.com/ansible/latest/modules/ec2_vpc_nacl_module.html
```

Deployment validation using Ansible

In this recipe, we will outline how to collect the operational state of the different networking components within AWS, such as VPCs and subnets, and how to check that our deployment is being implemented as per our design.

Getting ready

The Ansible control machine must have internet reachability and all the networking components that we have outlined in the previous recipes should be in place.

How to do it...

1. Create a new `pb_vpc_validate.yml` playbook and populate it with the tasks to validate the VPC build:

```
$ cat pb_vpc_validate.yml

- name: Validate VPC Build
  hosts: all
  gather_facts: no
  environment:
    AWS_ACCESS_KEY: "{{ aws_access_key }}"
    AWS_SECRET_KEY: "{{ aws_secret_key_id }}"
    AWS_REGION: "{{ aws_region }}"
  tasks:
    - name: Get VPC facts
      ec2_vpc_net_facts:
        filters:
          "tag:Name": "{{ vpc_name }}"
      register: vpc_facts

    - name: Validate VPC Info
      assert:
        that:
          - vpc_facts.vpcs[0].cidr_block == vpc_cidr
          - vpc_facts.vpcs[0].tags.Name == vpc_name
      when: vpc_facts.vpcs != []
```

2. Update the playbook with the following tasks to collect the facts for the AWS subnets:

```
- name: Extract VPC ID
  set_fact:
    vpc_id: "{{ vpc_facts.vpcs[0].id }}"

- name: Get Subnet facts
  ec2_vpc_subnet_facts:
    filters:
      vpc-id: "{{ vpc_id }}"
  register: vpc_subnet_facts
  tags: subnet
```

3. Update the playbook with the following task to validate the state of the AWS subnets:

```
- name: Validate VPC Subnets Info
  assert:
```

```
      that:
        - vpc_subnet_facts.subnets |
          selectattr('tags.Name','equalto',item.key) |
          map(attribute='cidr_block') |
          list | first == item.value.cidr

        - vpc_subnet_facts.subnets |
          selectattr('tags.Name','equalto',item.key) |
          map(attribute='availability_zone') |
          list | first == item.value.az

    with_dict: "{{ vpc_subnets }}"
```

How it works...

We can create a new playbook to collect the VPC and subnet's facts using the `ec2_vpc_net_facts` and `ec2_vpc_subnet_facts` Ansible modules. We can collect the data returned from these modules and use the `assert` module to validate the state, as follows:

1. VPCs:
   - Check that the name assigned to the VPC is provisioned as per our design.
   - Check that the CIDR block assigned to the VPC is deployed as per our design.

2. Subnets:
   - Check that the CIDR assigned to the subnets is provisioned correctly.
   - Check that the subnet is provisioned in the correct availability zone.

We can perform all of the preceding validation by comparing the operational state returned by the facts modules with the metadata that we have defined for each VPC in either of the `group_vars` or `host_vars` variables.

> In the `ec2_vpc_net_facts` task, we used the `filters` parameter to select our VPC based only on its `Name` tag. By default, this module will return the facts for all of the VPCs within this region.
>
> In the `ec2_vpc_subnet_facts` task, we used the `filters` parameter to only retrieve the subnets data for our VPC, since by default this module will return all the subnets' facts for all of our VPCs within the region.

See also

For more information regarding the modules for fact collection for the different network resources in AWS, use the following links:

- https://docs.ansible.com/ansible/latest/modules/ec2_vpc_net_facts_module.html#ec2-vpc-net-facts-module

- https://docs.ansible.com/ansible/latest/modules/ec2_vpc_subnet_facts_module.html#ec2-vpc-subnet-facts-module

- https://docs.ansible.com/ansible/latest/modules/ec2_vpc_igw_facts_module.html#ec2-vpc-igw-facts-module

Decommissioning resources on AWS using Ansible

In this recipe, we will outline how to decommission a complete network within AWS with all the associated network resources. This outlines how we can easily build and tear down resources on the cloud with a simple playbook execution using Ansible.

Getting ready

The Ansible control machine must have internet reachability and all the networking components that we have outlined in the previous recipes should be in place.

How to do it...

1. Create a new `pb_delete_vpc.yml` playbook with the following tasks to collect the facts for the VPC:

```
$ cat pb_delete_vpc.yml

- name: Delete all VPC resources
  hosts: all
  gather_facts: no
  environment:
    AWS_ACCESS_KEY: "{{ aws_access_key }}"
    AWS_SECRET_KEY: "{{ aws_secret_key_id }}"
```

```
            AWS_REGION: "{{ aws_region }}"
        tasks:
          - name: Get VPC facts
            ec2_vpc_net_facts:
              filters:
                "tag:Name": "{{ vpc_name }}"
            register: vpc_facts

          - name: Extract VPC ID
            set_fact:
              vpc_id: "{{ vpc_facts.vpcs[0].id }}"
```

2. Update the playbook with the following tasks to remove all the subnets and IGW nodes within the VPC:

```
          - name: Start Delete VPC Resources
            block:
              - name: Delete Subnets
                ec2_vpc_subnet:
                  cidr: "{{ item.value.cidr }}"
                  vpc_id: "{{ vpc_id }}"
                  state: absent
                with_dict: "{{ vpc_subnets }}"

              - name: Delete IGW
                ec2_vpc_igw:
                  vpc_id: "{{ vpc_id }}"
                  state: absent
```

3. Update the playbook with the following task to remove all the NACLs:

```
          - name: Delete NACLs
            ec2_vpc_nacl:
              name: "{{ item.name }}"
              vpc_id: "{{ vpc_id }}"
              state: absent
            loop: "{{ network_acls }}"
```

4. Update the playbook with the final task to remove all the VPCs:

```
          - name: Delete VPC
            ec2_vpc_net:
              cidr_block: "{{ vpc_cidr }}"
              name: "{{ vpc_name }}"
              state: absent
        when: vpc_id is defined
```

How it works...

We can start our new playbook with a collection of facts for our VPC to get the VPC ID for our deployed VPC. Once we have this information, we can start to delete the resources. However, the order in which we delete the resources is important. We need to remove any dependent resources first, so we must remove the subnets before we can remove the VPC. So, for example, if there are EC2 instances attached to the subnet, we must remove these EC2 instances before we can remove the subnets. So, in our case, we need to remove the subnets, then the IGW node, and then, finally, remove the VPC.

In all of these tasks, we are using the same exact modules that we have outlined in the previous recipes. The only change is that we are setting the state to be absent and we are supplying the required VPC ID to uniquely identify the VPC that we need to remove the required resources from.

Finally, when we start removing the resources within the VPC, we are validating first whether a VPC ID is present. If the resources have already been deleted and we run the playbook again, the deletion step would be skipped since no VPC ID would be retrieved by the facts task.

8
Deploying and Operating Azure Networking Resources with Ansible

In the previous chapter, we explored how to provision network resources on the AWS cloud and how to use Ansible as the orchestration engine to deploy those resources on AWS. In this chapter, we will look at another major cloud provider, Microsoft, and its Azure cloud offering.

Azure provides multiple networking services to facilitate the deployment of highly scalable cloud solutions on the Azure cloud. Ansible provides multiple modules to interact with multiple services within the Azure cloud and is an excellent tool to automate cloud deployments on the Azure cloud. We will explore the basic networking constructs available in Azure and outline how to use several modules in Ansible to build and validate the following basic network setup in the Azure cloud:

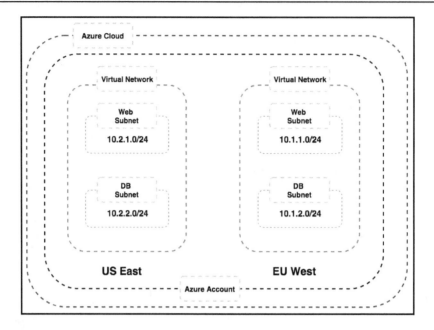

The main recipes covered in this chapter are as follows:

- Installing the Azure SDK
- Building an Ansible inventory
- Authenticating to your Azure account
- Creating a resource group
- Creating virtual networks
- Creating subnets
- Building user-defined routes
- Deploying network security groups
- Deployment validation using Ansible
- Decommissioning Azure resources using Ansible

Technical requirements

To be able to start working with Azure, you need to create an account. You can set up a free account at `https://Azure.microsoft.com/en-au/free/`.

The following link is to the GitHub code used in this chapter:

```
https://github.com/PacktPublishing/Network-Automation-Cookbook/tree/master/ch8_
azure
```

The software releases that this chapter is based on are as follows:

- An Ansible machine running CentOS 7
- Ansible 2.9
- Python 3.6.8

Check out the following video to see the Code in Action:
```
https://bit.ly/3esy3fS
```

Installing the Azure SDK

In this recipe, we will outline how to install the Python libraries required to start interacting with the Azure orchestration system using Ansible. This step is mandatory as these Python libraries must be installed on the Ansible control machine in order for all of the Ansible Azure modules to work.

Getting ready

You will need to have sudo access on the machine in order to install the Azure Python library. You also need to have Python installed with a Python PIP package, which we will use to install the Azure package.

How to do it...

1. Install the `boto3` package, as follows:

   ```
   $ sudo pip3 install 'Ansible[Azure]'
   ```

2. Create a new folder, entitled `ch8_Azure`, to host all of the code for this chapter:

   ```
   $ mkdir ch8_Azure
   ```

How it works...

The default installation of Ansible doesn't include all of the Python modules needed to run the Ansible Azure modules. That is why our first step is to install the required Python libraries. We install all of these packages using the Python pip program. We can verify that all of the Azure modules were installed with the following code:

```
$ pip3 list | grep Azure

Azure-cli-core            2.0.35

Azure-cli-nspkg           3.0.2

Azure-common              1.1.11

Azure-graphrbac           0.40.0

Azure-keyvault            1.0.0a1


  <<  ---  Output Omitted for brevity  -- >>
```

As previously outlined, multiple Python packages need to be installed to be able to begin interacting with the Azure API from Ansible. With this step complete, we are now ready to build our playbooks and infrastructure in Azure.

See also...

For more information about how to start interacting with the Azure cloud using Ansible, refer to the following link:

https://docs.Ansible.com/Ansible/latest/scenario_guides/guide_Azure.html

Building an Ansible inventory

In this recipe, we will outline how to build an Ansible inventory to describe the network infrastructure setup that we will build across the Azure public cloud. This is a necessary step as we will define all of our virtual networks across all of the regions in which we will deploy our infrastructure.

How to do it...

1. Create the `hosts` file inside the `ch8_Azure` directory with the following data:

```
$ cat hosts

[az_net]

eu_az_net

us_az_net

[eu]

eu_az_net

[us]

us_az_net
```

2. Create the `Ansible.cfg` file with the following content:

```
$ cat Ansible.cfg

[defaults]

inventory=hosts

retry_files_enabled=False

gathering=explicit

host_key_checking=False

action_warnings=False
```

3. Create the `group_var` folder and the `eu.yml` and `us.yml` files with the following code:

```
$ cat group_var/eu.yml

---

region: westeurope

$ cat group_var/us.yml
```

```
---

region: eastus
```

How it works...

We created the host's Ansible inventory file and declared the different virtual networks that we will provide in the Azure cloud. We also created two groups that describe the location of each virtual network.

In short, we created the following groups to define and group our virtual networks:

- az_net: This groups all of our virtual networks across the Azure cloud.
- eu: This lists all of the virtual networks in the EU region (and will map to a specific region in the Azure cloud, as we will outline later).
- us: This lists all of the virtual networks in the US region (and will map to a specific region in the Azure cloud, as we will outline later).

We can use this regional grouping to specify the exact region where this virtual network will be used across the Azure cloud. We can declare the exact region in a variable called region, which can be defined in both the eu.yml and us.yml files under the group_vars directory.

We are going to use this variable in the subsequent recipes to deploy our resources in the respective Azure regions.

Authenticating to your Azure account

In this recipe, we will outline how to create the credentials required to programmatically authenticate to our Azure account from Ansible. We will also learn how to secure those credentials using Ansible Vault. This step is required in order to be able to run any Ansible modules in the following recipes.

Getting ready

The Ansible controller must have internet access and the Ansible inventory must be set up as outlined in the previous recipe. The user performing these steps must have administrative access to the Azure portal to be able to create the required resources that will enable programmatic interaction with the Azure APIs.

How to do it...

1. Log in to the Azure portal with an account that has administrative rights: `https://portal.Azure.com/`

2. On the home page, select **Azure Active Directory**:

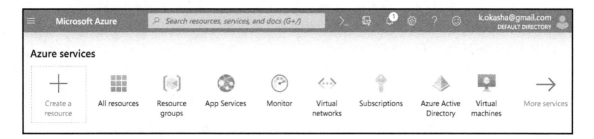

3. From the left panel, select **App registrations**:

4. Click the **New Registration** option and supply the following information to create a new application. The option highlighted in blue is the active option here:

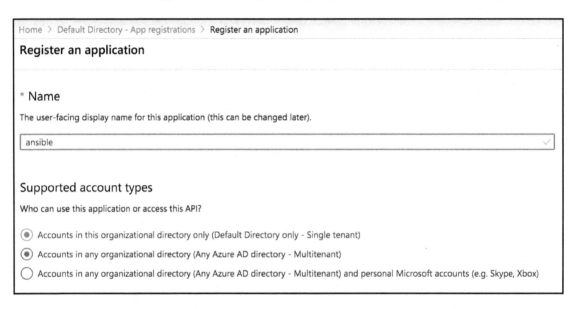

5. Once you click on the **register** button, the new application will be created and its information displayed, as in the following screenshot (we need the **client_id** and **tenant_id** data):

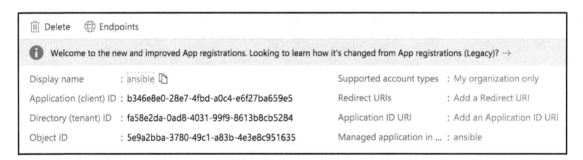

6. Select **Certificates & secrets** in the left panel:

7. Click on **New client secret**:

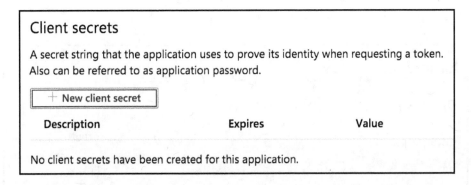

8. Specify a name for the password for this app and select its expiry date:

9. Once created, keep a record of the secret string that is displayed (this is the only time that we will be able to see this password in plain text):

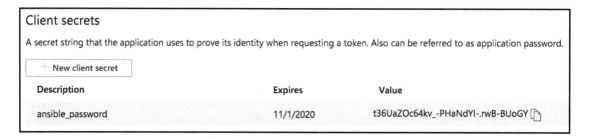

10. Go to **All Services** and select **Subscriptions**:

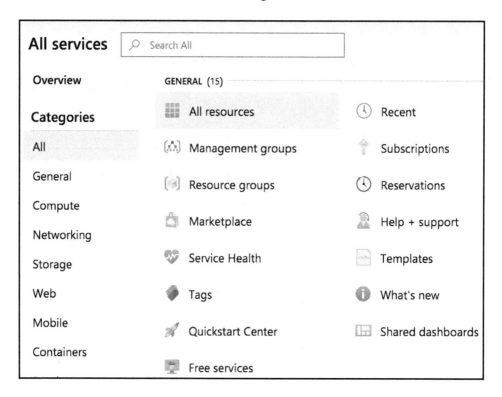

11. Click on **Subscription name** (**Free Trial**, in my case):

12. Record the **Subscription ID** string (as we need it for authentication), and then click on the **Access control (IAM)** tab on the left:

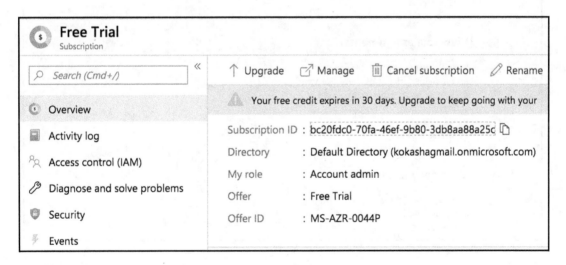

13. Click on **Add role assignment** and assign the **Contributor** role to the Ansible app that we created:

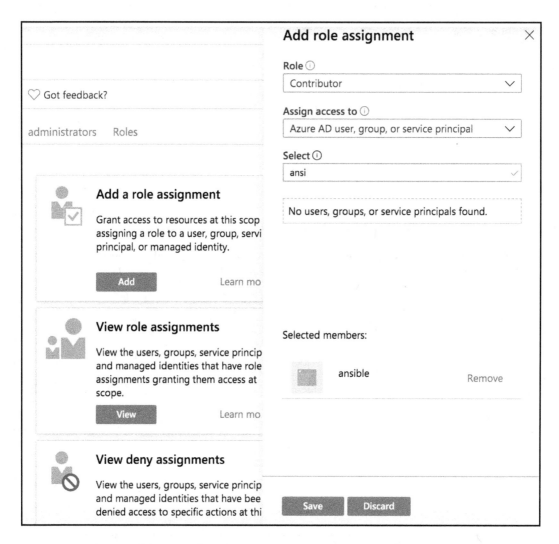

14. On the Ansible control node, create a new file that will hold our Ansible Vault password:

```
$ echo 'AzureV@uLT2019' > .vault_pass
```

15. Create a new file called `Azure_secret.yml` using Ansible Vault, as in the following code:

    ```
    $ Ansible-vault create Azure_secret.yml --vault-password-
    file=.vault_pass
    ```

16. Populate the `Azure_secret.yml` file with the data that we got from the Azure portal for `client_id`, `tenant_id`, and `subscription_id`, and the secret we created for our app:

    ```
    ---

    tenant_id: XXX-XXXXXXXX

    client_id: XXX-XXXX

    subscription_id: XXX-XXXXX

    secret: XXX-XXXX
    ```

How it works...

To be able to have programmatic access to the Azure API (this is how Ansible communicates with the Azure cloud to provision resources), we need to create a construct known as a *service principal* in our Azure account. This service principal is similar to a user but only has API access to the Azure account. We can create this service principal and call it Ansible. We can then assign the contributor role to it in access management in order to be able to create resources in our account. To authenticate to the Azure API using this service principal, we need to supply the following four components:

- `Client_id`
- `Tenant_id`
- `Subscription_id`
- `Service principal password`

We can locate all of this information in the Azure portal using the steps outlined in this recipe. We can create a new file, called `Azure_secrets.yml`, which we will encrypt using Ansible Vault, and place all of the preceding variables in this file.

We will use these parameters in all the subsequent recipes to authenticate to our Azure account and create the required infrastructure.

See also...

For more information about how to create a new service principal, use the following URL:

```
https://docs.microsoft.com/en-au/Azure/active-directory/develop/howto-create-
service-principal-portal
```

For more information about the Azure built-in roles that can be assigned to users/apps, use the following URL:

```
https://docs.microsoft.com/en-au/Azure/role-based-access-control/built-in-roles
```

Creating a resource group

In this recipe, we will outline how to deploy resource groups in Azure. Resource groups are a part of the Azure Resource Manager deployment model, which is the preferred method for deploying resources in the Azure cloud. This is because it allows us to group similar resources (such as the VM, the VM NIC, and the VM IP address) that share the same life cycle in a single container, which is the resource group. We are going to deploy all of the related resources that we will provision using resource groups.

Getting ready

The Ansible control machine must be connected to the internet with reachability to the Azure public API endpoints. The Azure account should be configured as outlined in the previous recipes.

How to do it...

1. Update the eu.yml and us.yml files under group_vars with the following data to define the resource group's name:

   ```
   $ cat group_vars/eu.yml

   rg_name: "rg_{{ inventory_hostname }}"

   $ cat group_vars/eu.yml

   rg_name: "rg_{{ inventory_hostname }}"
   ```

2. Create a new `pb_build_Azure_net.yml` playbook with the following content:

```yaml
---
- name: Build Azure Network Infrastructure
  hosts: all
  connection: local
  vars_files:
    - Azure_secret.yml
  tasks:
    - name: Create Resource group
     Azure_rm_resourcegroup:
        tenant: "{{ tenant_id }}"
        client_id: "{{ client_id }}"
        secret: "{{ secret }}"
        location: "{{ region }}"
        subscription_id: "{{ subscription_id }}"
        name: "{{ rg_name }}"
        state: "{{ state | default('present') }}"
```

How it works...

We declare the name of the resource group that we will deploy in each region in the YAML file that describes each region. We use the `rg_name` parameter to hold the name of the resource group. We use the `Azure_rm_resourcegroup` Ansible module to create the resource group on Azure. It takes the following parameters to authenticate to the Azure API and deploy the resource group:

- The `location` parameter, which describes the region into which we will deploy this resource group
- The `tenant`, `secret`, `client_id`, and `subscription_id` parameters to authenticate to our Azure account
- The `name` parameter, which is the name of our resource group

In our playbook, we read the `Azure_secrets.yml` file, using the `vars_files` parameter, in order to capture all the parameters stored in this file. We set the connection to `local` to instruct Ansible to run the playbook locally on the Ansible control machine and to not attempt to SSH to the hosts defined in our inventory. This is mandatory as all Azure modules need to run from the Ansible control machine to invoke the **REST API** calls to the Azure orchestration system.

Once we run our playbook, we can see that the resource groups are provisioned on the Azure portal, as in the following screenshot:

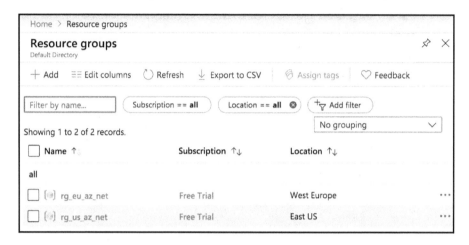

See also...

For more information about the Azure resource module in Ansible, and all the other parameters supported by this module, use the following URL:

```
https://docs.Ansible.com/Ansible/latest/modules/Azure_rm_resourcegroup_module.
html
```

Creating virtual networks

Virtual networks in the Azure cloud are our virtual data center, which groups all of our infrastructure in a similar manner to a physical data center. We can have multiple virtual networks in the same and across different regions, and we can deploy our infrastructure inside these virtual networks. In this recipe, we will outline how to define and provision a virtual network in Azure.

Getting ready

The Ansible control machine must be connected to the internet with reachability to the Azure public API endpoints and the Azure account should be configured as outlined in the previous recipes. The resource group should also be provisioned as in the previous recipe.

How to do it...

1. Update the `eu.yml` and `us.yml` files under `group_vars` with the virtual network's name and **CIDR** address:

```
$ cat group_vars/eu.yml
vnet_name: "vn_{{ inventory_hostname }}"
vnet_cidr: 10.1.0.0/16
$ cat group_vars/us.yml
vnet_name: "vn_{{ inventory_hostname }}"
vnet_cidr: 10.2.0.0/16
```

2. Update the `pb_build_Azure_net.yml` playbook with the task to create the virtual networks:

```
- name: Create Virtual Networks
  Azure_rm_virtualnetwork:
    tenant: "{{ tenant_id }}"
    client_id: "{{ client_id }}"
    secret: "{{ secret }}"
    location: "{{ region }}"
    subscription_id: "{{ subscription_id }}"
    resource_group: "{{ rg_name}}"
    name: "{{ vnet_name }}"
    address_prefixes_cidr: "{{ vnet_cidr }}"
    state: "{{ state | default('present') }}"
```

How it works...

In order to create the virtual network, we need to supply its name, along with the CIDR IP range that this virtual network will take. We define these two parameters in the region YAML files as `vnet_name` and `vnet_cidr`. We use the `Azure_rm_virtualnetwork` Ansible module to create all of the required virtual networks and we supply the following parameters:

- The resource group name in `resource_group`.
- The `location` parameter, which describes the region into which we will deploy this resource group.
- The name of each subnet in the `name` parameter, along with the CIDR IP range in the `address_prefixes_cidr` parameter.
- The `tenant`, `secret`, `client_id`, and `subscription_id` parameters are all used to authenticate to our Azure account.

Once we run the playbook, we can see that the virtual networks are created, as in the following screenshot:

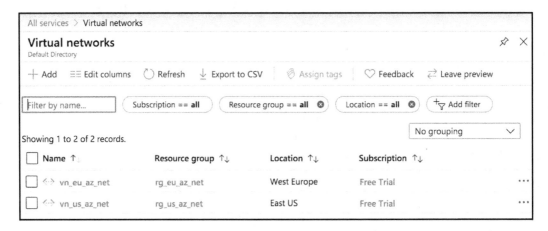

See also...

For more information regarding the Azure virtual network module in Ansible, and all the other parameters supported by this module, use the following URL:

```
https://docs.Ansible.com/Ansible/latest/modules/Azure_rm_virtualnetwork_module.
html
```

Creating subnets

A subnet is the networking construct within the Azure cloud that is used to segment the virtual network. It is used to provide us with the tools to segregate our virtual network into distinct routing and security domains that we can control in order to provide different routing and security behaviors within each subnet. In this recipe, we will outline how to define and provision subnets within the Azure cloud.

Getting ready

The Ansible control machine must be connected to the internet, with reachability to the Azure public API endpoints. The Azure account should be configured as outlined in the previous recipes. The resource group and virtual networks should also be provisioned as outlined in the previous recipe.

How to do it...

1. Update the eu.yml and us.yml files under group_vars with the subnet information:

```
$ cat group_vars/eu.yml
subnets:
  - name: web_tier
    cidr: 10.1.1.0/24
  - name: db_tier
    cidr: 10.1.2.0/24

$ cat group_vars/us.yml
subnets:
  - name: web_tier
    cidr: 10.2.1.0/24
  - name: db_tier
    cidr: 10.2.2.0/24
```

2. Update the pb_build_Azure_net.yml playbook with the task to create the subnets:

```
- name: Create Subnets
  Azure_rm_subnet:
    tenant: "{{ tenant_id }}"
    client_id: "{{ client_id }}"
    secret: "{{ secret }}"
    subscription_id: "{{ subscription_id }}"
    resource_group: "{{ rg_name}}"
    name: "{{ item.name}}"
    virtual_network_name:  "{{ vnet_name }}"
    address_prefix_cidr: "{{ item.cidr }}"
    state: "{{ state | default('present') }}"
  loop: "{{ subnets }}"
  loop_control:
    label: "{{ item.name }}"
```

How it works...

In order to create the subnets within the virtual network, we need to supply the virtual network and the CIDR prefix for the subnet, which must be within the CIDR of the virtual network. We define these in the subnet's data structure, which includes the name and CIDR for each subnet we want to provision. We can use the `Azure_rm_subnet` Ansible module to create all of the required subnets and we can loop over the subnet's data structure to supply the required parameters.

Once we run the playbook, we can see the subnets created within each virtual network, as in the following screenshot:

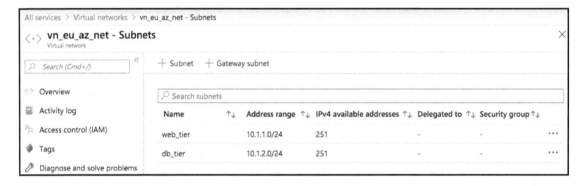

See also...

For more information regarding the Azure subnets module in Ansible, and all the other parameters supported by this module, use the following URL:

```
https://docs.Ansible.com/Ansible/latest/modules/Azure_rm_subnet_module.html
```

Building user-defined routes

In this recipe, we will outline how to control routing within a subnet using user-defined routers. This user-defined routes object can be associated with a specific subnet. We can define custom routes to adjust the forwarding behavior within a subnet in the Azure cloud.

Getting ready

The Ansible control machine must be connected to the internet, with reachability to the Azure public API endpoints. The Azure account should be configured as outlined in the previous recipes. The resource group, virtual networks, and subnets should also be provisioned as outlined in the previous recipes.

How to do it...

1. Update the `eu.yml` and `us.yml` files under `group_vars` with the `route_tables` data, as shown here:

```
$ cat group_vars/eu.yml  group_vars/us.yml
route_tables:
  - name: db_tier_rt
    subnet: db_tier
    routes:
      - name: Default Route
        prefix: 0.0.0.0/0
        nh: none
```

2. Update the `pb_build_Azure_net.yml` playbook with the following task to create the custom route table:

```
- name: Create Custom Route Table
  Azure_rm_routetable:
    tenant: "{{ tenant_id }}"
    client_id: "{{ client_id }}"
    secret: "{{ secret }}"
    subscription_id: "{{ subscription_id }}"
    resource_group: "{{ rg_name}}"
    name: "{{ item.name}}"
    state: "{{ state | default('present') }}"
  loop: "{{ route_tables }}"
  tags: routing
```

3. Update the playbook with the following task to provision the routes within the custom route table:

```
- name: Provision Routes
  Azure_rm_route:
    tenant: "{{ tenant_id }}"
    client_id: "{{ client_id }}"
    secret: "{{ secret }}"
    subscription_id: "{{ subscription_id }}"
```

```
      resource_group: "{{ rg_name}}"
      route_table_name: "{{ item.0.name }}"
      name: "{{ item.1.name}}"
      address_prefix: "{{ item.1.prefix }}"
      next_hop_type: "{{ item.1.nh }}"
      state: "{{ state | default('present') }}"
    with_subelements:
      - "{{ route_tables }}"
      - routes
    tags: routing
```

4. Update the playbook with the following task to associate the custom route with the subnet:

```
- name: Attach Route Table to Subnet
  Azure_rm_subnet:
    tenant: "{{ tenant_id }}"
    client_id: "{{ client_id }}"
    secret: "{{ secret }}"
    subscription_id: "{{ subscription_id }}"
    resource_group: "{{ rg_name}}"
    name: "{{ item.subnet}}"
    virtual_network_name:  "{{ vnet_name }}"
    route_table: "{{ item.name }}"
    state: "{{ state | default('present') }}"
  loop: "{{ route_tables }}"
  loop_control:
    label: "{{ item.name }}"
  tags: routing
```

How it works...

In our setup, we have two subnets (web and DB) and we need to provide a different routing treatment for the DB subnet so that it does not have public internet access. We can do this by creating a new custom route table and installing a default route with next-hop set to none in order to drop all the traffic destined for the internet.

We need to define our custom route table that we will deploy in the route_tables variable and include it in each region definition. We can then use the Azure_rm_routetable Ansible module to create the route table in the specific resource group and use the Azure_rm_route module to create the required routes within each route table. Finally, we can attach the route table to the specific subnet using the Azure_rm_subnet module in order to modify the default routing behavior for this subnet.

The following screenshot outlines the new route table that was created:

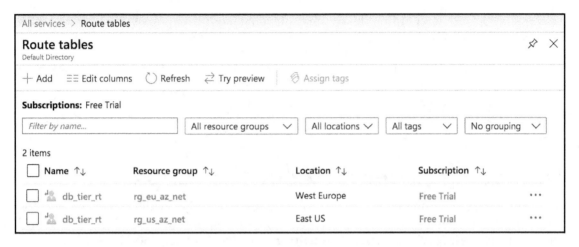

The following screenshot outlines the exact details for one of the route tables, the custom routes, and the subnet this custom route is attached to:

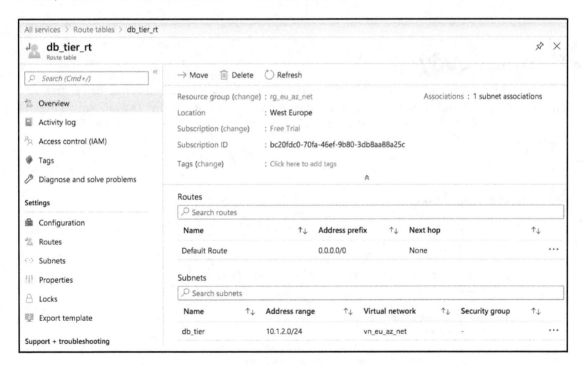

See also...

For more information regarding the Azure route table modules in Ansible, and all the other parameters supported by this module, use the following URLs:

- `https://docs.Ansible.com/Ansible/latest/modules/Azure_rm_routetable_module.html#Azure-rm-routetable-module`
- `https://docs.Ansible.com/Ansible/latest/modules/Azure_rm_route_module.html#Azure-rm-route-module`

Deploying network security groups

Security in cloud environments is critical, and the Azure cloud provides different tools and services to help build a secure cloud environment for the application. In this recipe, we will look at one of these services: **network security groups** (**NSGs**). An NSG is a stateful firewall that can be attached to a virtual machine or subnet in order to restrict the traffic flowing through the virtual machine or subnet. In this recipe, we will outline how to define and provision an NSG on the Azure cloud.

Getting ready

The Ansible control machine must be connected to the internet, with reachability to the Azure public API endpoints. The Azure account should be configured as outlined in the previous recipes. The resource group, virtual networks, and subnets should also be provisioned as outlined in the previous recipes.

How to do it...

1. Update the `eu.yml` and `us.yml` files under `group_vars` with the ACL data, as shown here:

```
$ cat group_vars/eu.yml  group_vars/us.yml
acls:
  - name: Inbound_Web_Tier
    subnet: web_tier
    rules:
      - name: Allow_HTTP_Internet
        destination_address_prefix: 10.1.1.0/24
        direction: Inbound
```

```
access: Allow
protocol: Tcp
destination_port_range:
  - 80
  - 443
priority: 101
```

2. Update the `pb_build_Azure_net.yml` playbook with the following task to create the security group and populate all of its rules:

```
- name: Create new Security Group
  Azure_rm_securitygroup:
    tenant: "{{ tenant_id }}"
    client_id: "{{ client_id }}"
    secret: "{{ secret }}"
    subscription_id: "{{ subscription_id }}"
    resource_group: "{{ rg_name}}"
    name: "{{ item.name }}"
    purge_rules: yes
    rules: "{{ item.rules }}"
  loop: "{{ acls }}"
  Tags: security
```

3. Update the playbook with the following task to attach the security group with the corresponding subnet:

```
- name: Attach Security Group to Subnet
  Azure_rm_subnet:
    tenant: "{{ tenant_id }}"
    client_id: "{{ client_id }}"
    secret: "{{ secret }}"
    subscription_id: "{{ subscription_id }}"
    resource_group: "{{ rg_name}}"
    name: "{{ item.subnet}}"
    virtual_network_name:  "{{ vnet_name }}"
    security_group: "{{ item.name }}"
    state: "{{ state | default('present') }}"
  loop: "{{ acls }}"
  tags: security
```

How it works...

Azure provides default NSGs that are attached to subnets. These provide basic security controls to the computer resources deployed in these subnets. The default policy includes these default rules for inbound traffic:

- Allow inbound traffic between virtual network CIDR ranges (inter-subnet communication).
- Allow inbound traffic from Azure load balancers.
- Deny any other traffic.

In the outbound direction, the default rules are as follows:

- Allow outbound traffic between the virtual network CIDR (inter-subnet communication).
- Allow outbound traffic to the internet.
- Deny any other traffic.

Azure NSGs provide a mechanism to augment the default NSG applied by Azure by defining a custom NSG that is appended to the default one. The resultant NSG is evaluated based on the priority value for each rule (a rule with a lower value is evaluated first) and once a rule is matched, the rule is applied to the traffic traversing the subnet.

As we are deploying a web application in the Web_tier subnet, we need to allow inbound HTTP and HTTPs traffic to this subnet. So, we can create an ACL definition to create a custom NSG and define the required parameters in order to allow this traffic in the inbound direction.

We can use the Azure_rm_securitygroup Ansible module to loop over all of our custom ACLs and create the NSG and respective rules. We can use Azure_rm_subnet to attach the security group to the subnet.

The following screenshot shows the new NSG that is defined:

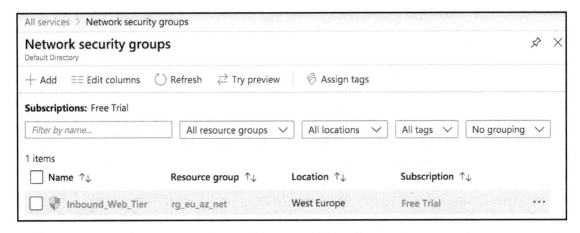

The following screenshot shows the resultant NSG rules that are defined (both custom and default) for the inbound and outbound directions:

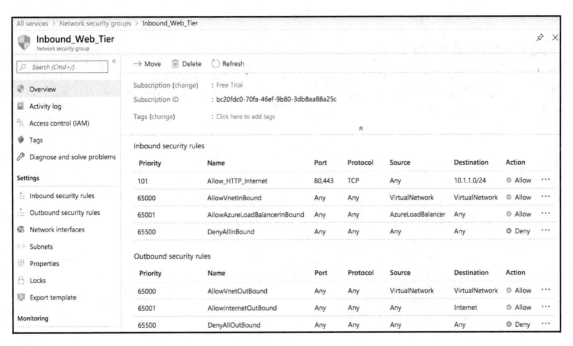

See also...

For more information regarding the Azure NSG module in Ansible, and all the other parameters supported by this module, use the following URL:

```
https://docs.Ansible.com/Ansible/latest/modules/Azure_rm_securitygroup_module.
html
```

Deployment validation using Ansible

Ansible provides multiple modules to collect the operational state of the different resources deployed in Azure. We can use these modules to validate the current state of our network in the Azure cloud. This provides a programmatic approach to validating a deployment, without the need to log in via a GUI to the portal to check the status of the different components within the infrastructure of Azure. In this recipe, we will outline how to use multiple modules to validate the resource groups and virtual networks that we have deployed.

Getting ready

The Ansible control machine must be connected to the internet, with reachability to the Azure public API endpoints. The Azure account should also be configured as outlined in the previous recipes.

How to do it...

1. Create a new file, `~/.Azure/credentials`, to host all of the credentials to authenticate to Azure, as in the following code:

```
$ cat ~/.Azure/credentials
[default]
subscription_id=XXX-XXXX-XXXX
client_id=XXX-XXXX-XXXX
secret=XXX-XXXX-XXXX
tenant=XXX-XXXX-XXXX
```

2. Create a new playbook, `pb_validate_Azure_net.yml`, to validate our deployment and include the following tasks to collect resource group facts and validate it:

```
$ cat pb_validate_Azure_net.yml
- name: Build Azure Network Infrastructure
  hosts: all
  connection: local
  tasks:
    - name: Get Resource Facts
      Azure_rm_resourcegroup_facts:
        name: "{{ rg_name }}"
      register: rg_facts
      tags: rg_facts
    - name: Validate Resource Group is Deployed
      assert:
        that:
          - rg.name == rg_name
          - rg.properties.provisioningState == 'Succeeded'
          - rg.location == region
      loop: "{{ Azure_resourcegroups }}"
      loop_control:
        loop_var: rg
      tags: rg_facts
```

3. Update the `pb_validate_Azure_net.yml` playbook to include the tasks that will collect the virtual network's facts and validate its state:

```
- name: Validate Virtual Network is Deployed
  Azure_rm_virtualnetwork_facts:
    resource_group: "{{ rg_name }}"
  register: vnet_facts
  tags: vnet_facts
- name: Validate Virtual Networks are Deployed
  assert:
    that:
      - vnet.name == vnet_name
      - vnet.properties.provisioningState == 'Succeeded'
      - vnet.properties.addressSpace.addressPrefixes | length == 1
      - vnet.properties.addressSpace.addressPrefixes[0] == vnet_cidr
  loop: "{{ Azure_virtualnetworks }}"
  loop_control:
  loop_var: vnet
  tags: vnet_facts
```

How it works...

In this recipe, we outline an alternative method to authenticate to the Azure cloud. We create the ~/.Azure/credentials file and we put the same information into it that is needed to authenticate to the Azure API (tenant_id, client_id, and so on). As we have this information in the file, we don't need to include these parameters in our Ansible modules.

In order to validate our deployment, Ansible provides multiple fact modules to collect the operational state of multiple objects in the Azure cloud. In this example, we are outlining two of these modules to collect the facts for resource groups and virtual networks. We can use the Azure_rm_resourcegroup_facts module to collect resource group facts and Azure_rm_virtualnetwork_facts to collect virtual network facts. All the Azure fact modules register the data retrieved by these modules as Ansible facts— that is why we don't need to register the data returned by the module in a custom-defined variable.

The Azure_rm_resourcegroup_facts module saves the output in the Azure_resourcegroups Ansible fact and we use the assert module to loop over all the resource groups within this variable. We can then confirm that it is created with the correct parameters.

The following is a snippet from Azure_resourcegroups:

```
ok: [eu_az_net] => {
    "Azure_resourcegroups": [
        {
            "id":
"/subscriptions/bc20fdc0-70fa-46ef-9b80-3db8aa88a25c/resourceGroups/rg_eu_a
z_net",
            "location": "westeurope",
            "name": "rg_eu_az_net",
            "properties": {
                "provisioningState": "Succeeded"
            }
        }
    ]
}
```

We can use the exact same technique to collect the facts for virtual networks deployed using Azure_rm_virtualnetwork_facts and use the assert module to validate its state.

See also...

For more information about the multiple modules for fact collection for different network resources in Azure, use the following links:

- **Resource group** facts: `https://docs.Ansible.com/Ansible/latest/modules/Azure_rm_resourcegroup_info_module.html#Azure-rm-resourcegroup-info-module`
- **Virtual network** facts: `https://docs.Ansible.com/Ansible/latest/modules/Azure_rm_virtualnetwork_info_module.html#Azure-rm-virtualnetwork-info-module`
- **Subnet** facts: `https://docs.Ansible.com/Ansible/latest/modules/Azure_rm_subnet_info_module.html#Azure-rm-subnet-info-module`
- **Route table** facts: `https://docs.Ansible.com/Ansible/latest/modules/Azure_rm_routetable_info_module.html#Azure-rm-routetable-info-module`
- **Security group** facts: `https://docs.Ansible.com/Ansible/latest/modules/Azure_rm_securitygroup_info_module.html#Azure-rm-securitygroup-info-module`

Decommissioning Azure resources using Ansible

Similar to how we can create resources at scale using automation, we can also destroy those resources once we decide we don't need them. This is simplified with Ansible and the resource groups implemented by Azure – with a single API call with the correct parameters, we can decommission all the resources within a resource group that we have defined. In this recipe, we will outline how to perform this action to destroy all the resources we have provisioned so far.

Getting ready

The Ansible control machine must be connected to the internet, with reachability to the Azure Public API endpoints. The Azure account should also be configured as outlined in the previous recipes.

How to do it...

1. Create a new `pb_destroy_Azure_net.yml` playbook and add the following
   task to delete all the resource groups:

```
$ cat pb_destroy_Azure_net.yml
---- name: Decomission Azure Infrastructure
  hosts: all
  connection: local
  vars:
    state: absent
  vars_files:
    - Azure_secret.yml
  tasks:
    - name: Delete Resource group
      Azure_rm_resourcegroup:
        tenant: "{{ tenant_id }}"
        client_id: "{{ client_id }}"
        secret: "{{ secret }}"
        location: "{{ region }}"
        subscription_id: "{{ subscription_id }}"
        name: "{{ rg_name }}"
        force_delete_nonempty: yes
        state: "{{ state | default('present') }}"
```

How it works...

We can use the `Azure_rm_resourcegroup` Ansible module to destroy all the resources
within the resource group as well as to delete the resource group itself. We can supply two
important parameters to the module in order to perform the `delete` function:

- Set `state` to `absent`.
- Include the `force_delete_nonempty` parameter and set it to `yes`.

With these parameters set, all the resources within the resource group (the virtual
networks, subnets, and so on) will be deleted, along with the resource group itself.

The following output shows that our two resource groups are no longer present:

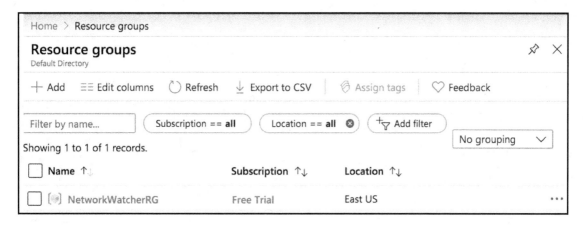

The following output also confirms that all of the virtual networks were deleted after running the playbook:

The preceding screenshot shows that all the virtual networks have been deleted.

Deploying and Operating GCP Networking Resources with Ansible

9

Google Cloud is one of the big players in the public cloud and it provides a comprehensive set of services and features on its **Google Cloud Platform** (**GCP**) cloud. In this chapter, we will explore how to automate the provisioning of resources on the GCP cloud using Ansible and how to use the various Ansible modules to orchestrate the building of virtual networks across the GCP cloud.

In this chapter, we will use a simple network setup to illustrate the use of different Ansible modules in building an example network across GCP. The following diagram outlines this sample network that we will build:

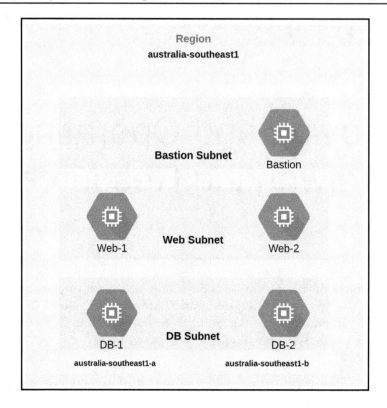

This chapter will cover the following recipes:

- Installing the GCP SDK
- Building an Ansible inventory
- Authenticating to your GCP account
- Creating GCP VPC networks
- Creating subnets
- Deploying firewall rules in GCP
- Deploying VMs in GCP
- Adjusting routing within a VPC
- Validating GCP deployment using Ansible
- Decommissioning GCP resources using Ansible

Technical requirements

In order to start working with GCP, we need to create an account. You can set up a free GCP account at `https://cloud.google.com/free/`.

The GitHub code used in this chapter can be found at `https://github.com/PacktPublishing/Network-Automation-Cookbook/tree/master/ch9_gcp`.

The following are the software releases that this chapter is based on:

- CentOS 7
- Ansible 2.9
- Python 3.6.8

Check out the following video to see the Code in Action: `https://bit.ly/3erVlSN`

Installing the GCP SDK

In this recipe, we will outline how to install the required Python libraries needed to start interacting with the GCP orchestration system using Ansible. This step is mandatory since the required Python libraries must be installed on the Ansible control machine in order for all the Ansible GCP modules to work.

Getting ready

You need to have `sudo` access on the machine in order to install the GCP Python libraries. You also need to have Python installed and the Python pip package, which we will use to install the GCP package.

How to do it...

1. Install the `requests` package as shown in the following code:

   ```
   $ sudo pip3 install requests
   ```

2. Install the Google authentication package as shown in the following code:

   ```
   $ sudo pip3 install google-auth
   ```

3. Create a new folder called `ch9_gcp` to host all the code for this chapter:

   ```
   $ mkdir ch9_gcp
   ```

How it works...

The default installation of Ansible doesn't include all the required Python modules needed to execute the GCP cloud modules. In this recipe, we installed the two required Python packages that are needed by all GCP modules. The first package is the `requests` package, which is used mainly to invoke REST API calls to the Google orchestration system, and the other package is the `google-auth` package to authenticate against the API.

See also...

For more information regarding how to start interacting with GCP using Ansible, please refer to `https://docs.ansible.com/ansible/latest/scenario_guides/guide_gce.html`.

Building an Ansible inventory

In this recipe, we will outline how to build an Ansible inventory to describe the network infrastructure setup that we will build across the GCP public cloud. This is a mandatory step that we need to take in order to define all our VPC networks across all the regions that we will deploy our infrastructure in.

How to do it...

1. Create the `hosts` file inside the `ch9_gcp` directory with the following data:

    ```
    $ cat hosts

    [gcp_vpc]
    demo_gcp_vpc
    ```

2. Create the `ansible.cfg` file with the following content:

    ```
    $ cat ansible.cfg

    [defaults]
    inventory=hosts
    retry_files_enabled=False
    gathering=explicit
    host_key_checking=False
    action_warnings=False
    ```

3. Create the `group_vars` folder and the `gcp_vpc.yml`, which will host all the variables that define our infrastructure in this VPC:

    ```
    $ mkdir -p group_var/gcp_vpc.yml
    ```

4. Create the `roles` directory within our main folder (`ch9_gcp`). This folder will include all the roles that we will use to create our GCP infrastructure:

    ```
    $ mkdir -p roles
    ```

How it works...

We created the `hosts` Ansible inventory file and we declared all the VPCs that we will provision in the GCP cloud. We have a single VPC in our sample setup, so we created a single group called the `gcp_vpc`, which includes our VPC (`demo_gcp_vpc`).

We created the `group_vars/gcp_vpc.yml` file, which will house all the variables that we will declare to define our infrastructure in this VPC.

At this time, our directory layout is as follows:

```
$ tree ch9_gcp
.
├── ansible.cfg
├── group_vars
```

```
|    └── gcp_vpc.yml
├── hosts
└── roles
```

Authenticating to your GCP account

In this recipe, we will outline how to create the required credentials to programmatically authenticate to our GCP account from Ansible. This is a mandatory step that you need to take in order to be able to run any Ansible module in the following recipes.

Getting ready

The Ansible controller must have internet access. In addition, the user performing these steps must have administrative access to the GCP console in order to create the required resources to enable programmatic interaction with the GCP APIs.

How to do it...

1. Log in to **GCP Console** with an administrative account.
2. From the main console, choose **IAM & admin** | **Manage Resources**. Create a new project within GCP that will house all the infrastructure that we will build in GCP:

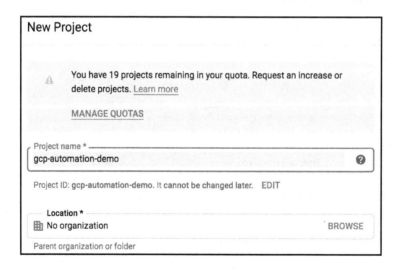

3. From the main console, go to **IAM & admin | Service accounts**:

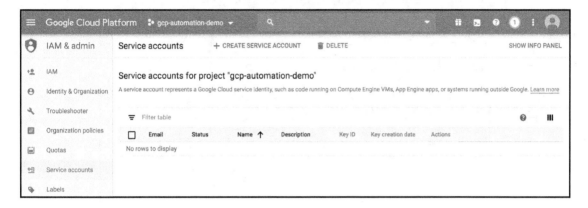

4. Create a **New Service** account for a new Ansible user:

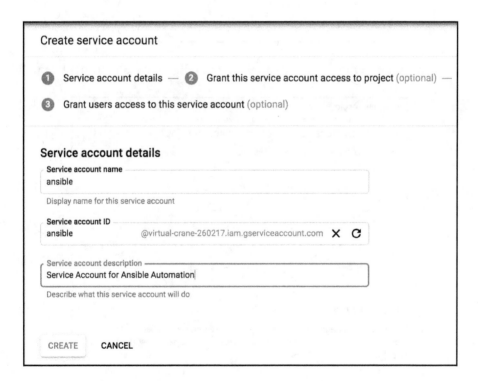

5. Assign the appropriate role to this new service account so that you can create/edit/delete the resources in this GCP project:

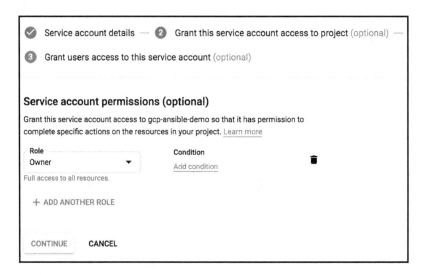

6. Create and download the private key that will be used to authenticate this user:

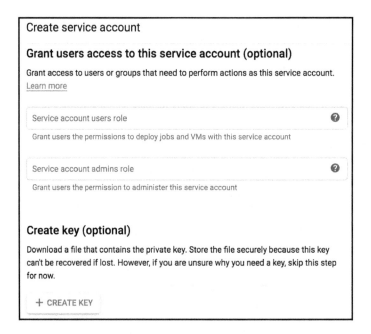

7. Copy the downloaded JSON key file to the project directory `ch9_gcp` and rename it as `gcp_ansible_secret.json`.

8. On the GCP console, select **API & Services** and enable the **Google Compute Engine API** for the current project:

How it works...

In order to have programmatic access to the GCP API (this is how Ansible communicates with the GCP cloud to provision resources), we need to create a special account called a service account within our GCP project. This service account is similar to a user, but with only API access to the GCP project. We created this service account and called it Ansible, and we provided it with the **Project Owner** role in order to have full privilege to create resources within the GCP project (in production, a more restrictive role should be assigned to this service account).

In order to authenticate to the GCP API using this service account, GCP provided us with a JSON file that has the identification information for this account. The main parameters included in this JSON file are as follows:

- The private SSH key for this service account
- The type of this account
- `Project_id`
- `Client_id`
- `client_email`

We save this JSON file and copy it to our directory, since we will refer to it in all our playbooks in order to provision the resources on the GCP cloud. The final step is to enable the API in our GCP project; we need to enable the GCP compute engine API in order to start interacting with this API since, by default, the API access is disabled within the GCP project.

There's more...

The JSON file that holds all the identification information to authenticate the GCP API again is a critical file that should be secured, and so we are going to use an Ansible vault in order to secure this file.

We create a new file called `vault_pass`, which holds our Ansible vault password and we update our `ansible.cfg` file to point to it, as shown in the following code:

```
$ cat ansible.cfg

[defaults]
 vault_password_file=vault_pass
```

We encrypt the JSON file using Ansible vault, as shown in the following code:

```
$ ansible-vault encrypt gcp-ansible-secret.json
```

At this stage, we have our JSON file secure and all its contents encrypted using the password declared in the `vault_pass` file.

See also...

For more information regarding how to create a new service account in GCP, go to `https:/ /cloud.google.com/iam/docs/creating-managing-service-accounts`.

Creating GCP VPC networks

In the GCP, VPCs are the main networking construct that are used to group all our resources. We can think of them as a virtual data center in the cloud. We need to define our VPCs in order to prepare our cloud environment to host our applications. In this recipe, we will outline how to define and provision a VPC in GCP.

Getting ready

The Ansible control machine must be connected to the internet with reachability to GCP public API endpoints, and the GCP account should be configured as outlined in the previous recipes.

How to do it...

1. Create a new YAML file called `gcp_account_info.yml` and include the following data for our GCP login parameters:

```
$ cat gcp_account_info.yml
---
service_account_file: gcp_credentials.json
project: "gcp-ansible-demo"
auth_kind: serviceaccount
```

2. Create a new Ansible role called `gcp_net_build`, as shown in the following code:

```
$ cd roles
$ ansible-galaxy init gcp_net_build
```

3. Update the `gcp_net_build/tasks/main.yml` file with the following task to create our VPC:

```
- name: Create a New GCP VPC
  gcp_compute_network:
    name: "{{ vpc_name | regex_replace('_','-') }}"
    routing_config:
      routing_mode: "REGIONAL"
    auto_create_subnetworks: no
    state: present
    auth_kind: "{{ auth_kind }}"
    project: "{{ project }}"
    service_account_file: "{{ service_account_file }}"
  register: gcp_vpc
  tags: gcp_vpc
```

4. Create the `group_vars` folder and create the `gcp_vpc.yml` file with the following data for the VPC:

```
$ cat group_vars/gcp_vpc.yml
---
vpc_name: ansible-demo-vpc
```

5. Create the `pb_gcp_env_build.yml` playbook with the following task to read the vault-encrypted JSON file:

```
---
- name: Build GCP Environment
  hosts: all
  connection: local
  gather_facts: no
  force_handlers: true
  vars_files:
    - gcp_account_info.yml
  tasks:
    - name: Read the Vault Encrypted JSON File
      copy:
        content: "{{ lookup('file','gcp-ansible-secret.json') }}"
        dest: "{{ service_account_file }}"
      notify: Clean tmp Decrypted Files
      tags: always
```

6. Update the `pb_gcp_env_build.yml` playbook with the following task to create the required VPCs:

```
- name: Build GCP Network
  import_role:
    name: gcp_net_build
  tags: gcp_net_build
```

7. Update the playbook with the following handlers to delete the temporary JSON credentials file, as shown in the following code:

```
handlers:
  - name: Clean tmp Decrypted Files
    file:
      path: "{{ service_account_file }}"
      state: absent
```

How it works...

In this recipe, we created and deployed the GCP VPC in the project that we created previously. We used an Ansible role in order to build all the components of the GCP network, and the first task was to create the VPC using the Ansible module `gcp_compute_network`.

In order to use any Ansible GCP module, we needed to authenticate every API call triggered by each module and we needed to provide the following information in order to authenticate the API calls:

- `Auth_kind`: The type of authentication—in our case, `serviceaccount`.
- `Project`: This is the project name for the current project that we created.
- `Service_account_file`: This is the JSON file that we downloaded when we created the service account.

Since we are using an Ansible vault in order to encrypt all the contents of the JSON file that holds all the authentication information, we needed to decrypt this file during playbook execution in order to use the data within this file. Furthermore, since we are not directly reading the contents of this JSON file but rather pointing to it using the `serivce_account_file` parameter in all our GCP Ansible modules, we created a task to read the contents of this JSON file using the `lookup` module and store this data in a temporary file. With this approach, we can read the encrypted data in this JSON file and create a new temporary JSON file with the data in plaintext. We can also use this temporary JSON file as the input to `service_account_file`. We used a handler task in order to delete this temporary file at the end of the play. On the play level, we used `force_handlers` in order to ensure the run of all the tasks within the handler section, even if any of the tasks within our play fails. This means that we are sure that the plaintext JSON file that holds our credentials is always deleted.

We grouped all the preceding parameters and placed them in the `gcp_account_info.yml` file, and we included this file in our playbook. We created the VPC using the `gcp_compute_network` module and we supplied the following information in order to deploy the VPC:

- `Name`: The name of our new VPC.
- `Auto_create_subnetwork`: Set it to `no`, since we want to create a custom VPC network, not an auto-mode VPC network.
- `Routing_config`: Set it to `Regional` in order to stop route propagation between subnets in different regions.

One clear point that we need to highlight is that VPCs within GCP have a global scope, which means that they are not bound to a specific region, but span all the regions in the GCP cloud. The subnets, on the other hand, are region-specific; however, since we created a custom VPC, no subnets are created by default in any region, and we have complete control over where to define our subnets. This logic is different when we compare it with AWS and GCP in terms of VPC scope.

When creating the VPC using the `gcp_compute_network` module, we must supply the VPC name. In this task, we used the `regex_replace` Ansible filter in order to make sure that the VPC name doesn't contain the underscore character (_), since it is not a valid character in the VPC name. We use this filter to replace any occurrence of the underscore with the dash (–) in order to make sure that the VPC name is compliant with GCP VPC naming standards.

Once we run our playbook with this single task, we can see that the VPC is created, as seen on the GCP console:

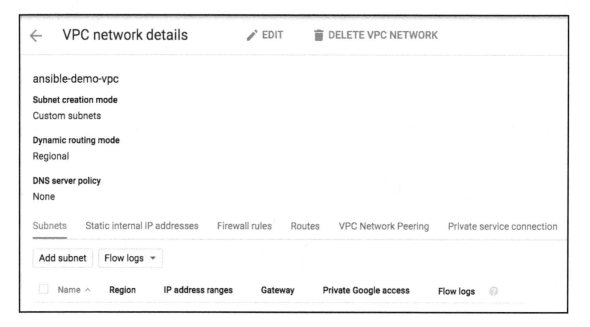

The following snippet outlines the parameters returned by the Ansible module after creating the VPC:

```
ok: [demo_gcp_vpc] => {
  "gcp_vpc": {
    "autoCreateSubnetworks": false,
    "changed": true,
    "creationTimestamp": "2019-11-26T12:49:51.130-08:00",
    "failed": false,
    "id": "8661055357091590400",
    "kind": "compute#network",
    "name": "demo-gcp-vpc",
    "routingConfig": {
```

```
        "routingMode": "REGIONAL"
    },
    "selfLink":
"https://www.googleapis.com/compute/v1/projects/gcp-ansible-demo/global/net
works/demo-gcp-vpc"
    }
}
```

This information is important, and we will use it in subsequent recipes in order to create subnets so that we can register the output of this task in the `gcp_vpc` variable in order to be able to refer to it in later tasks.

There is more...

By default, when we create a new project in GCP, an auto-mode VPC is created for this project named `default`. It is recommended that we delete this default network since we will rely on our custom VPC to house all of our compute workload.

We can see in our project that this default VPC is present and it has subnets in each region across the GCP cloud, as shown in the following screenshot:

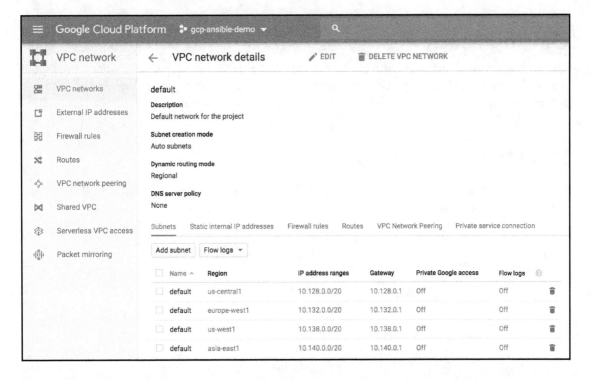

I have created a playbook called `pb_gcp_delete_default_vpc.yml` to delete this default VPC and all the default firewall rules attached to it.

See also...

For more information regarding the GCP Virtual Private Cloud module in Ansible and all the other parameters supported by this module, go to `https://docs.ansible.com/ ansible/latest/modules/gcp_compute_network_module.html#gcp-compute-network-module`.

Creating subnets

We segregate our GCP VPCs using subnets, which is the tool that allows us to place our compute workload into a specific region. Furthermore, subnets provide us with the tool to segregate our virtual network into distinct routing and security domains that we can control in order to provide differentiated routing and security behavior within each subnet. In this recipe, we will outline how to define and provision subnets within the GCP cloud.

Getting ready

The Ansible control machine must be connected to the internet with reachability to the GCP public API endpoints and the GCP account should be configured as outlined in the previous recipes. Also, the GCP VPC needs to be created as outlined in the previous recipe.

How to do it...

1. Update the `group_vars/gcp_vpc.yml` file with the subnets data, as shown in the following code:

   ```
   $ cat group_vars/gcp_vpc.yml

   subnets:
     - name: anz-web
       cidr: 10.1.1.0/24
       region: australia-southeast1

     - name: anz-db
       cidr: 10.1.2.0/24
   ```

```
    region: australia-southeast1

  - name: anz-bastion
    cidr: 10.1.3.0/24
    region: australia-southeast1
```

2. Update the `gcp_net_build/tasks/main.yml` file with the following task to create our subnets:

```
- name: Create Subnets
  gcp_compute_subnetwork:
    name: "{{ subnet.name }}"
    ip_cidr_range: "{{ subnet.cidr }}"
    network: "{{ gcp_vpc}}"
    region: "{{ subnet.region }}"
    state: present
    auth_kind: "{{ auth_kind }}"
    project: "{{ project }}"
    service_account_file: "{{ service_account_file }}"
  loop: "{{ subnets }}"
  loop_control:
    loop_var: subnet
  register: gcp_subnets
```

How it works...

In this recipe, we created the subnets that we are going to use in our deployment. The first thing to notice in our subnet definition is that we defined a region for each subnet. This is mandatory since, as we discussed, a subnet in GCP has regional scope compared to VPCs, which have global scope. We defined a CIDR range for each subnet, along with its name.

We used the `gcp_compute_subnet` module in order to create all our subnets. We used the same parameters that we discussed before for authentication. To create the subnets, we specified the following parameters:

- Name: The name of our subnet.
- Region: The region where this subnet will be deployed.
- Ip_cidr_range: The CIDR block for this subnet.
- Network: The reference for our VPC that we want this subnet to be part of. We get this parameter from the output of creating the VPC. We supply the `gcp_vpc` variable, which is the registered variable from our VPC creation task.

Once we run the playbook, we can see that all subnets are created as shown in the following screenshot:

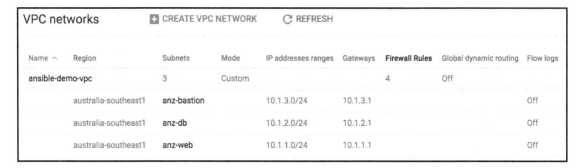

See also...

For more information regarding the GCP subnets module in Ansible and all the other parameters supported by this module, go to `https://docs.ansible.com/ansible/latest/modules/gcp_compute_subnetwork_module.html`.

Deploying firewall rules in GCP

GCP provides many tools in order to enforce security within the customer environment of the GCP cloud. Firewall rules are one of the most basic security tools supported in GCP in order to implement the first level of defense for all the workloads within a VPC. In this recipe, we will outline how to define and provision firewall rules on the GCP cloud.

Getting ready

The Ansible control machine must be connected to the internet with reachability to GCP public API endpoints, and the GCP account should be configured as outlined in the previous recipes. Also, VPC and subnets should be provisioned as outlined in the previous recipes.

How to do it...

1. Update `group_vars/gcp_vpc.yml` with the following firewall rules to secure traffic between the web and DB layers.

```
$ cat group_vars/gcp_vpc.yml

fw_rules:
  - name: allow_sql_from_anz-web_to_anz-db
    type: allow
    direction: ingress
    priority: 10
    apply_to: anz-db
    src_tag: anz-web
    dest_tag:
    protocol: tcp
    port: 3389
    state: present
```

2. Update `group_vars/gcp_vpc.yml` with the following firewall rules to secure traffic toward the web layer:

```
  - name: allow_internet_to-anz-web
    type: allow
    direction: ingress
    priority: 10
    src: 0.0.0.0/0
    apply_to: anz-web
    protocol: tcp
    port: 80,443
    state: present
```

3. Update `group_vars/gcp_vpc.yml` with the following firewall rules to allow `ssh` to only bastion hosts:

```
  - name: allow_ssh_to_anz-bastion
    type: allow
    direction: ingress
    priority: 10
    src: 0.0.0.0/0
    apply_to: anz-bastion
    protocol: tcp
    port: 22
    state: present

  - name: allow_ssh_from_bastion_only
    type: allow
```

```
          direction: ingress
          priority: 10
          src_tag: anz-bastion
          apply_to: anz-web,anz-db
          protocol: tcp
          port: 22
          state: present
```

4. Update the `roles/gcp_net_build/tasks.main.yml` file with the following task to create all the required firewall rules:

```
- name: Create Allow Firewall Rules
  gcp_compute_firewall:
    name: "{{ rule.name | regex_replace('_','-') }}"
    network: {selfLink: "{{ gcp_vpc.selfLink }}"}
    priority: "{{ rule.priority | default(omit) }}"
    direction: "{{ rule.direction | upper | mandatory }}"
    allowed:
      - ip_protocol: "{{ rule.protocol }}"
        ports: "{{ (rule.port|string).split(',') }}"
    source_ranges: "{{ rule.src | default(omit) }}"
    source_tags: "{{ omit if rule.src_tag is not defined else
rule.src_tag.split(',') }}"
    destination_ranges: "{{ rule.dest | default(omit) }}"
    target_tags: "{{ omit if rule.apply_to is not defined else
rule.apply_to.split(',') }}"
    auth_kind: "{{ auth_kind }}"
    project: "{{ project }}"
    service_account_file: "{{ service_account_file }}"
  loop: "{{ fw_rules | selectattr('type','equalto','allow') | list
}}"
  loop_control:
    loop_var: rule
  tags: gcp_fw_rules
```

How it works...

The firewall rules in GCP are stateful firewall rules that are applied to hosts within the VPC. Firewall rules within GCP can be applied on the ingress or the egress direction, and there are some default firewall rules that are defined and applied to all hosts within a VPC, as shown here:

- On the ingress direction, there is a default `deny all` for all traffic destined to any host within a new custom VPC.

- On the egress direction, there is a default `allow all` for all traffic from any host within a new custom VPC.

With the preceding default rules, and since all the firewall rules are stateful, any communication initiated from any host within the VPC to the outside world will be allowed; however, any initiated traffic from outside the VPC will be rejected.

GCP firewall rules can match traffic based on the following criteria:

- Source/destination IPv4 ranges
- IP protocol numbers
- TCP/UDP port numbers
- Network tags

All the preceding criteria are quite obvious except for network tags. Network tags are special metadata that can be applied to any host within a VPC to identify and group these hosts. We can use these network tags in order to use them as match criteria in firewall rules, as well as to apply the firewall rules only to a subset of our hosts within the VPC.

With all this information, we want to implement the following security policy on our hosts within our sample network:

- All HTTP/HTTPs traffic should be allowed only to all our web servers.
- SSH access from outside should be limited to only our bastion hosts.
- SSH access to our web and DB servers is limited to only bastion hosts.
- Only allow SQL traffic from the web to DB servers.

We defined our firewall rules in a new data structure, `fw_rules`, which is a list of all our rules that need to be applied to our VPC. We used the network tags in all our policies in order to apply the correct firewall rule to the hosts where this rule should be enforced.

We used the Ansible module `gcp_compute_firewall` in order to iterate over all the firewall policies and apply them. In this module, we can define the match criteria to be either based on source/destination IPv4 address ranges or based on source and target network tags. We defined our task so that if a parameter is not defined in our firewall rule (for example, source IPv4 ranges), we should remove this parameter from the list of parameters supplied to the module. We use the `omit` filter in order to accomplish this logic.

All firewall rules within GCP have the priority field, which defines the priority of the rule compared to other rules and its precedence in terms of processing. Any rule with no specific priority gets the priority value of 1,000. The default firewall rules applied by GCP to the VPC have the priority value of `65535`, so any rule we define will have precedence over them. In all our rules, we specify the priority value of `10`.

Once we run the following task, we can see that the following rules are applied to our VPC, as shown in the following screenshot:

See also...

For more information regarding the GCP firewall modules in Ansible and all the other parameters supported by this module, go to `https://docs.ansible.com/ansible/latest/modules/gcp_compute_firewall_module.html`.

Deploying VMs in GCP

In this recipe, we will outline how to deploy virtual machines (using Google Compute Engine) in GCP within our VPCs using the correct subnets that we have deployed. We will also assign the correct network tags in order to enforce the correct security policy on these machines.

Getting ready

The Ansible control machine must be connected to the internet with reachability to GCP public API endpoints, and the VPCs, subnets, and firewall rules need to be deployed as outlined in the previous chapters.

How to do it...

1. Update the `group_vars/gcp_vpc.yml` file to include the required information to describe the flavor and OS that we will use on all our VMs:

```
$ cat group_vars/gcp_vpc.yml

compute_node_flavor: f1-micro
compute_node_images: projects/centos-
cloud/global/images/family/centos-7
compute_node_image_size: 10
```

2. Update the `group_vars/gcp_vpc.yml` file to include the required information that describes our compute nodes:

```
$ cat group_vars/gcp_vpc.yml
compute_nodes:
  - name: web-server-1
    network: anz-web
    has_internet: yes
    zone: australia-southeast1-a

< -- Output Omitted for Brevity -- >

  - name: db-server-1
    network: anz-db
    has_internet: no
    zone: australia-southeast1-a

< -- Output Omitted for Brevity -- >

  - name: bastion-host
    network: anz-bastion
    ip: 10.1.3.253
    has_internet: yes
    ip_forwarding: yes
    zone: australia-southeast1-a
```

3. Create a new Ansible role (`gcp_vm_build`) to deploy the VM workload on GCP:

    ```
    $ cd roles
    $ ansible-galaxy init gcp_vm_build
    ```

4. Update the `gcp_vm_build/tasks/main.yml` file with the following task to create the disks for the VMs:

    ```
    - name: create a disk for {{ node.name }}
      gcp_compute_disk:
        name: "{{ node.name | regex_replace('_','-') }}-disk"
        size_gb: "{{compute_node_image_size }}"
        source_image: "{{ compute_node_images }}"
        zone: "{{ node.zone }}"
        auth_kind: "{{ auth_kind }}"
        project: "{{ project }}"
        service_account_file: "{{ service_account_file }}"
        state: present
      register: gcp_vm_disk
    ```

5. Update the `gcp_vm_build/tasks/main.yml` file with the following task to create a VM with no public IP address:

    ```
    - name: create a {{ node.name }} instance with no Internet
      gcp_compute_instance:
        name: "{{ node.name | regex_replace('_','-') }}"
        machine_type: "{{ compute_node_flavor }}"
        disks:
          - source: "{{ gcp_vm_disk }}"
            boot: 'true'
        network_interfaces:
          - network: "{{ gcp_vpc }}"
            subnetwork: "{{ gcp_subnets.results |
              selectattr('name','equalto',node.network) |
              list | first }}"
        metadata:
          tier: "{{ node.name.split('-')[0] }}"
        tags:
          items: "{{ node.network }}"
        zone: "{{ node.zone }}"
        auth_kind: "{{ auth_kind }}"
        project: "{{ project }}"
        service_account_file: "{{ service_account_file }}"
        state: present
      when: not node.has_internet
    ```

6. Update the `gcp_vm_build/tasks/main.yml` file with the following task to create a VM with a public IP address:

```
- name: create an {{ node.name }} instance with Internet
  gcp_compute_instance:
    name: "{{ node.name | regex_replace('_','-') }}"
    machine_type: f1-micro
    can_ip_forward: "{{ node.ip_forwarding if node.ip_forwarding is
defined else 'no' }}"
    disks:
      - source: "{{ gcp_vm_disk }}"
        boot: 'true'
    network_interfaces:
      - network: "{{ gcp_vpc }}"
        network_ip: "{{ node.ip if node.ip is defined else omit }}"
        subnetwork: "{{ gcp_subnets.results |
          selectattr('name','equalto',node.network) |
          list | first }}"
        access_configs:
          - name: External NAT
            type: ONE_TO_ONE_NAT
    metadata:
      tier: "{{ node.name.split('-')[0] }}"
    zone: "{{ node.zone }}"
    tags:
      items: "{{ node.network }}"
    auth_kind: "{{ auth_kind }}"
    project: "{{ project }}"
    service_account_file: "{{ service_account_file }}"
    state: present
  register: vm_data
  when: node.has_internet
```

7. Update the `pb_gcp_env_build.yml` playbook with the following task to create all the required VMs that we have defined:

```
- name: Build VM Instances
  include_role:
    name: gcp_vm_build
  loop: "{{ compute_nodes }}"
  loop_control:
    loop_var: node
```

How it works...

As per our example network's design, we will deploy two web servers and two database servers in two different availability zones. Then we will build a bastion host in a single AZ since it is only used for management. We defined all our required machines in the `compute_nodes` variable and, for each machine, we specified the following parameters, which we will use during the provisioning:

- `Name`: The name of the machine
- `Network`: Specifies the subnet in which we will deploy this machine and enforce the correct network tag
- `Zone`: Specifies the zone in which we want to deploy this machine
- `has_internet`: Signifies whether this machine should get a public IP address

We created a new role to deploy our compute workload and we defined the following main sections:

- **Create disk for VMs**: The initial task is to create the disk that will house the OS for these machines. We used the `gcp_compute_disk` Ansible module to define these disks and we specified the following parameters:
    - `Name`: This is the name of this disk.
    - `Image_source`: Specifies the OS that the machine will run—in our example, all our machines will run CentOS.
    - `Zone`: Specifies the availability zone where this disk will be created.
    - `Size_gb`: Specifies the disk size that will be deployed.

- **Create VMs**: After creating the disks, we created the VMs using the `gcp_compute_instance` module, which takes the following parameters in order to provision the VM:
    - `Name`: The name of this VM.
    - `Machine_type`: Specifies the instance type that we use for these machines.

- `Disks`: A dictionary that specifies the disk that we will use with this machine. We supply the `gcp_vm_disk` variable, which we obtained when we provisioned the disks in the previous task.
- `Network_interfaces`: A dictionary that specifies which subnet and VPC that we need to deploy this instance on. For the VPC, we supply the `gcp_vpc` variable, which is the value that we get when we provision the VPC.
- `Zone`: Specifies which availability zone we will deploy our VM in.
- `Tags`: Specifies the network tags that we will assign to these VMs. These are the same tags that we used in our firewall rules in order to reference our compute nodes.

On top of the preceding parameters, we have the `access_configs` parameter (which is a dictionary), and it is used to specify whether a compute node will get a public IP address. If the VM gets a public IP address, we set the name parameter in `access_configs` as external NAT and the type parameter as `ONE_TO_ONE_NAT`. If the machine doesn't require a public IP address, we omit the `access_configs` dictionary.

In our setup, all our web servers and bastion hosts should get a public IP address; however, our DB servers shouldn't have direct internet connectivity, and so no public IP address should be assigned to them. We differentiated this using the `has_internet` parameter in our compute node definition, and we used this parameter to choose the correct task to use during the VM provisioning.

Once we run the playbook with the new role to create the VMs, we will see that all the disks for each VM are created, as shown in the following screenshot:

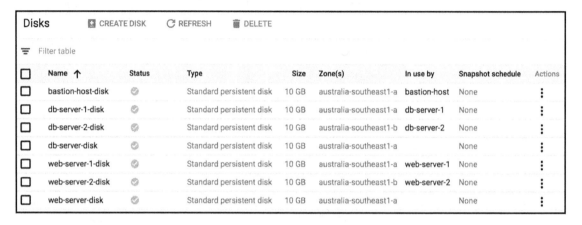

Also, all the VMs are created in the correct subnet, as shown in the following screenshot:

Once our VMs are created with the correct network tags, we can verify that our firewall rules are applied only on those VMs that are based on the network tags assigned to those VMs. The following snippet outlines the firewall rule `allow-internet-to-anz-web` and how it is applied only to web servers:

See also...

For more information regarding the GCP instance and disk modules in Ansible, and all the other parameters supported by these modules, please go to the following links:

- https://docs.ansible.com/ansible/2.8/modules/gcp_compute_instance_module.html#gcp-compute-instance-module
- https://docs.ansible.com/ansible/latest/modules/gcp_compute_disk_module.html#gcp-compute-disk-module

Adjusting routing within a VPC

In this recipe, we will outline how to control routing within the GCP VPC to enforce custom routing decisions for hosts. This allows us to have full control of the routing for our hosts within the VPC.

Getting ready

The Ansible control machine must be connected to the internet with reachability to GCP public API endpoints and the GCP account should be configured as outlined in the previous recipes. In addition, the resource group, virtual networks, and subnets should be provisioned as outlined in the previous recipes.

How to do it...

1. Update the `group_vars/gcp_vpc.yml` file to include the required routing data, as shown in the following code:

```
$ cat group_vars/gcp_vpc.yml
route_tables:
  - name: db_tier_rt
    subnet: db_tier
    routes:
      - name: Default Route
        prefix: 0.0.0.0/0
        nh: none
```

2. Update the `pb_gcp_env_build.yml` playbook with the following task to create the routes in GCP:

```
- name: Create the Route
  gcp_compute_route:
    name: "{{ route.name }}"
    dest_range: "{{ route.dest}}"
    network: {selfLink: "{{ gcp_vpc.selfLink }}"}
    next_hop_ip: "{{ route.nh }}"
    tags: "{{ route.apply_to.split(',') | default(omit) }}"
    state: present
    auth_kind: "{{ auth_kind }}"
    project: "{{ project }}"
    service_account_file: "{{ service_account_file }}"
  loop: "{{ cutom_routes }}"
  loop_control:
    loop_var: route
  tags: gcp_route
```

How it works..

In our example setup, with the current routing and firewall rules, our DB servers have no internet connectivity; however, we need to have the ability to access the internet from these servers in order to install software or perform patches. In order to achieve this goal, we are going to use our bastion hosts as NAT instances to provide internet access to our DB servers. In order to achieve this, we need to adjust the routing for all the DB servers in our VPC.

In GCP, we have a default route that is pointing to our internet gateway in the VPC. This default route is present in the VPC and is applied to all the hosts within the VPC. The following is the routing table for our VPC:

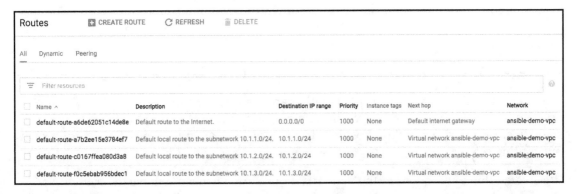

However, because of the firewall rules in place and the fact that all the DB servers have no external public IP addresses, the DB servers will not be able to access the internet. We need to adjust the routing for the DB servers to point to the bastion hosts (which are performing NAT). We also need to leave the original default route since this is the main path that is used by our web and bastion hosts in order to reach the internet.

We defined the custom routes that we need to apply using the `custom_routes` list data structure, and we used the `gcp_compute_route` Ansible module to loop across this data structure to create all the required routes. We used the network tag applied on the DB hosts in order to enforce this route only on the hosts with this network tag. Once we run this new task, the updating routing table for the VPC is as shown in the following screenshot:

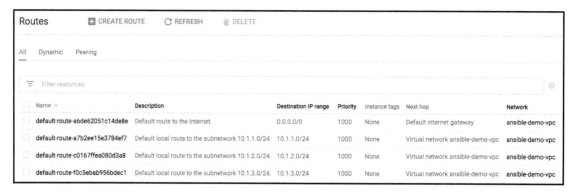

We can set the next hop for the route to either an IP address or an instance identification; however, we used the IP address for simplicity, and in our VM definition, we selected a static IP address for our bastion host in order to make it easy to reference this IP address in our routing setup.

We created this routing task in the main playbook since we need to have the bastion VM provisioned in order to set up the route with the next hop set to its IP address. If we created the route before the VM is provisioned, the route will be created; however, the task will fail with a warning that the next hop IP address for our route is not present.

See also...

For more information regarding the GCP routing modules in Ansible and all the other parameters supported by this module, go to `https://docs.ansible.com/ansible/latest/modules/gcp_compute_route_module.html#gcp-compute-route-module`.

Validating GCP deployment using Ansible

Ansible provides multiple modules to collect the operational state of the different resources that we created in GCP, and we can use these modules to validate the current state of our network resources in the GCP cloud. This provides a programmatic approach for validating a deployment without the need to log in to the portal via the **Graphical User Interface (GUI)** to check the status of the different components provisioned in GCP. In this recipe, we will outline how to use some Ansible modules to validate the network subnets that we have deployed.

Getting ready

The Ansible control machine must be connected to the internet with the ability to reach GCP public API endpoints, and the GCP account should be configured as outlined in the previous recipes.

How to do it...

1. Create a new `pb_gcp_net_validate.yml` playbook and add the following task to collect VPC subnet information:

```
$ cat pb_gcp_net_validate.yml

---
- name: Build GCP Environment
  hosts: all
  connection: local
  gather_facts: no
  force_handlers: True
  vars_files:
    - gcp_account_info.yml
  tasks:
    - name: Get Subnet Facts
      gcp_compute_subnetwork_facts:
        region: "{{ subnets | map(attribute='region') | list |
first }}"
        auth_kind: "{{ auth_kind }}"
        project: "{{ project }}"
        service_account_file: "{{ service_account_file }}"
      register: gcp_vpc_subnets
```

2. Update the playbook with the following task to validate the IP prefix provisioned on all the deployed subnets:

```
- name: Validate all Subnets are Deployed
  assert:
    that:
      - gcp_vpc_subnets['items'] |
  selectattr('name','equalto',item.name) |
        map(attribute='ipCidrRange') | list | first
        == item.cidr
  loop: "{{ subnets }}"
```

How it works...

We created a new playbook that we will use to validate all the subnets that we have deployed in our GCP project. Ansible provides multiple modules to collects the operational state or facts for the different resources in GCP (subnets, VPC, virtual machines, and so on). In this example, we are using the `gcp_compute_subnetwork_facts` module in order to collect the subnet facts for our deployment. We registered all the data returned by this module in a new variable, `gcp_vpc_subnets`. Finally, we used the `assert` module to loop across all our subnet definitions to validate whether the IP prefixes provisioned on all these subnets are correct and aligned with our design.

We can use the other fact-gathering modules in order to validate the other aspect of our deployment and to use the same approach using multiple `assert` statements in order to make sure that all the resources deployed are aligned with our design.

See also...

For more information regarding the other GCP fact-gathering modules, please visit the following links:

- https://docs.ansible.com/ansible/2.8/modules/gcp_compute_network_facts_module.html
- https://docs.ansible.com/ansible/2.8/modules/gcp_compute_subnetwork_facts_module.html

Decommissioning GCP resources using Ansible

Similar to creating resources at scale using automation, we can destroy these resources once we decide we don't need them. We use the same Ansible modules that we used to create the resources in GCP in order to destroy these resources.

Getting ready

The Ansible control machine must be connected to the internet and be able to reach GCP public API endpoints, and the GCP account should be configured as outlined in the previous recipes.

How to do it...

1. Create a new `pb_gcp_env_destroy.yml` playbook and add the following task to read the vault-encrypted JSON file:

```
$ cat pb_gcp_env_destroy.yml

---
- name: Decommission GCP Resources
  hosts: all
  connection: local
  force_handlers: True
  environment:
    GCP_SERVICE_ACCOUNT_FILE: "{{ service_account_file }}"
    GCP_AUTH_KIND: 'serviceaccount'
  vars_files:
    - gcp_account_info.yml
  tasks:
    - name: Read the Vault Encrypted JSON File
      copy:
        content: "{{ lookup('file','gcp-ansible-secret.json') }}"
        dest: "{{ service_account_file }}"
      notify: Clean tmp Decrypted Files
      tags: always
```

2. Update the `pb_gcp_env_destroy.yml` playbook and add the following task to collect VPC information:

```
- name: Get VPC Facts
  gcp_compute_network_facts:
    project: "{{ project }}"
  register: gcp_vpc
```

3. Update the playbook with the following task to delete all the VMs:

```
- name: Delete Instance {{ node.name }}
  gcp_compute_instance:
    name: "{{ node.name | regex_replace('_','-') }}"
    zone: "{{ node.zone }}"
    project: "{{ project }}"
    state: absent
  loop: "{{ compute_nodes }}"
  loop_control:
    loop_var: node
```

4. Update the playbook with the following task to delete all the disks that we created for all the VMs in our VPC:

```
- name: Delete disks for {{ node.name }}
  gcp_compute_disk:
    name: "{{ node.name | regex_replace('_','-') }}-disk"
    zone: "{{ node.zone }}"
    project: "{{ project }}"
    state: absent
  loop: "{{ compute_nodes }}"
  loop_control:
    loop_var: node
```

5. Update the playbook with the following task to delete all the firewall rules within our VPC:

```
- name: Delete All Firewall Rules
  gcp_compute_firewall:
    name: "{{ rule.name | regex_replace('_','-') }}"
    network: "{{ gcp_vpc }}"
    project: "{{ project }}"
    state: absent
  loop: "{{ fw_rules }}"
  loop_control:
    loop_var: rule
  tags: gcp_fw_rules
```

6. Update the playbook with the following task to delete all the custom routes within our VPC:

```
- name: Delete all Routes
  gcp_compute_route:
    name: "{{ route.name }}"
    dest_range: "{{ route.dest}}"
    network: "{{ gcp_vpc }}"
    project: "{{ project }}"
    state: absent
  loop: "{{ custom_routes }}"
  loop_control:
    loop_var: route
  when:
    - custom_routes is defined
```

7. Update the playbook with the following task to delete all the subnets within our VPC:

```
- name: Delete GCP Subnets
  gcp_compute_subnetwork:
    name: "{{ subnet.name }}"
    ip_cidr_range: "{{ subnet.cidr }}"
    network: "{{ gcp_vpc }}"
    region: "{{ subnet.region }}"
    project: "{{ project }}"
    state: absent
  loop: "{{ subnets }}"
  loop_control:
    loop_var: subnet
```

8. Update the playbook with the following task to delete all the VPCs:

```
- name: Delete GCP VPC
  gcp_compute_network:
    name: "{{ vpc_name | regex_replace('_','-') }}"
    project: "{{ project }}"
    state: absent
```

How it works...

We created a new playbook that we will use to destroy all our resources within our sample network design. We used the same modules that we utilized to provision the resources across the GCP cloud; however, we used the `state: absent` in order to delete all these resources.

The only thing that we need to take care when decommissioning the resources is the order by which we delete these resources. We can't delete any resource if there is a dependent resource still active that depends on the resource that we are trying to delete. For example, we can't delete a disk without deleting the VM that utilizes this disk first.

Once we run our playbook, we can see that all the VMs are deleted, as shown in the following screenshot:

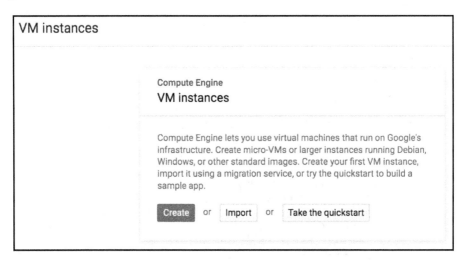

Also, all our VPCs and subnets are deleted as well, as shown in the following screenshot:

The preceding screenshot shows that there are no local VPC networks in the current project.

Network Validation with Batfish **10** and Ansible

In all previous chapters of this book, we have used multiple recipes to outline how to perform network validation using Ansible—we have done this by utilizing the different modules available within Ansible. In all of these cases, we performed network validation after pushing the configuration into the network devices. We then collected the network state and validated that it was aligned with our intended state. However, we may want to validate the network state *prior* to pushing the configuration on the devices. As well as this, it might be necessary to validate that the intended network state is as desired without even touching our network. But how do we do this?

Batfish is an open source project that targets this use case. Its main aim is to provide an offline network validation tool to validate multiple aspects of the network configuration. Batfish can provide a validation and correctness guarantee for security, compliance, and traffic forwarding for the network. It uses the device configuration from our network devices to build a neutral data model and forwarding tree for our network, which we can then use to validate the network state and validate the correct traffic forwarding within our network. The following diagram outlines the high-level architecture of Batfish, and how it works:

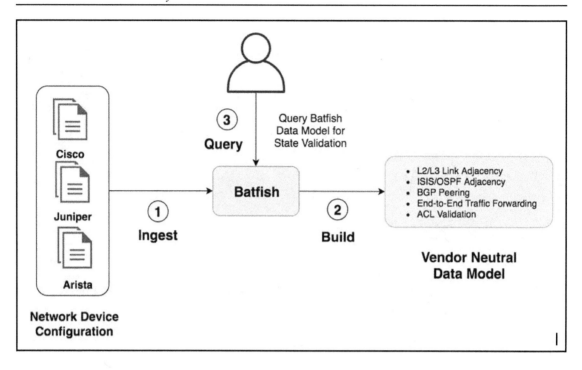

Batfish uses a client/server model. With this, we run a Batfish server instance (written in Java), and we communicate with the server using a client-side **software development kit (SDK)** called **Pybatfish** (written in Python). We then initialize a snapshot of our network using our network configuration files, and, based on this network snapshot, the Batfish server computes a data model for our network. Using the client, we can start to ask questions to validate our network using this vendor-neutral data model.

The Batfish team has developed multiple Ansible modules that wrap around the **Pybatfish** client library to retrieve the data model generated by the Batfish server. The modules allow us to perform different queries against this network model to validate our network state. The diagram that appears next outlines the interaction between Ansible, Pybatfish, and the Batfish server.

In this chapter, we will outline how to install Batfish and how to integrate it with Ansible in order to start using it to validate the network state, prior to pushing the configuration to our devices. This combination is very powerful, and can easily be extended to build complete **continuous integration/continuous deployment (CI/CD)** pipelines for network configuration changes. Batfish can be an integral part to provide pre-validation prior to pushing the configuration to network devices in production.

We are going to use the following network topology, which we used in Chapter 4, *Building Data Center Networks with Arista and Ansible,* to outline how we can validate this sample leaf-spine network topology using Ansible and Batfish:

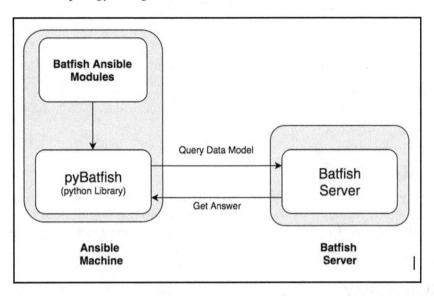

The main recipes covered in this chapter are:

- Installing Batfish
- Integrating Batfish with Ansible
- Generating the network configuration
- Creating a network snapshot for Batfish
- Initializing the network snapshot with Ansible
- Collecting network facts from Batfish
- Validating traffic forwarding with Batfish
- Validating **access control lists** (**ACLs**) with Batfish

Technical requirements

All the code described in this chapter can be found at this URL: https://github.com/ PacktPublishing/Network-Automation-Cookbook/tree/master/ch10_batfish.

This chapter is based on the following software releases:

- Ansible machine running CentOS 7.7
- A CentOS 7.7 machine hosting a Batfish container
- Python 3.6.8
- Ansible 2.9
- Arista **virtualized extensible operating system** (**vEOS**) running EOS 4.20.1F

Check out the following video to see the Code in Action:
`https://bit.ly/3bhke1A`

Installing Batfish

In this recipe, we will outline how to install the Batfish container (the server component in the Batfish architecture) and start it, in order to start to interact with it from Ansible. This is a mandatory foundation step in order to start validating our network using Batfish.

Getting ready

As outlined in this chapter introduction, we will install Batfish on a separate Linux machine. This machine needs to have internet connectivity in order to be able to install Docker and pull down the Batfish container.

How to do it...

1. Install Docker on the CentOS Linux machine, as demonstrated at the following URL:

   `https://docs.docker.com/install/linux/docker-ce/centos/`

2. Once Docker is installed and operational, download the Docker container, as shown in the following code snippet:

   ```
   $ sudo docker pull batfish/batfish
   ```

3. Start the Batfish container, as shown in the following code snippet:

   ```
   $ sudo docker run -d -p 9997:9997 -p 9996:9996 batfish/batfish
   ```

How it works...

Batfish provides multiple options for installing and running the Batfish server. However, the simplest and most recommended method is to run a Docker container that houses the Batfish server. In order to run this Docker container, we first need to install Docker on the CentOS Linux machine. In our case, Docker can be installed on different Linux distributions, and also on macOS and Windows.

Once Docker is installed, we download the Batfish container to our Linux machine using the `docker pull` command and start the Docker container using the `docker run` command. We must expose **Transmission Control Protocol (TCP)** ports `9996` and `9997` from the container and map them on the Linux machine, using the `-p` directive. We map these ports to the same ports on the Linux machine. These ports are used to interact with the Batfish server from the remote client (the *Pybatfish* client library installed on the Ansible control machine).

Batfish provides two Docker containers: `batfish/batfish` and `batfish/allinone`. The `batfish/allinone` container has the Batfish server and the Pybatfish client library. It also has the Jupyter Notebook Python library installed, along with some sample notebooks, to start interacting with the Batfish server. However, we will not be using this approach. Instead, we will be using the `batfish/batfish` container, which only has the Batfish server.

See also...

For more information regarding Batfish and how to install it, please visit the following URLs:

- `https://github.com/batfish/docker`
- `https://github.com/batfish/batfish/blob/master/README.md`

Integrating Batfish with Ansible

In order to integrate Batfish with Ansible, we need to install the required Python packages. Doing so will allow Ansible to communicate with the Batfish server. In this recipe, we will outline how to install these Python packages, as well as how to install the required Ansible roles needed to run the required Batfish Ansible modules.

Getting ready

In order to follow along with this recipe, the Ansible controller must have internet connectivity. This will allow us to install the required dependencies for Batfish.

How to do it...

1. Install the Batfish client python3 package on the Ansible controller, as shown in the following code snippet:

```
$ sudo python3 -m pip install --upgrade
git+https://github.com/batfish/pybatfish.git
```

2. Download the batfish Ansible roles to the roles folder, as shown in the following code snippet:

```
$ ansible-galaxy install batfish.base
```

How it works...

In this recipe, we are setting up the integration between Ansible and Batfish. This is accomplished through two steps:

1. On the Ansible controller, we need to install the pybatfish Python library, which is the Batfish client-side SDK that interacts with the Batfish server. This package is required by the Ansible modules. These will be used to interact with the Batfish server in our playbooks.

2. Secondly, we install the batfish roles that the Batfish team has developed in order to interact with the Batfish server and validate network device configuration. This Ansible role contains all the required Python scripts to run the custom Ansible modules for Batfish. In order to install this role onto the Ansible control machine, we are using ansible-galaxy.

We can validate that pybatfish is installed correctly like so:

```
$ pip3 freeze | grep batfish
pybatfish==0.36.0
```

We can now explore the installed role downloaded by `ansible-galaxy`:

```
$ ansible-galaxy list batfish.base
# /home/ansible/.ansible/roles
```

Here is the list of Python source code for this role, which is found in the `library` folder for this role:

```
$tree ~/.ansible/roles/batfish.base/library/
/home/ansible/.ansible/roles/batfish.base/library/
├──── bf_assert.py
├──── bf_extract_facts.py
├──── bf_init_snapshot.py
├──── bf_session.py
├──── bf_set_snapshot.py
├──── bf_upload_diagnostics.py
└──── bf_validate_facts.py
```

With these two steps covered, the Ansible controller is ready to start interacting with the Batfish server that we deployed in the previous recipe.

Since we didn't specify any additional arguments on the `ansible-galaxy install` command, the roles will be installed on the `~/.ansible/roles` path by default.

See also...

For more information on Pybatfish and the Ansible roles developed by Batfish and to be used with Ansible, please check this page: `https://github.com/batfish/batfish/blob/master/README.md`.

Generating the network configuration

To start our analysis and validation with Batfish, we need to provide the configuration for our network devices to the Batfish server. In this recipe, we will outline how to generate this configuration using Ansible. Batfish is an offline network validation tool, and having a complete network configuration is one of the mandatory steps for achieving the correct network validation.

Getting ready

There are no specific requirements here, other than having Ansible installed on the Ansible control machine.

How to do it...

1. Create a new folder named `ch10_batfish` that will hold all our variables and playbooks.
2. Populate all the variables to describe our network in the `group_vars/all.yml` file and the `host_vars` folder. Here, we are using the exact same variables that were outlined in *Chapter 4, Building Data Center Networks with Arista and Ansible.*
3. Create a `roles` folder inside the `ch10_batfish` folder, in order to house all the roles that we will create.
4. Create a new role named `generate_fabric_config`, like so:

   ```
   $ cd ch10_batfish
   $ ansible-galaxy init --init-path roles generate_fabric_config
   ```

5. Build all the Jinja2 templates inside the `templates` folder to create the interfaces, management, and **Border Gateway Protocol (BGP)** configuration.
6. Include all the required tasks to build the configuration in the `tasks/main.yml` file. Again, we are using the exact same steps and modules already discussed in *Chapter 4, Building Data Center Networks with Arista and Ansible,* to build the configuration for this sample network.
7. Create the `ansible_host` inventory, as shown in the following code block:

   ```
   $ cat hosts

   [leaf]
   leaf01    ansible_host=172.20.1.41
   leaf02     ansible_host=172.20.1.42
   leaf03     ansible_host=172.20.1.43
   leaf04     ansible_host=172.20.1.44


   [spine]
   spine01      ansible_host=172.20.1.35
   spine02      ansible_host=172.20.1.36

   [arista:children]
   ```

```
      leaf
      spine
```

8. Now, create a new playbook named `pb_build_fabric_config.yml`, like so:

```
$ cat pb_build_fabric_config.yml
---
- name: Build DC Fabric Config
  hosts: all
  connection: local
  gather_facts: no
  vars:
    tmp_dir: tmp
    config_dir: configs
  roles:
    - generate_fabric_config
```

How it works...

In this recipe, we are using Ansible to generate the configuration for the network devices in our sample topology. We are also using the exact same data and variables structure that we have discussed in Chapter 4, *Building Data Center Networks with Arista and Ansible*. We group all our infrastructure definition using the YAML files inside the `group_vars` and `host_vars` folders. We are also using the exact same Jinja2 templates that have been used in Chapter 4, *Building Data Center Networks with Arista and Ansible*, in order to generate the configuration snippet for interfaces, BGP, and the management configuration for our devices.

We use the `ansible-galaxy init` command to build the role skeleton, and we use the `--init-path` directive to specify where to create this new role.

The following output outlines the structure of our new role to generate the configuration for our devices:

```
$ tree roles/generate_fabric_config
roles/generate_fabric_config
├── meta
│   └── main.yml
├── tasks
│   └── main.yml
└── templates
    ├── intf.j2
    ├── mgmt.j2
    ├── overlay_bgp.j2
    └── underlay_bgp.j2
```

At this point, we create a new playbook to generate the device configuration, and we use the `connection` local parameter since we need to capture the configuration of the network devices on the Ansible controller node. Once we have run the playbook, we are left with the configuration for all our devices on the `configs` folder, as shown in the following code block:

```
$ tree ch10_batfish/configs
configs
├──── leaf01.cfg
├──── leaf02.cfg
├──── leaf03.cfg
├──── leaf04.cfg
├──── spine01.cfg
└──── spine02.cfg
```

Creating a network snapshot for Batfish

To allow Batfish to analyze the network using the devices' configuration files, these files need to be structured in a specific order. This makes it easy for the Batfish server to ingest this data.

In this recipe, we will outline how to properly structure and prepare our network configuration files to be consumed by the Batfish service.

Getting ready

The device configuration should already be generated, as demonstrated in the previous recipe.

How to do it...

1. Create a new playbook named `pb_batfish_analyis.yml`, and add the following task to create a new folder. This folder will house the network configuration that will be analyzed by `batfish`:

```
$ cat pb_batfish_analyis.yml
---
- name: Extract network device facts using Batfish and Ansible
  hosts: all
  gather_facts: no
```

```
    roles:
      - batfish.base
    vars:
      ansible_connection: local
      batfish_host: 172.20.100.101
      config_dir: configs
      batfish_network_folder: batfish_net_snapshot
      batfish_analysis_folder: batfish_analysis
    tasks:

    - name: Create a Batfish Config Directory
      file:
        path: "{{ batfish_network_folder }}"
        state: directory     run_once: yes
```

2. Update the playbook named `pb_batfish_analyis.yml` with the following task to copy all the configuration files to the new folder:

```
    - name: copy All configs to Batfish Directory
      copy:
        src: "{{ config_dir }}"
        dest: "{{ batfish_network_folder }}"
      run_once: yes
```

How it works...

In order to start our analysis of our network, we create a new playbook that is used to execute all the required tasks and validate the network configuration with Batfish. In this playbook, we use the following parameters:

- We run the playbook on all the nodes in our network. This is because we will need to reference the parameters for each node in subsequent tasks (such as loopback **internet protocols (IPs)**).
- We set the `ansible_connection` parameter to `local` as we don't need to connect to our devices, and all the tasks will run locally on the Ansible machine.
- We specify the IP address of the Batfish server machine hosting the `batfish` container. This will be used in all subsequent tasks to communicate with the Batfish server.

For Batfish to start analyzing the configuration of our devices, the configuration files for our devices need to be structured in a specific order in one directory. This step is often referred to as preparing the network snapshot for Batfish analysis.

Here, we create a new playbook for the Batfish analysis. In the first task, we create the `configs` folder, which will be the base used by Batfish to retrieve the configuration for our network devices.

In the second task, we use the `copy` module to copy the configuration files of our network devices over to the `configs` folder. Once we run the playbook with the tasks specified, we will get the following directory structure needed for Batfish analysis:

```
$ tree ch10_batfish/batfish_net_snapshot/

batfish_net_snapshot
└── configs
    ├── leaf01.cfg
    ├── leaf02.cfg
    ├── leaf03.cfg
    ├── leaf04.cfg
    ├── spine01.cfg
    └── spine02.cfg
```

 In all the tasks, we are using the `run_once` parameter as we want to create the folder and copy the files only once. If we omit this option, we will run these tasks per each node in our inventory, which is not optimal in this case.

See also...

For more information on the directory structure needed by Batfish for network snapshots, please visit this link: `https://pybatfish.readthedocs.io/en/latest/notebooks/interacting.html#Uploading-configurations`.

Initializing the network snapshot with Ansible

In this recipe, we will outline how to open a session between Ansible and the Batfish server. In addition to this, we will look at how to initialize the network snapshot that we prepared in the previous step, as well as how to send it to the Batfish server.

Getting ready

As outlined in the previous recipe, the device configuration is generated, and the network snapshot is packaged at this point. Furthermore, IP reachability is now also provided between the Ansible controller and the Batfish server on TCP ports 9996 and 9997.

How to do it...

1. Update the `pb_batfish_analyis.yml` playbook with the following task to start the session with the Batfish server:

```
- name: Setup connection to Batfish service
  bf_session:
    host: "{{ batfish_host }}"
    name: local_batfish
  register: bf_session
  run_once: yes
```

2. Update the `pb_batfish_analyis.yml` playbook to initialize the network snapshot on the Batfish server:

```
- name: Initialize the Network Snapshot
  bf_init_snapshot:
    network: arista_dc_fabric
    snapshot: arista_dc_fabric_config
    snapshot_data: "{{ batfish_network_folder }}"
    overwrite: true
  run_once: yes
  register: bf_snapshot
```

How it works...

In the playbook, we are using the `batfish.base` Ansible role (which we have downloaded from `ansible-galaxy`) that interacts with the Batfish server. This role provides multiple modules that we use to start the integration between the Ansible control machine and the Batfish server.

The first module is `bf_session`. This module opens the session between the Batfish client (Ansible, in this case) and the Batfish server, in order to start to exchange data between the two. The second module, `br_init_snapshot`, initializes the network snapshot (device configuration files) that we have created on the Ansible controller. It then sends them to the Batfish server in order to start analysis on the Batfish server and for the Batfish server to build the neutral data model for our network, based on these configuration files.

The `bf_init_session` module returns the status of how Batfish parsed the configuration and whether there was any problem in decoding the configuration. We capture this return value in the `bf_snapshot` variable. The following snippet outlines the status of parsing that was performed by Batfish on the supplied network snapshot:

```
ok: [localhost] => {
  "bf_snapshot": {
    "ansible_facts": {
      "bf_network": "arista_dc_fabric",
      "bf_snapshot": "arista_dc_fabric_config"
    },
    "result": {
      "network": "arista_dc_fabric",
      "snapshot": "arista_dc_fabric_config"
    },
    "summary": "Snapshot 'arista_dc_fabric_config' created in network
'arista_dc_fabric'",
    "warnings": [
      "Your snapshot was successfully initialized but Batfish failed to
fully recognize some lines in one or more input files. Some unrecognized
configuration lines are not uncommon for new networks, and it is often fine
to proceed with further analysis.
    ]
  }
}
```

 We can ignore the warning we received since it will not impact our analysis.

Collecting network facts from Batfish

Batfish can generate a vendor-neutral data model that represents the critical facts discovered from the configuration files supplied to Batfish. In this recipe, we will outline how to collect these facts discovered by Batfish and how to use this information to validate the network configuration on the devices as per the intended state.

Getting ready

The network configuration is already generated and the network snapshot is already synced with the Batfish server.

How to do it...

1. Update the `pb_batfish_analyis.yml` playbook with the following task to collect facts generated by Batfish:

```
- name: Retrieve Batfish Facts
  bf_extract_facts:
    output_directory: "{{ batfish_analysis_folder }}/bf_facts"
  run_once: yes
  register: bf_facts
```

2. Update the `pb_batfish_analysis.yml` playbook with the following task to validate the interface configuration that was generated:

```
 - name: Validate all Interfaces are Operational and Have correct
IP
   assert:
     that:
       -
bf_facts.result.nodes[inventory_hostname].Interfaces[item.port].Act
ive
== true
       -
bf_facts.result.nodes[inventory_hostname].Interfaces[item.port].Pri
mary_Address ==
         item.ip + '/' + global.p2p_prefix | string
     loop: "{{ p2p_ip[inventory_hostname] }}"
```

How it works...

Batfish processes the network snapshot (device configuration) and generates a vendor-neutral data model for the different sections of the configuration. These are considered to be the facts that Batfish has generated and collected from the input configuration files. We use the `bf_extract_facts` Ansible module to extract the facts, and we can then save it to a directory for further analysis.

In our case, we saved the Batfish analysis in the `bf_facts` folder, and the module generated a unique YAML file that contains this neutral data model for each device. The following snippet outlines the interface data model for one of the devices (`leaf01`) in our sample topology:

```
nodes:
  leaf01:
    Interfaces:
      Ethernet8:
        Active: true
        All_Prefixes:
        - 172.31.1.1/31
    < --- Output Omitted for brevity --->
        Declared_Names:
        - Ethernet8
        Description: '"DC1 | Rpeer: spine01 | Rport: Ethernet1"'
    < --- Output Omitted for brevity --->
        MTU: 1500
    < --- Output Omitted for brevity --->
        Primary_Address: 172.31.1.1/31
        Primary_Network: 172.31.1.0/31
    < --- Output Omitted for brevity --->
        Speed: 1000000000.0
```

This same data structure is returned by the module, and we save this result in a new variable called `bf_facts`. We use the data in this variable to validate the intended network state of our devices, based on the configuration that we have generated. We also use the `assert` module to loop through all our interfaces for each node that we have declared in our data model. We then compare the value for these parameters from the generated data model of Batfish to make sure that all our interfaces are operational and that all the IP addresses are configured correctly.

There's more...

Batfish also provides different built-in `assert` tests to perform validation on the data model that it generates. This allows it to provide a more simple and robust validation for the critical issues that might affect the network. Here is a task that uses these built-in `assert` that are already available with Batfish:

```
- name: Validate BGP Sessions and Undefined References
  bf_assert:
    assertions:
      - type: assert_no_undefined_references
        name: Confirm we have no undefined references
      - type: assert_no_incompatible_bgp_sessions
        name: Confirm we have no incompatible BGP sessions
  run_once: yes
```

We can see two assertions in the preceding code block:

- `assert_no_undefined_references`: This validates that all configuration blocks are present and valid. For example, all prefix lists are present and there is no undefined reference to a missing prefix list. This ensures that the configuration generated is sane and doesn't include any undefined reference to an object that is not declared.
- `Assert_no_incompatible_bgp_sessions`: This assertion validates that all the BGP sessions are configured correctly and there is no mismatch between the configuration of the BGP peers. This also ensures that the generated configuration is valid and the resulting BGP session will be operational.

If we need to validate that these tests will catch errors in the configuration, we can do so by shutting down a link between a leaf and spine switch in our master configuration files, as shown in the following code block:

```
$ cat configs/leaf01.cfg

!
interface Ethernet8
   description "DC1 | Rpeer: spine01 | Rport: Ethernet1"
   no switchport
   shutdown
   ip address 172.31.1.1/31
!
```

This configuration change should bring down the underlay BGP session between the `leaf01` and `spine01` nodes.

When we run our playbook again with the preceding task, we will see the following error message:

```
TASK [Validate BGP Sessions and Undefined References]
**************************************************************************
************************          "result": [

        {
            "details": "Assertion passed",
            "name": "Confirm we have no undefined references",
            "status": "Pass",
            "type": "assert_no_undefined_references"
        },
        {
            "details": "Found incompatible BGP session(s), when none
were expected\n[{'Node': 'leaf01', 'VRF': 'default', 'Local_AS': 65001,
'Local_Interface': None, 'Local_IP': '172.31.1.1', 'Remote_AS': '65100',
'Remote_Node': None, 'Remote_Interface': None, 'Remote_IP': '172.31.1.0',
'Session_Type': 'EBGP_SINGLEHOP', 'Configured_Status':
'INVALID_LOCAL_IP'}]",
            "name": "Confirm we have no incompatible BGP sessions",
            "status": "Fail",
            "type": "assert_no_incompatible_bgp_sessions"
        }
    ],
    "summary": "1 of 2 assertions failed"
}
```

From the output, we can see that the first assertion was successful, meaning that there were no undefined references in our configuration. However, the second assertion failed, since there is now a BGP session that is failing.

See also...

For more information regarding all the available assertions supported by Batfish Ansible modules, please check the following links:

- https://github.com/batfish/ansible/blob/master/docs/bf_assert.rst
- https://github.com/batfish/ansible/blob/master/docs/assertions.rst

Validating traffic forwarding with Batfish

In this recipe, we will outline how to validate traffic forwarding in the network. This is accomplished in Batfish using the forwarding tables that Batfish generates from the device configuration. It is very useful to validate proper traffic forwarding within the network prior to any change.

Getting ready

The network configuration is already generated and the network snapshot is already synced with the Batfish server.

How to do it...

1. Update the `pb_batfish_analyis.yml` playbook with the following task to validate traffic forwarding within our topology:

```
- name: Validate Traffic Forwarding in the Fabric
  bf_assert:
    assertions:
      - type: assert_all_flows_succeed
        name: confirm host is reachable for traffic received
        parameters:
          startLocation: "{{ item.0 }}"
          headers:
            dstIps: "{{ item.1.value.ip }}"
            srcIps: "{{ lo_ip[item.0].ip }}"
  with_nested:
    - "{{ play_hosts }}"
    - "{{ lo_ip | dict2items }}"
  run_once: yes
```

How it works...

Batfish provides a built-in validation method to validate the proper traffic forwarding between endpoints within your network topology. This is achieved using the `assert_all_flows_succeed` method. This method validates that all the flows between given endpoints are successful. In order for Batfish to validate the traffic flow for any given flow, we need to provide the following information:

- The start node location
- The source IP for the flow
- The destination IP addresses for the flow

Batfish will use the data model that it generated to build the forwarding table for all the nodes in our network topology and to validate that the flows we are testing will be forwarded within the network.

In our sample topology, we want to validate that all the flows from all the nodes' loopback IP addresses can reach the destination loopback IP address on all the remote nodes. We use the `with_nested` looping construct to loop across all the nodes in our inventory and to loop across all the loopback IP addresses within the `lo_ip` data structure. This will test from all the nodes within our inventory if we can reach the remote loopbacks of all the other nodes.

When we run this test, we will see that all the flows are working fine except for traffic from `spine01` to `spine02` and the reverse traffic from `spine02` to `spine01`, as shown in the following code block:

```
### Traffic from Spine01 to Spine02 Failing


                        "msg": "1 of 1 assertions failed",
                        "result": [
                            {
                                "details": "Found a flow that failed, when expected
to succeed\n[{'Flow': Flow(dscp=0, dstIp='10.100.1.253', dstPort=0, ecn=0,
fragmentOffset=0, icmpCode=0, icmpVar=8, ingressInterface=None,
ingressNode='spine01', ingressVrf='default', ipProtocol='ICMP',
packetLength=0, srcIp='10.100.1.254', srcPort=0, state='NEW', tag='BASE',
tcpFlagsAck=0, tcpFlagsCwr=0, tcpFlagsEce=0, tcpFlagsFin=0, tcpFlagsPsh=0,
tcpFlagsRst=0, tcpFlagsSyn=0, tcpFlagsUrg=0), 'Traces':
ListWrapper([[((ORIGINATED(default), NO_ROUTE))]]), 'TraceCount': 1}]",
                                "name": "confirm host is reachable for traffic
received",
                                "status": "Fail",
                                "type": "assert_all_flows_succeed"
```

```
            }
        ],
        "summary": "1 of 1 assertions failed"
    }
```

On the live network, we can check the routing on the live nodes to validate our findings from Batfish:

```
dc1-spine01#sh ip route 10.100.1.253

VRF: default
Codes: C - connected, S - static, K - kernel,
       O - OSPF, IA - OSPF inter area, E1 - OSPF external type 1,
       E2 - OSPF external type 2, N1 - OSPF NSSA external type 1,
       N2 - OSPF NSSA external type2, B I - iBGP, B E - eBGP,
       R - RIP, I L1 - IS-IS level 1, I L2 - IS-IS level 2,
       O3 - OSPFv3, A B - BGP Aggregate, A O - OSPF Summary,
       NG - Nexthop Group Static Route, V - VXLAN Control Service,
       DH - Dhcp client installed default route


Gateway of last resort is not set
```

After checking our network configuration, we can see that the preceding output is correct. This is possible since we are using a route-map on all the `leaf` switches to only advertise the local loopback IP address, and we are not re-advertising any other IP address from the `leaf` nodes.

Furthermore, there is no BGP session between the `spine` nodes, thus there is no traffic path between them. So, in order to complete our test and make it successful, we will only test all flows originating from the `leaf` nodes toward all the destinations.

We will not test traffic originating from the `spine` nodes. Here, you can see the modified task:

```
- bf_assert:

    assertions:
      - type: assert_all_flows_succeed
        name: confirm host is reachable for traffic received
        parameters:
          startLocation: "{{ item.0 }}"
          headers:
            dstIps: "{{ item.1.value.ip }}"
            srcIps: "{{ lo_ip[item.0].ip }}"
    with_nested:
      - "{{ play_hosts }}"
```

```
      - "{{ lo_ip | dict2items }}"
    when: '"spine" not in item.0'
    run_once: yes
```

After running the test again, all the flows pass and the task is successful.

Validating ACLs with Batfish

In this recipe, we will outline how to use Batfish to validate ACL entries and validate the correct traffic handling by these ACLs' definition. This allows us to use Batfish and Ansible as auditing tools to enforce correct security compliance for our infrastructure.

Getting ready

The device configuration is generated and the network snapshot is packaged, as outlined in the previous recipe.

How to do it...

1. Update our network configuration on `leaf03` and `leaf04` with the following ACLs' entries to secure the web **virtual local area network** (**VLAN**):

```
!
ip access-list WEB_VLAN_IN
   10 deny ip host 172.20.10.10 any
   20 permit tcp 172.20.10.0/24 any eq https


!
ip access-list WEB_VLAN_OUT
   10 permit tcp any 172.20.10.0/24 eq https
!
```

2. Update the `pb_batfish_analyis.yml` playbook with the following task to validate correct egress ACL behavior for our web VLAN:

```
- name: Validate Internet to Web Servers
  bf_assert:
    assertions:
      - type: assert_filter_permits
        name: Confirm Internet Access to Web Servers
        parameters:
```

```
              filters: "{{ web_acl }}"
              headers:
                dstIps: "{{ web_server_subnet}}"
                srcIps: "0.0.0.0/0"
                dstPorts: '443'
                ipProtocols: 'TCP'
        vars:
          web_acl: WEB_VLAN_OUT
          web_server_subnet: 172.20.10.0/24
        run_once: yes
```

3. Update the `pb_batfish_analyis.yml` playbook with the following task to validate correct ingress ACL behavior for our VLAN:

```
    - name: Validate Server {{ web_server }} is Denied
      bf_assert:
        assertions:
          - type: assert_filter_denies
            name: Confirm Traffic is Denied
            parameters:
              filters: "{{ web_acl_in }}"
              headers:
                dstIps: "0.0.0.0/0"
                srcIps: "{{ web_server}}"
        vars:
          web_acl_in: WEB_VLAN_IN
          web_server: 172.20.10.10
        run_once: yes
```

How it works...

Batfish is yet another great tool for validating the correct traffic handling of traffic processed by ACLs. This allows us to validate whether or not a specific flow is permitted or denied by a specific ACL. Batfish also provides a powerful tool to validate network changes involving ACLs. Furthermore, it can be used as a safeguard against implementing rogue ACL changes that could impact the live traffic on the network or lead to violations in our security policy.

We use the `bf_assert` Batfish module again—however, in this case, for validating ACL. We use two other `assert` methods implemented in this module, which are as follows:

- The `assert_filter_permits` method tests and validates that a specific flow is correctly allowed by our ACL.
- The `assert_filter_denies` method tests and validates that a specific flow is denied by our ACL.

In our playbook, we create two separate tasks. The first one uses the `assert_filter_permits` method to validate that all traffic from the internet to our web server's subnet is permitted. We use the `headers` parameter in order to specify the IP header information for all the flows that we want to be validated.

We then create the second task using the `assert_filter_denies` method, and this tests that a specific web server is blocked from communicating with any destination.

When we run our playbook with the newly updated tasks, we can see that all of them are completed successfully, which outlines that the ACL behavior in our sample network is as expected.

In order to validate that our filters are working correctly, we will introduce a problem in one of our ACL filters by allowing **Hypertext Transfer Protocol Secure (HTTPS)** traffic to our denied web servers (`172.20.10.10`), as shown in the following code snippet:

```
!
ip access-list WEB_VLAN_IN
    05 permit tcp host 172.20.10.10 any eq ssh
    10 deny ip host 172.20.10.10 any
    20 permit tcp 172.20.10.0/24 any eq https
!
```

When we run our playbook again, we can see that we have an error in the last task. This error shows that specific traffic flow has been allowed when it was expected to be denied by our ACL, as shown in the following code block:

```
        "result": [
            {
                "details": "Found a flow that was permitted, when expected
    to be denied\n[{'Node': 'leaf03', 'Filter_Name': 'WEB_VLAN_IN', 'Flow':
    Flow(dscp=0, dstIp='0.0.0.0', dstPort=22, ecn=0, fragmentOffset=0,
    icmpCode=0, icmpVar=0, ingressInterface=None, ingressNode='leaf03',
    ingressVrf='default', ipProtocol='TCP', packetLength=0,
    srcIp='172.20.10.10', srcPort=0, state='NEW', tag='BASE', tcpFlagsAck=0,
    tcpFlagsCwr=0, tcpFlagsEce=0, tcpFlagsFin=0, tcpFlagsPsh=0, tcpFlagsRst=0,
    tcpFlagsSyn=0, tcpFlagsUrg=0), 'Action': 'PERMIT', 'Line_Content': '05
```

```
permit tcp host 172.20.10.10 any eq ssh', 'Trace':
AclTrace(events=[AclTraceEvent(class_name='org.batfish.datamodel.acl.Permit
tedByIpAccessListLine', description='Flow permitted by extended ipv4
access-list named WEB_VLAN_IN, index 0: 05 permit tcp host 172.20.10.10 any
eq ssh', lineDescription='05 permit tcp host 172.20.10.10 any eq
ssh')])}]",
                    "name": "Confirm Traffic is Denied",
                    "status": "Fail",
                    "type": "assert_filter_denies"
            }
        ]
```

This simple example shows that we can create more sophisticated assertion rules in order to enforce the correct security policy within our network. Furthermore, we can utilize Batfish to validate the correct enforcement of this policy across our network.

11
Building a Network Inventory with Ansible and NetBox

In the previous chapters of this book, we described network infrastructure using Ansible variables stored in YAML files. While this approach is perfectly acceptable, it is not the optimal solution for adopting automation across an organization. We need to have our network inventory, IP addresses, and VLANs in a central system, which will act as the authoritative source of truth for our network. This system should have a robust and powerful API that can be queried by other automation and OSS/BSS systems to retrieve and update the network inventory.

NetBox is an open source inventory system for network infrastructure, which was initially developed by the network engineering team at DigitalOcean to document their data center infrastructure. It is a simple yet powerful and highly extensible inventory system, which can act as a source of truth regarding our network. It allows us to document and describe the following features on any network infrastructure:

- **IP address management (IPAM)**: IP networks and addresses, VRFs, and VLANs
- **Equipment racks**: Organized by groups and sites
- **Devices**: Types of devices and where they are installed
- **Connections**: Network, console, and power connections between devices
- **Virtualization**: Virtual machines and clusters
- **Data circuits**: Long-haul communication circuits and providers
- **Secrets**: Encrypted storage of sensitive credentials

NetBox is a Django-based Python application that uses PostgreSQL as backend data storage and NGINX as a frontend web server, along with other optional components that work together to deliver the NetBox system. It has a powerful REST API, which can be used to retrieve or update the data stored in the NetBox database.

In this chapter, we will outline the following three main use cases for integration between Ansible and NetBox:

- Ansible can be used to populate data in NetBox for the various types of network information that are modeled by NetBox, such as sites, devices, and IP addresses. The following diagram outlines the high-level integration between Ansible and NetBox in this use case:

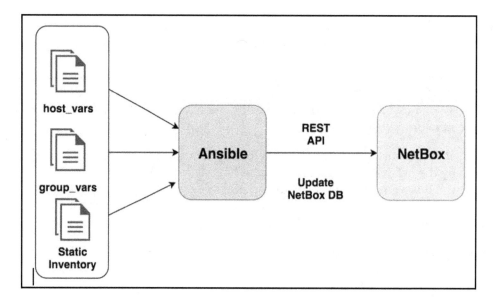

- NetBox can be used as the dynamic inventory source for Ansible to retrieve and build an Ansible inventory. The following diagram outlines this integration:

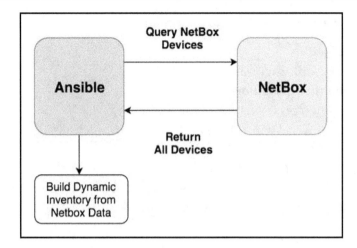

- NetBox can be used as the source of information for data required by Ansible to provision and configure network devices. The following diagram outlines this use case:

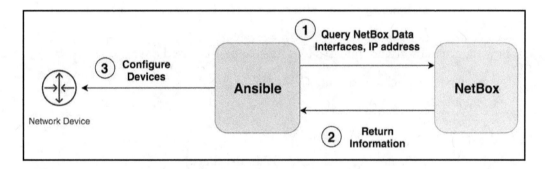

We are going to use a sample network composed of two data center sites with a spine or leaf fabric in each site. We will model all the information and populate it in NetBox. The following table captures this sample network infrastructure:

Site	Device	Role
DC1	dc1-spine01	Spine switch
DC1	dc1-spine02	Spine switch
DC1	dc1-leaf01	Leaf switch
DC1	dc1-leaf02	Leaf switch
DC2	dc2-spine01	Spine switch
DC2	dc2-spine02	Spine Switch
DC2	dc2-leaf01	Leaf switch
DC2	dc2-leaf02	Leaf switch

The main recipes covered in this chapter are as follows:

- Installing NetBox
- Integrating NetBox with Ansible
- Populating sites in NetBox
- Populating devices in NetBox
- Populating interfaces in NetBox
- Populating IP addresses in NetBox
- Populating IP prefixes in NetBox
- Using NetBox as a dynamic inventory source for Ansible
- Generating a configuration using NetBox data

Technical requirements

All of the code used in this chapter can be found in the following GitHub repository:

```
https://github.com/PacktPublishing/Network-Automation-Cookbook/tree/master/
ch11_netbox
```

The following are the software releases that this chapter is based on:

- An Ansible machine running CentOS 7
- Ansible 2.9
- Python 3.6.8
- Arista vEOS running EOS 4.20.1F
- NetBox v2.6.5 running on a CentOS 7 Linux machine

Installing NetBox

In this recipe, we will outline how to install NetBox using Docker containers and how to start all the required containers to have a functional NetBox server. Using Docker containers to install NetBox is the simplest way of getting started.

Getting ready

In order to start installing NetBox on a Linux machine, the machine needs to have internet connectivity to pull the required Docker image for NetBox operation from Docker Hub.

How to do it...

1. Install Docker on your CentOS Linux machine using the following URL:

   https://docs.docker.com/install/linux/docker-ce/centos/

2. Install Docker Compose using the following URL:

   https://docs.docker.com/compose/install/

3. Clone the NetBox repository into a new directory (netbox_src), as follows:

   ```
   $ git clone https://github.com/netbox-community/netbox-docker.git
   netbox_src
   ```

4. Change to the netbox_src directory and pull all the required Docker images using docker-compose, as follows:

   ```
   $ cd netbox_src
   $ /usr/local/bin/docker-compose pull
   ```

5. Update the docker-compose.yml file to set the correct port for the NGINX web server:

   ```
   $ cat docker-compose.yml
    ß--- Output Omitted for brevity -->
   nginx:
       command: nginx -c /etc/netbox-nginx/nginx.conf
       image: nginx:1.17-alpine
       depends_on:
       - netbox
       ports:
       - 80:8080  >>  # This will make NGINX listen on port 80 on the
   host machine
   ```

6. Start all the Docker containers, as follows:

   ```
   $ /usr/local/bin/docker-compose up -d
   ```

How it works...

As outlined in this chapter's introduction, NetBox is composed of multiple services that integrate together to deliver the required NetBox application. The simplest installation method for NetBox is by using Docker containers. We use a single `docker-compose` definition file to describe the interaction between the different Docker containers needed to deliver the NetBox application. The following diagram outlines the high-level architecture of NetBox and how each service runs in its own container:

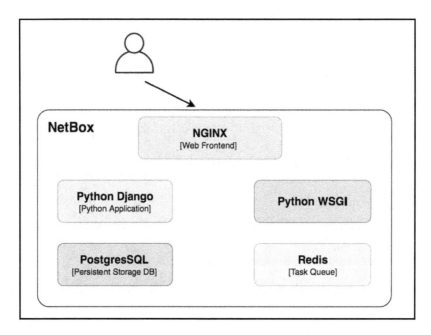

In this recipe, we described the steps required to install NetBox using Docker and `docker-compose`, which greatly simplifies the installation steps that lead to a functional NetBox server. The developers behind NetBox created the Docker images required to run NetBox using Docker and the `docker-compose` file, which describes the overall interaction between the different NetBox components in order to set up a NetBox server. All the NetBox setup instructions, along with the Docker files and the `docker-compose` file to build and deploy NetBox using Docker containers, can be found at `https://github.com/netbox-community/netbox-docker`.

After installing Docker and `docker-compose` on our Linux machine, we cloned the GitHub repository and edited the `docker-compose.yml` file to set the port that the NGINX web server will listen to on the host machine. Finally, we ran the `docker-compose pull` command to download all the Docker containers defined in the `docker-compose.yml` file and we ran `docker-compose` to start up all the Docker containers.

Once all the Docker containers are downloaded and started, we can access NetBox at `https://<netbox-server-ip>/`.

This will take us to the following page:

The default username is `admin` and the password is `admin`.

There's more

To simplify the installation of NetBox, I have created an Ansible role within this chapter's code to deploy NetBox. To use this role, we need to perform the following steps:

1. On the Ansible control machine, clone the following chapter code:

    ```
    git clone git@github.com:PacktPublishing/Network-Automation-
    Cookbook.git
    ```

2. Update the `hosts` file with the correct IP address for your NetBox server:

    ```
    $ cat hosts
    < --- Output omitted for bevitry --- >
    [netbox]
    netbox  ansible_host=172.20.100.111
    ```

3. Run the `pb_deploy_netbox.yml` Ansible playbook:

```
$ ansible-playbook pb_deploy_netbox.yml
```

See also...

For more information about how to install NetBox using Docker containers, go to `https://github.com/netbox-community/netbox-docker`.

Integrating NetBox with Ansible

In this recipe, we will outline how to integrate Ansible and NetBox via the NetBox API. This integration is mandatory as it will allow us to populate the NetBox database through Ansible playbooks, as well as to use NetBox as our dynamic inventory source to create an Ansible inventory in later recipes.

Getting ready

NetBox should be installed as outlined in the previous recipe, and the IP needs to stretch between the Ansible control machine and the NetBox server. Ansible will communicate with NetBox over port 80, so this port needs to be open on the NetBox server.

How to do it...

1. On the Ansible control machine, install the `pynetbox`Python package:

```
$ sudo pip3 install pynetbox
```

2. Log in to the NetBox server using the admin user details and click on the **Admin** tab to create a new user, as shown here:

3. Create a new user and set its username and password:

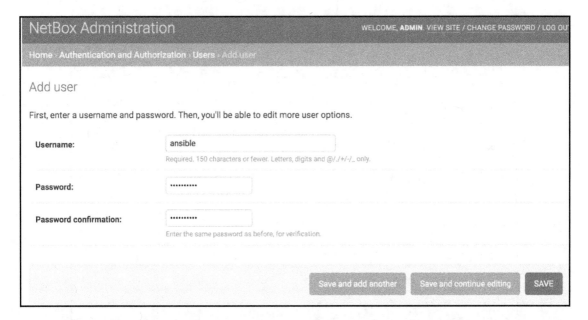

4. Assign superuser privileges to this new user so that you will be able to write to the NetBox **Database (DB)**:

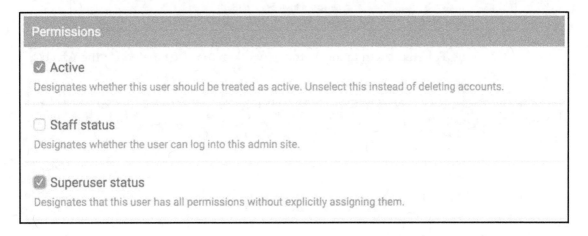

5. Create a new token for this new user:

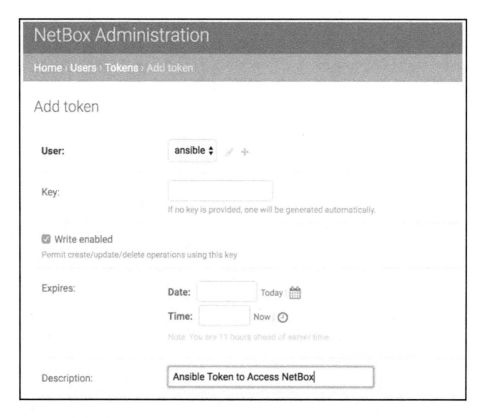

6. Go to the **Tokens** screen to locate the new token that we created for the Ansible user:

7. In the `ch11_netbox` project directory, create our `hosts` Ansible inventory file, as follows:

```
$ cat hosts
[dc1]
dc1-spine01      ansible_host=172.20.1.41
dc1-spine02      ansible_host=172.20.1.42dc1-leaf01
ansible_host=172.20.1.35
dc1-leaf02       ansible_host=172.20.1.3

[dc2]
dc2-spine01      ansible_host=172.20.2.41dc2-spine02
ansible_host=172.20.2.42dc2-leaf01      ansible_host=172.20.2.35
dc2-leaf02       ansible
host=172.20.2.36

[leaf]
dc[1:2]-leaf0[1:2]

[spine]
dc[1:2]-spine0[1:2]
```

8. Create the `group_vars` folder and the `all.yml` file and populate the file, as follows:

```
---
netbox_url: http://172.20.100.111
netbox_token: 08be88e25b23ca40a9338d66518bd57de69d4305
```

How it works...

In this recipe, we are setting up the integration between Ansible and NetBox. In order to start using Ansible modules to populate the NetBox DB, we installed the `pynetbox` Python module. This module is mandatory for all the NetBox Ansible modules that we are going to use in this chapter.

On the NetBox site, we started by creating a new user with complete admin rights. This granted the user the full privileges to create, edit, or delete any object within the NetBox DB. Then, we created a token, which will be used to authenticate all the API requests from Ansible to NetBox.

Finally, we created our Ansible inventory and declared two parameters in our Ansible variables, `netbox_url` and `netbox_token`, to hold the API endpoint and the token for the Ansible user on NetBox.

See also...

For more information about the `pynetbox` Python library that interacts with NetBox, go to `https://pynetbox.readthedocs.io/en/latest/`.

Populating sites in NetBox

In this recipe, we will outline how to create sites in NetBox. Sites are a logical construct within NetBox that allow us to group our infrastructure based on their physical location. We need to define our sites before we can start declaring our devices and place them in these sites.

Getting ready

Ensure integration between Ansible and NetBox is in place, as outlined in the previous recipe.

How to do it...

1. Update the `group_vars/all.yml` file with the following data about our physical sites:

```
sites:
  - name: DC1
    description: "Main Data Center in Sydney"
    location: Sydney
  - name: DC2
    description: "Main Data Center in KSA"
    location: Riyadh
```

2. Create a new `roles` directory under `ch11_netbox`.
3. Create a new Ansible role, called `build_netbox_db`, and populate the `tasks/main.yml` file, as follows:

```
$ cat roles/build_netbox_db/tasks/main.yml
---
- name: Create NetBox Sites
  netbox_site:
    netbox_token: "{{ netbox_token }}"
    netbox_url: "{{ netbox_url }}"
```

```
      data:
        name: "{{ item.name | lower }}"
        description: "{{ item.description | default(omit) }}"
        physical_address: "{{ item.location | default(omit) }}"
      state: "{{ netbox_state }}"
    loop: "{{ sites }}"
    run_once: yes
    tags: netbox_sites
```

4. Update the `defaults/main.yml` file with the following data:

```
$ cat roles/build_netbox_db/defaults/main.yml
---
netbox_state: present
```

5. Create a new playbook, called `pb_build_netbox_db.yml`, with the following contents:

```
$ cat pb_build_netbox_db.yml
---
- name: Populate NetBox DataBase
  hosts: all
  gather_facts: no
  vars:
    ansible_connection: local
  tasks:
    - import_role:
        name: build_netbox_db
```

How it works...

In this recipe, we began by populating the sites in our sample network and defining the `sites` data structure, which describes the physical locations of our data centers in the `all.yml` file under `group_vars`. We created an Ansible role in order to populate the NetBox database and the first task we performed within this role was to use the `netbox_site` module to create all the sites within our network. We looped across all the sites defined in the `sites` data structure and pushed the data to NetBox using the `netbox_site` module.

We created a new playbook, which will be our master playbook, to populate the contents of our network inventory into NetBox and we referenced the role that we created in order to start executing all the tasks within this role.

Once we run this playbook, the sites are populated in NetBox, as shown here:

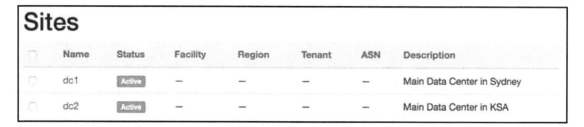

See also...

For more information about the `netbox_site` module, go to `https://docs.ansible.com/ansible/latest/modules/netbox_site_module.html`.

Populating devices in NetBox

In this recipe, we will outline how to create and populate network devices in NetBox. This will include declaring the device model and manufacturer, along with their role in our network. This will help us to build an accurate inventory of our network infrastructure, which we can use later on in the last recipe of this chapter to build a dynamic inventory for Ansible using NetBox.

Getting ready

The Ansible and NetBox integration should be in place and the sites should be defined and populated in NetBox, as outlined in the previous recipe. This is critical since when we start to populate devices in NetBox, we need to tie them to an existing site.

How to do it...

1. Update the `group_vars/all.yml` file with the `devices` information, as follows:

```
$ cat group_vars/all.yml

< --- Output Omitted for brevity --- >
```

```
devices:
  - role: Leaf_Switch
    type: 7020SR
    vendor: Arista
    color: 'f44336'  # red
  - role: Spine_Switch
    type: 7050CX3
    ru: 2
    vendor: Arista
    color: '2196f3'  # blue
```

2. Create the group_vars/leaf.yml and group_vars/spine.yml files, then update them with the following information:

```
$ cat group_vars/leaf.yml


---
device_model: 7020SR
device_role: Leaf_Switch
vendor: Arista
$ cat group_vars/spine.yml
---
device_model: 7050CX3
device_role: Spine_Switch
vendor: Arista
```

3. Create a new task to create the manufacturer for all of the devices in our inventory under the tasks/create_device_vendors.yml file, as shown here:

```
$ cat roles/build_netbox_db/tasks/create_device_vendors.yml

- name: NetBox Device  // Get Existing Vendors
  uri:
    url: "{{ netbox_url }}/api/dcim/manufacturers/?name={{ device }}"
    method: GET
    headers:
      Authorization: "Token {{ netbox_token }}"
      Accept: 'application/json'
    return_content: yes
    body_format: json
    status_code: [200, 201]
  register: netbox_vendors
  run_once: yes
  tags: device_vendors
- name: NetBox Device  // Create Device Vendors
  uri:
```

```
    url: "{{ netbox_url }}/api/dcim/manufacturers/"
    method: POST
    headers:
      Authorization: "Token {{ netbox_token }}"
      Accept: 'application/json'
    return_content: yes
    body_format: json
    body:
      name: "{{ device }}"
      slug: "{{ device | lower }}"
    status_code: [200, 201]
  when:
    - netbox_vendors.json.count == 0
    - netbox_state == 'present'
  run_once: yes
  tags: device_vendors
```

4. Update the `tasks/main.yml` file to include the
   `create_device_vendors.yml` file, as follows:

```
$ cat roles/build_netbox_db/tasks/main.yml
< --- Output Omitted for brevity --- >
- name: Create NetBox Device Vendors
  include_tasks: create_device_vendors.yml
  loop: "{{ devices | map(attribute='vendor') | list | unique}}"
  loop_control:
    loop_var: device
  run_once: yes
  tags: device_vendors
```

5. Create a new task to create all the device models for all of the network devices in
   our inventory under the `tasks/create_device_types.yml` file, as follows:

```
$ cat roles/build_netbox_db/tasks/create_device_types.yml
- name: NetBox Device  // Get Existing Device Types
  uri:
    url: "{{ netbox_url }}/api/dcim/device-types/?model={{
device.type }}"
    method: GET
    headers:
      Authorization: "Token {{ netbox_token }}"
      Accept: 'application/json'
    return_content: yes
    body_format: json
    status_code: [200, 201]
  register: netbox_device_types
  run_once: yes
  tags: device_types
```

```
- name: NetBox Device  // Create New Device Types
  uri:
    url: "{{ netbox_url }}/api/dcim/device-types/"
    method: POST
    headers:
      Authorization: "Token {{ netbox_token }}"
      Accept: 'application/json'
    return_content: yes
    body_format: json
    body:
      model: "{{ device.type }}"
      manufacturer: { name: "{{ device.vendor }}"}
      slug: "{{ device.type | regex_replace('-','_') | lower  }}"
      u_height: "{{ device.ru | default(1) }}"
    status_code: [200, 201]
  when:
    - netbox_device_types.json.count == 0
    - netbox_state != 'absent'
  register: netbox_device_types
  run_once: yes
  tags: device_types
```

6. Update the `tasks/main.yml` file to include the
   `create_device_types.yml`files, as follows:

```
$ cat roles/build_netbox_db/tasks/main.yml
< --- Output Omitted for brevity --- >
- name: Create NetBox Device Types
  include_tasks: create_device_types.yml
  loop: "{{ devices }}"
  loop_control:
    loop_var: device
  run_once: yes
  tags: device_types
```

7. Create a new task to create all the device roles for all of the network devices in
   our inventory under the `tasks/create_device_roles.yml` file, as follows:

```
$ cat roles/build_netbox_db/tasks/create_device_roles.yml
- name: NetBox Device  // Get Existing Device Roles
  uri:
    url: "{{ netbox_url }}/api/dcim/device-roles/?name={{
device.role}}"
    method: GET
    headers:
      Authorization: "Token {{ netbox_token }}"
      Accept: 'application/json'
    return_content: yes
```

```
      body_format: json
      status_code: [200, 201]
    register: netbox_device_role
    tags: device_roles
  - name: NetBox Device   // Create New Device Roles
    uri:
      url: "{{ netbox_url }}/api/dcim/device-roles/"
      method: POST
      headers:
        Authorization: "Token {{ netbox_token }}"
        Accept: 'application/json'
      return_content: yes
      body_format: json
      body:
        name: "{{ device.role }}"
        slug: "{{ device.role | lower }}"
        color: "{{ device.color }}"
      status_code: [200, 201]
    when:
      - netbox_device_role.json.count == 0
      - netbox_state != 'absent'
    register: netbox_device_role
    tags: device_roles
```

8. Update the `tasks/main.yml` file to include the
`create_device_roles.yml` file, as follows:

```
$ cat roles/build_netbox_db/tasks/main.yml
< --- Output Omitted for brevity --- >
- name: Create NetBox Device Roles
  include_tasks: create_device_roles.yml
  loop: "{{ devices }}"
  loop_control:
    loop_var: device
  run_once: yes
  tags: device_roles
```

9. Create a new task to populate all of the devices in our inventory under the
`tasks/create_device.yml` file, as follows:

```
---
- name: Provision NetBox Devices
  netbox_device:
    data:
      name: "{{ inventory_hostname }}"
      device_role: "{{ device_role }}"
      device_type: "{{ device_model }}"
      status: Active
```

```
        site: "{{ inventory_hostname.split('-')[0] }}"
      netbox_token: "{{ netbox_token }}"
      netbox_url: "{{ netbox_url }}"
      state: "{{ netbox_state }}"
    register: netbox_device
    tags: netbox_devices
```

10. Update the `tasks/main.yml` file to include the `create_device.yml` file, as follows:

```
$ cat roles/build_netbox_db/tasks/main.yml
< --- Output Omitted for brevity --- >
- name: Create NetBox Device
  include_tasks: create_device.yml
  tags: netbox_devices
```

How it works...

In order to populate our network devices in NetBox, we first need to populate the following parameters related to the devices in NetBox:

- All the manufacturers for all of our network devices
- All the device models for our network equipment
- All the device roles that will be assigned to each network device

There is no pre-built module in Ansible that will populate all of this information and build these objects in NetBox. So, in order to populate this information in NetBox, we need to use the URI module, which allows us to trigger REST API calls to the correct API endpoint responsible for each of these objects. To carry out all of these tasks, follow these steps:

1. First, query the API endpoint using the GET method to get a matching object in the NetBox DB.
2. If an object is not present, we can create one by using a POST REST call and supplying the necessary data.
3. If an object is already present, we can skip the previous step.

Using the previous approach, we are simulating the idempotent nature of Ansible modules. When we run our playbook, we can see that all the device types have been populated in NetBox:

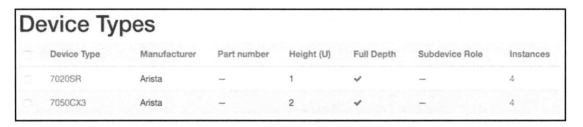

Device Types

	Device Type	Manufacturer	Part number	Height (U)	Full Depth	Subdevice Role	Instances
	7020SR	Arista	—	1	✔	—	4
	7050CX3	Arista	—	2	✔	—	4

Also, all the device roles for our equipment are populated, as shown here:

Device Roles

	Name	Devices	VMs	Label	VM Role	Slug
	Leaf_Switch	4	0	Leaf_Switch	✔	leaf_switch
	Spine_Switch	4	0	Spine_Switch	✔	spine_switch

Once we have built all the objects required to define a device in NetBox (such as the device role and device types), we can use the `netbox_device` Ansible built-in module to create all of the devices in our Ansible inventory. The following screenshot outlines all of the devices that have been correctly populated in the NetBox DB:

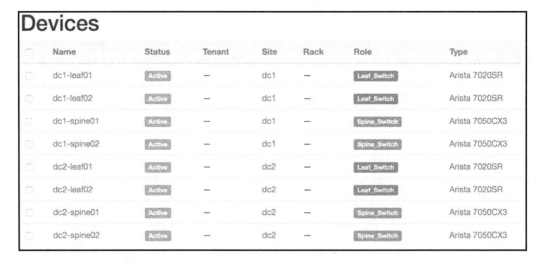

Devices

	Name	Status	Tenant	Site	Rack	Role	Type
	dc1-leaf01	Active	—	dc1	—	Leaf_Switch	Arista 7020SR
	dc1-leaf02	Active	—	dc1	—	Leaf_Switch	Arista 7020SR
	dc1-spine01	Active	—	dc1	—	Spine_Switch	Arista 7050CX3
	dc1-spine02	Active	—	dc1	—	Spine_Switch	Arista 7050CX3
	dc2-leaf01	Active	—	dc2	—	Leaf_Switch	Arista 7020SR
	dc2-leaf02	Active	—	dc2	—	Leaf_Switch	Arista 7020SR
	dc2-spine01	Active	—	dc2	—	Spine_Switch	Arista 7050CX3
	dc2-spine02	Active	—	dc2	—	Spine_Switch	Arista 7050CX3

In this recipe, we used the URI module to trigger API calls to the NetBox API in order to create objects within its DB. In order to understand more about what APIs are available and which parameters need to be passed in each API call, we need to check the API documentation for NetBox. The documentation for the API is contained within the NetBox installation and can be accessed at `http:///api/docs/`.

See also...

- For more information about the NetBox API, go
  to `https://netbox.readthedocs.io/en/stable/api/overview/`.

- For more information about the Ansible module to create devices on NetBox, go
  to `https://docs.ansible.com/ansible/latest/modules/netbox_device_module.html`.

Populating interfaces in NetBox

In this recipe, we will outline how to populate interfaces on network devices in NetBox. This provides us with a complete inventory for our devices and will allow us to assign IP addresses for each interface on our network device, as well as to model the network links within our network.

Getting ready

In order to create the network interfaces, the devices need to already be created, as outlined in the previous recipe.

How to do it...

1. Update the `group_vars/all.yml` file with the point-to-point links within our network fabric in each data center, as follows:

```
p2p_ip:
  dc1-leaf01:
    - {port: Ethernet8, ip: 172.10.1.1/31, peer: dc1-spine01,
pport: Ethernet1,
peer_ip: 172.10.1.0/31}
```

```
        - {port: Ethernet9, ip: 172.10.1.5/31, peer: dc1-spine02,
pport: Ethernet1,
peer_ip: 172.10.1.4/31}
< --- Output Omitted for brevity --- >
  dc2-leaf01:
        - {port: Ethernet8, ip: 172.11.1.1/31, peer: dc2-spine01,
pport: Ethernet1, peer_ip: 172.11.1.0/31}
        - {port: Ethernet9, ip: 172.11.1.5/31, peer: dc2-spine02,
pport: Ethernet1, peer_ip: 172.11.1.4/31}
```

2. Create a new task to create all the interfaces for all of the network devices in our inventory under the `tasks/create_device_intf.yml` file, as follows:

```
$ cat roles/build_netbox_db/tasks/create_device_intf.yml
---
- name: Create Fabric Interfaces on Devices
  netbox_interface:
    netbox_token: "{{ netbox_token }}"
    netbox_url: "{{ netbox_url }}"
    data:
      device: "{{ inventory_hostname }}"
      name: "{{ item.port }}"
      description: "{{ item.type | default('CORE') }} | {{
item.peer }}| {{
item.pport }}"
      enabled: true
      mode: Access
    state: "{{ netbox_state }}"
  loop: "{{ p2p_ip[inventory_hostname] }}"
  when: p2p_ip is defined
  tags: netbox_intfs
```

3. Update the `tasks/main.yml` file to include the `create_device_intfs.yml` file, as follows:

```
$ cat roles/build_netbox_db/tasks/main.yml
< --- Output Omitted for brevity --- >
- name: Create NetBox Device Interfaces  include_tasks:
create_device_intf.yml
  tags: netbox_intfs
```

How it works...

In order to populate all the point-to-point interfaces in our data center fabric, we first created the p2p_ip data structure, which holds all the parameters needed to model these point-to-point links. We then used the netbox_interface module to create all of these links in NetBox. Using the same module and following the exact same procedures, we can model the management (out-of-band management) and the loopback interface on our network devices.

The following screenshot shows the interfaces on one of our devices in NetBox and how the interfaces are populated:

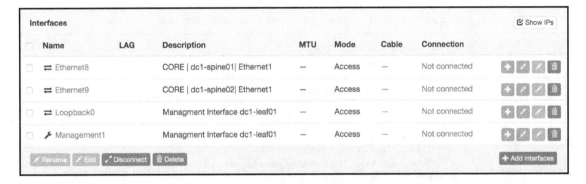

See also...

For more information about the Ansible module used to create interfaces on NetBox, go to https://docs.ansible.com/ansible/latest/modules/netbox_interface_module.html#netbox-interface-module.

Populating IP addresses in NetBox

In this recipe, we will outline how to create IP addresses in NetBox and how to bind these addresses to the interfaces on each of our network devices.

Getting ready

The network interfaces on each device within our inventory need to be defined and populated in NetBox, as outlined in the previous recipe.

How to do it...

1. Create a new task to create all the IP addresses attached to the network interfaces. This is carried out for all of the network devices in our inventory under the `tasks/create_device_intf_ip.yml` file, as follows:

```
$ cat roles/build_netbox_db/tasks/create_device_intf.yml
---
- name: Create Fabric IPs
  netbox_ip_address:
    netbox_token: "{{ netbox_token }}"
    netbox_url: "{{ netbox_url }}"
    data:
      address: "{{ item.ip }}"
      interface:
        name: "{{ item.port }}"
        device: "{{ inventory_hostname }}"
    state: "{{ netbox_state }}"
  loop: "{{ p2p_ip[inventory_hostname] }}"
  tags: netbox_ip
```

2. Update the `tasks/main.yml` file to include the `create_device_intf_ip.yml` file, as follows:

```
$ cat roles/build_netbox_db/tasks/main.yml
< --- Output Omitted for brevity ---


- name: Create NetBox Device Interfaces IP Address
  include_tasks: create_device_intf_ip.yml
  tags: netbox_ip
```

How it works...

In order to populate all the point-to-point IP addresses used on each data center fabric, we captured this information in the p2p_ip data structure, which holds all of the IP addresses assigned on each interface within our data center fabric. We used the netbox_ip_address module to loop across this data structure and populate all the IP addresses assigned to each interface on each device within our data center fabric. The same process is used for the management and loopback interfaces.

The following screenshot shows the IP addresses assigned to the interfaces for one of our devices (**dc1-leaf01**):

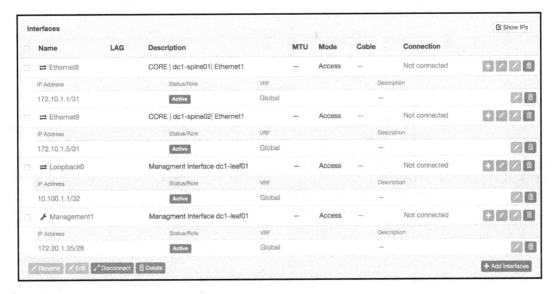

See also...

For more information about the Ansible module used to create IP addresses on NetBox, go to https://docs.ansible.com/ansible/latest/modules/netbox_ip_address_module. html#netbox-ip-address-module.

Populating IP prefixes in NetBox

In this recipe, we will look at how to create IP prefixes in NetBox. This allows us to utilize NetBox as our IPAM solution to manage IP address assignments within our network.

Getting ready

No specific requirements are needed to be able to populate IP subnets or prefixes in NetBox, as long as we don't bind these prefixes to a specific site. If we bind some subnets to a specific site, then these sites need to be defined in NetBox prior to this assignment.

How to do it...

1. Update the group_vars/all.yml file with the IP prefix information, as follows:

```
$ cat group_vars/all.yml

< --- Output Omitted for brevity --- >
subnets:
  -    prefix: 172.10.1.0/24
       role: p2p_subnet
       site: dc1
  -    prefix: 172.11.1.0/24
       role: p2p_subnet
       site: dc2
  -    prefix: 10.100.1.0/24
       role: loopback_subnet
       site: dc1
  -    prefix: 10.100.2.0/24
       role: loopback_subnet
       site: dc2
  -    prefix: 172.20.1.0/24
       role: oob_mgmt_subnet
       site: dc1
  -    prefix: 172.20.2.0/24
       role: oob_mgmt_subnet
       site: dc2
```

2. Update the tasks/main.yml file in our role definition to include the following task:

```
$ cat roles/build_netbox_db/tasks/main.yml
< --- Output Omitted for brevity --- >
- name: Create IP Prefixes
  netbox_prefix:
    netbox_token: "{{ netbox_token }}"
    netbox_url: "{{ netbox_url }}"
    data:
      prefix: "{{ item.prefix }}"
      site: "{{ item.site | default(omit) }}"
```

```
      status: Active
    state: "{{ netbox_state }}"
loop: "{{ subnets }}"
loop_control:
  label: "{{ item.prefix }}"
run_once: yes
tags: netbox_prefix
```

How it works...

We defined our subnets in the `group_vars/all.yml` file under the `subnets` data structure and then used the `netbox_prefix` module to loop over this data structure and populate the prefixes in NetBox.

The following screenshot shows the populated prefixes within NetBox and their respective utilization:

Prefixes

Prefix	Status	VRF	Utilization	Tenant	Site	VLAN	Role	Description
10.100.1.0/24	Active	Global	1%	—	dc1	—	—	—
10.100.2.0/24	Active	Global	1%	—	dc2	—	—	—
172.10.1.0/24	Active	Global	3%	—	dc1	—	—	—
172.11.1.0/24	Active	Global	3%	—	dc2	—	—	—
172.20.1.0/24	Active	Global	1%	—	dc1	—	—	—
172.20.2.0/24	Active	Global	1%	—	dc2	—	—	—

See also...

For more information about the Ansible module used to create IP prefixes on NetBox, go to `https://docs.ansible.com/ansible/latest/modules/netbox_prefix_module.html#netbox-prefix-module`.

Using NetBox as a dynamic inventory source for Ansible

In this recipe, we will outline how to use NetBox as a dynamic inventory source. With this approach, NetBox will have the inventory for our network infrastructure and we will use the different groupings available (such as sites, device roles, and so on) to build a dynamic inventory for Ansible and group them according to NetBox.

Getting ready

Integration between NetBox and Ansible needs to be in place, as outlined in the previous recipes.

How to do it...

1. In your main directory, create a new folder called `netbox_dynamic_inventory`.

2. In this new directory, create a new YAML file, called `netbox_inventory_source.yml`, with the following content:

```
$ cat netbox_dynamic_inventory/netbox_inventory_source.yml
---
plugin: netbox
api_endpoint: http://172.20.100.111
token: 08be88e25b23ca40a9338d66518bd57de69d4305
group_by:
  - device_roles
  - sites
```

3. Create a new playbook, called `pb_create_report.yml`, with the following content:

```
$ cat netbox_dynamic_inventory/pb_create_report.yml

---
- name: Create Report from Netbox Data
  hosts: all
  gather_facts: no
  connection: local
  tasks:
    - name: Build Report
```

```
        blockinfile:
          block: |
              netbox_data:
              {% for node in play_hosts %}
                  - { node: {{ node }} , type: {{
hostvars[node].device_types[0] }} , mgmt_ip: {{
hostvars[node].ansible_host }} }
              {% endfor %}
          path: ./netbox_report.yaml
          create: yes
        delegate_to: localhost
        run_once: yes
```

How it works...

In all of the examples and recipes that we have outlined in this book so far, we have used a static inventory file (in most cases `hosts`) where we defined our inventory, which Ansible will parse before executing our playbooks. In this recipe, we will use a different inventory source: a dynamic inventory. In this situation, we don't have a static file that holds our inventory, but we will build our inventory dynamically when we run our playbooks at execution time. All of our inventories, in this example, are maintained in NetBox and we have used NetBox as our inventory source.

For Ansible to use a dynamic inventory source, a plugin must be in place to talk to this inventory source in order to retrieve our inventory and any variables associated with it. Ansible, as of version 2.9, has introduced NetBox as a plugin that can be used as an inventory source. In order to use this plugin, we need to define a YAML file that outlines the different parameters needed by Ansible to communicate with the NetBox API. The mandatory parameters are as follows:

- The **Plugin** name: In our case, `NetBox`
- `Api_endpoint`: The API endpoint for our NetBox server
- The **Token**: The authentication token that we have created to establish communication between Ansible and our NetBox server

In the YAML declaration file, we can specify how we will group our inventory that is coming from NetBox. We can use the `group_by` attribute to outline the parameters that we will use to group our infrastructure. In our case, we are using `device_roles` and `sites` to group our infrastructure.

There's more

We can test our dynamic inventory by executing the following command to see how Ansible generates the inventory:

```
$ ansible-inventory --list -i netbox_inventory_source.yml
```

The following is a snippet of the output for the preceding command. It outlines the host variables that were retrieved from NetBox for a single device:

```
{
    "_meta": {
        "hostvars": {
            "dc1-leaf01": {
                "ansible_host": "172.20.1.35",
                "device_roles": [
                    "Leaf_Switch"
                ],
                "device_types": [
                    "7020SR"
                ],
                "manufacturers": [
                    "Arista"
                ],
                "primary_ip4": "172.20.1.35",
                "sites": [
                    "dc1"
                ]
            },
```

The following snippet shows the groups that Ansible built based on the grouping from NetBox:

```
"all": {
    "children": [
        "device_roles_Leaf_Switch",
        "device_roles_Spine_Switch",
        "sites_dc1",
        "sites_dc2",
        "ungrouped"
    ]
},
"device_roles_Leaf_Switch": {
    "hosts": [
        "dc1-leaf01",
        "dc1-leaf02",
        "dc2-leaf01",
        "dc2-leaf02"
```

```
            ]
    },
```

We have created a new playbook to test the integration between Ansible and NetBox and ensured that we can use the data retrieved from NetBox as a dynamic inventory source. Using our new playbook, we can create a simple report for each device in the NetBox dynamic inventory along with some of the parameters sent from NetBox.

When we run the playbook, we get the following report:

```
$ ansible-playbook pb_create_report.yml -i netbox_inventory_source.yml
$ cat netbox_report.yml
# BEGIN ANSIBLE MANAGED BLOCK
netbox_data:
  - { node: dc1-leaf01 , type: 7020SR , mgmt_ip: 172.20.1.35 }
  - { node: dc1-leaf02 , type: 7020SR , mgmt_ip: 172.20.1.36 }
  - { node: dc2-leaf01 , type: 7020SR , mgmt_ip: 172.20.2.35 }
  - { node: dc2-leaf02 , type: 7020SR , mgmt_ip: 172.20.2.36 }
  - { node: dc1-spine01 , type: 7050CX3 , mgmt_ip: 172.20.1.41 }
  - { node: dc1-spine02 , type: 7050CX3 , mgmt_ip: 172.20.1.42 }
  - { node: dc2-spine01 , type: 7050CX3 , mgmt_ip: 172.20.2.41 }
  - { node: dc2-spine02 , type: 7050CX3 , mgmt_ip: 172.20.2.42 }
# END ANSIBLE MANAGED BLOCK
```

See also...

For more information about the NetBox plugin, go to `https://docs.ansible.com/ansible/latest/plugins/inventory/netbox.html`.

To learn more about the Ansible dynamic inventory, go to `https://docs.ansible.com/ansible/latest/user_guide/intro_dynamic_inventory.html`.

Generating a configuration using NetBox

In this recipe, we will outline how to generate a configuration and push the configuration to network devices using the data retrieved from NetBox.

Getting ready

In this recipe, we will continue to use NetBox as our dynamic inventory source, so all of the configurations outlined in the previous recipe need to be implemented.

How to do it...

1. Under the `netbox_dynamic_inventory` directory, create the `netbox_data.yml` file with the following content:

```
$ cat netbox_data.yml
---
netbox_url: http://172.20.100.111
netbox_token: 08be88e25b23ca40a9338d66518bd57de69d4305
```

2. Create the `pb_build_config.yml` playbook with an initial task to read the `netbox_data.yml` file, as follows:

```
$ cat pb_build_config.yml
---
- name: Create Report from Netbox Data
  hosts: all
  gather_facts: no
  connection: local
  tasks:
    - name: Read netbox Data
      include_vars: netbox_data.yml
      run_once: yes
```

3. Update the `pb_build_config.yml` playbook to include a task to query NetBox for all interfaces in its DB for the current device:

```
- name: Get Data from Netbox
  uri:
  url: "{{ netbox_url }}/api/dcim/interfaces/?device={{
  inventory_hostname
  }}"
  method: GET
  headers:
  Authorization: "Token {{ netbox_token }}"
  Accept: 'application/json'
  return_content: yes
  body_format: json
  status_code: [200, 201]
  register: netbox_interfaces
  delegate_to: localhost
  run_once: yes
```

4. Update the playbook with the following task to push the configuration to the device:

```
- name: Push Config
  eos_config:
    lines:
      - description {{ port.description }}
    parent: interface {{ port.name }}
  loop: "{{ netbox_interfaces.json.results }}"
  loop_control:
    loop_var: port
  vars:
    ansible_connection: network_cli
    ansible_network_os: eos
```

How it works...

In order to run our playbook, we need to use the NetBox dynamic inventory script as our inventory source and execute the playbook, as follows:

```
$ ansible-playbook pb_build_config.yml -i netbox_inventory_source.yml
```

In this recipe, we will use NetBox as our source of truth to both construct our inventory as well as to retrieve interfaces on a given device. We will use a GET API call to the interface endpoints on NetBox and filter this API call by specifying only the interfaces for this specific device. The API call to achieve this is api/dcim/interfaces/?device=<deivce-name>/.

The following snippet shows the response we get from NetBox:

```
ok: [dc1-spine01] => {
    "netbox_interfaces": {
        "api_version": "2.6",
        "changed": false,
        "connection": "close",
        "json": {
            "results": [
                {
                    "description": "CORE | dc1-leaf01| Ethernet8",
                    "device": {
                        "display_name": "dc1-spine01",
                        "id": 44,
                        "name": "dc1-spine01",
                        "url": "http://172.20.100.111/api/dcim/devices/44/"
                    },
```

```
                     "enabled": true,
   <-- Output Omitted for Brevity -->
                     "name": "Ethernet1",
   <-- Output Omitted for Brevity -->
                },
```

We will use the data retrieved from the API to configure the description on all the ports on all the devices in our network, as per the data in the NetBox DB. In this case, we will use `eos_config` to push this data to our Arista EOS boxes. We can loop over the data returned from NetBox, which is stored in `netbox_interfaces.json.results`, and extract the interface name and description from this data. We can also push this information using the `eos_config` module to set up the correct description on all the devices in our network.

12
Simplifying Automation with AWX and Ansible

In all the previous chapters in this book, we have been using Ansible and, more specifically, Ansible Engine, and we have carried out different automation tasks using the **command-line interface (CLI)** options provided by Ansible. However, consuming Ansible in this approach at a large scale, and in an IT enterprise across multiple teams, can be challenging. This is why we will introduce the **Ansible Web eXecutable (AWX)** framework. AWX is an open source project, and it is the upstream project from which Red Hat Ansible Tower is derived.

AWX is a wrapper around Ansible Engine, and it provides extra features in order to simplify running Ansible at scale in an enterprise, across different teams. It provides multiple additional features, the following:

- **A graphical user interface (GUI)-based interface**

  AWX provides a visual dashboard to execute Ansible playbooks and to monitor their status, as well as providing different statistics regarding the different objects within AWX.

- **Role-based access control (RBAC)**

  AWX provides RBAC over all the objects within the AWX interface, such as Ansible playbooks, Ansible inventories, and machine credentials. This RBAC provides fine-grained control regarding who can create/edit/delete the different components within AWX. This provides a very powerful framework for delegating simple automation tasks to operations teams, and design teams can focus on developing the playbooks and the workflows. AWX provides the ability to define different users and assign them privileges according to their job role.

- **Inventory management**

  AWX provides a GUI to define inventories as either static or dynamic and has the ability to define hosts and groups, similar to the structure followed by Ansible.

- **Credential management**

  AWX provides central management for credentials such as passwords and **Secure Shell (SSH)** keys used to access the different systems in an organization, such as servers and network devices. All the credentials, once created, are encrypted, and can't be retrieved in plaintext format. This provides more security control regarding this sensitive information.

- **Centralized logging**

  AWX collects logs for all the automation tasks run on the AWX node, thus audits can be completed to understand who runs which playbooks on which nodes, and what the status of these playbooks is.

- **Representational State Transfer (RESTful) application programming interface (API)**

  AWX provides a rich API, which allows us to execute automation tasks from the API; this simplifies integrating Ansible with other orchestration and ticketing systems that are already in place in a typical enterprise environment. Also, you can use the API to retrieve all the information accessible from the GUI, such as the inventory.

The AWX Project is comprised of multiple open source software projects bundled together to provide all the features listed previously and to construct the AWX automation framework. The following diagram outlines the different components that are inside the AWX framework:

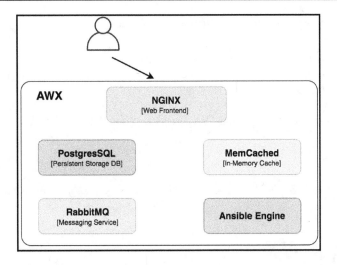

AWX can be deployed using different deployment tools, such as Docker Compose, Docker Swarm, or Kubernetes. It can be deployed as a standalone application or in a cluster (using Kubernetes or Docker Swarm). Using a cluster is more complex; however, it provides extra resiliency to the overall AWX deployment.

These are the main recipes covered in this chapter:

- Installing AWX
- Managing users and teams on AWX
- Creating a network inventory on AWX
- Managing network credentials on AWX
- Creating projects on AWX
- Creating templates on AWX
- Creating workflow templates on AWX
- Running automation tasks using the AWX API

Technical requirements

All the code presented in this chapter can be found at this URL:

```
https://github.com/PacktPublishing/Network-Automation-Cookbook/tree/master/
ch12_awx
```

This chapter is based on the following software releases:

- Ansible/AWX machine running Ubuntu 16.04
- Ansible 2.9
- AWX 9.0.0

For more information regarding the AWX Project, please check the following links:

- `https://www.ansible.com/products/awx-project`
- `https://www.ansible.com/products/awx-project/faq`
- `https://www.redhat.com/en/resources/awx-and-ansible-tower-datasheet`

Installing AWX

AWX can be deployed in multiple different ways; however, the most convenient way is to deploy it using containers. In this recipe, we will outline how to install AWS using Docker containers, in order to start to interact with the AWX interface.

Getting ready

Prepare a fresh Ubuntu 16.04 machine, on which we will deploy AWX – it must have internet connectivity.

How to do it...

1. Ensure Python 3 is installed on the Ubuntu Linux machine and that pip is installed and upgraded to the latest version:

```
$ python -version
Python 3.5.2

$ sudo apt-get install python3-pip

$ sudo pip3 install --upgrade pip

$ pip3 --version
pip 19.3.1 from /usr/local/lib/python3.5/dist-packages/pip (python 3.5)
```

2. Install Ansible on the Linux machine, as shown in the following code snippet:

   ```
   $ sudo pip3 install ansible==2.9
   ```

3. Install Docker on the Ubuntu Linux machine, using the following URL: `https://docs.docker.com/install/linux/docker-ce/ubuntu/`.

4. Install Docker Compose on the Ubuntu machine, using the following URL: `https://docs.docker.com/compose/install/`.

5. Install the `docker` and `docker-compose` Python modules, as shown in the following code snippet:

   ```
   $ sudo pip3 install docker docker-compose
   ```

6. Install Node.js 10.x and **Node Package Manager** (**npm**) 6.x on the Ubuntu Linux machine as per the following URL, using the **Personal Package Archive** (**PPA***)* method to get the exact and updated version: `https://www.digitalocean.com/community/tutorials/how-to-install-node-js-on-ubuntu-16-04`.

7. Create a new directory called `ch12_awx`, and clone the AWX project GitHub repository to a new directory called `awx_src`:

   ```
   $ mkdir ch12_awx
   $ cd ch12_awx
   $ git clone https://github.com/ansible/awx awx_src
   ```

8. Change to the installation directory and run the installation playbook:

   ```
   $ cd awx_src/installer
   $ ansible-playbook -i inventory install.yml
   ```

How it works...

As outlined in the introduction, AWX consists of multiple components glued together in order to provide a complete framework. This means AWX can be deployed by installing each component and configuring them, then integrating all these distinct products to create the AWX framework. The other alternative is to use a container-based deployment, creating a container for each component, and gluing them together in a microservices architecture. The container-based approach is the recommended approach, and this is what we use to deploy AWX.

Since we are going to use containers, we need to orchestrate between these different components; thus, we need a container orchestration tool. AWX supports deployment over Kubernetes, OpenShift, and `docker-compose`, and the simplest of these is `docker-compose`. For this reason, this is the method outlined in this recipe.

The AWX installer requires Ansible to be present on the deployment node since the installer is based on Ansible playbooks. These playbooks build/download the containers for the different components of AWX (PostgreSQL, NGINX, and so on), create the `docker-compose` declaration file, and start the containers. Thus, our first step is to install Ansible. Then, we need to install `docker` and `docker-compose`, as well as other required dependencies for the installation and the correct operation of the AWX containers.

Once we install all these prerequisites, we are ready to install AWX. We clone the AWX project GitHub repo, and, in this repo, there is the `installer` directory, which has all the Ansible roles and playbooks to deploy the containers. The `installer` directory has the `inventory` file, which defines the host to which we will deploy the AWX framework; in this case, it is the localhost. The `inventory` file also lists other variables such as the admin password, as well as the passwords for the PostgreSQL and RabbitMQ databases. Since this is a demo deployment, we will not change these variables, and we will deploy using these default parameters.

Once the installation is complete, we can verify that all the Docker containers are up and running, as shown here:

```
$ sudo docker ps
```

This gives us the following output:

CONTAINER ID STATUS	IMAGE PORTS	COMMAND	CREATED NAMES
225b95337b6d Up 2 hours	ansible/awx_task:7.0.0 8052/tcp	"/tini -- /bin/sh -c..."	30 hours ago awx_task
2ca06bd1cd87 Up 2 hours	ansible/awx_web:7.0.0 0.0.0.0:80->8052/tcp	"/tini -- /bin/sh -c..."	30 hours ago awx_web
66f560c62a9c Up 2 hours	memcached:alpine 11211/tcp	"docker-entrypoint.s..."	30 hours ago awx_memcached

fe4ccccdb511 Up 2 hours	postgres:10 5432/tcp	"docker-entrypoint.s..."	30 hours ago awx_postgres
24c997d5991c Up 2 hours	ansible/awx_rabbitmq:3.7.4 4369/tcp, 5671-5672/tcp, 15671-15672/tcp, 25672/tcp	"docker-entrypoint.s..."	30 hours ago awx_rabbitmq

We can log in to the AWX GUI by opening the web browser and connecting to the machine **internet protocol** (**IP**) address with the following credentials:

- **USERNAME:** admin
- **PASSWORD:** password

This can be seen in the following screenshot:

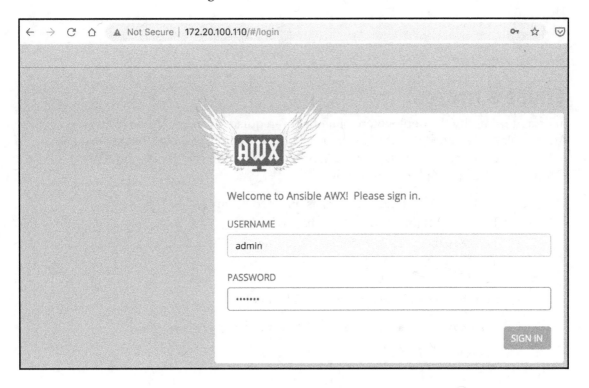

Once we log in to AWX, we will see the main dashboard, along with all the options available for configuration on the left panel (**Organizations**, **Teams**, **Projects**, and so on):

There's more...

In order to simplify the deployment of all the prerequisites for AWX, I have included an Ansible playbook called deploy_awx.yml, along with multiple roles that are used to orchestrate the deployment of all the AWX components. We can deploy the AWX components using this playbook, as follows:

1. Install Ansible on the machine, as outlined in this recipe.
2. Clone the GitHub repo for this chapter.
3. Change to the ch12_awx folder, as follows:

```
$ cd ch12_awx
```

4. From inside this directory, run the playbook:

```
$ ansible-playbook -i awx_inventory deploy_awx.yml
```

See also...

For more information regarding AWX installation, please check the following link:

```
https://github.com/ansible/awx/blob/devel/INSTALL.md
```

Managing users and teams on AWX

In this recipe, we will outline how to create users and teams in AWX. This is the way to implement RBAC and enforce privileges for the different teams within the organization, in order to provide more control over the different activities that can be carried out on the AWX platform.

Getting ready

AWX should be deployed as outlined in the previous recipe, and all the following tasks must be executed with the `admin` user account.

How to do it...

1. Create a new organization for all **Network** teams—as shown in the following screenshot—by selecting the organization from the left panel and pressing the **SAVE** button:

2. Create a new team within the **Network** organization for the **Design** team, by selecting the team from the left panel:

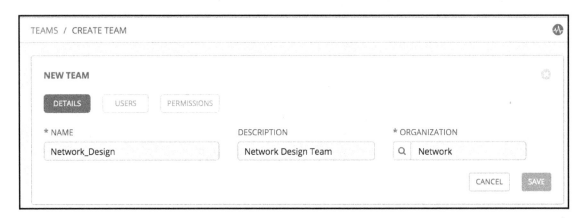

3. Create another team within the **Network** organization for the **Operation** team, as shown in the following screenshot:

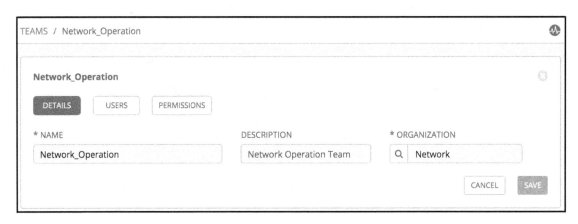

4. Create a `core` user within the **Network** organization by selecting the **USERS** button, as shown in the following screenshot:

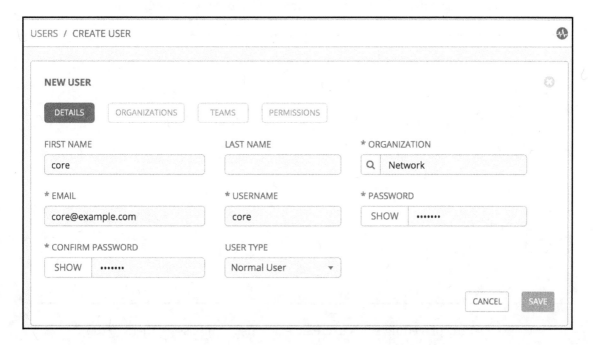

5. Assign this new user to the `Network_Design` team, click the **TEAMS** tab from the left panel, and then select the `Network_Design` team. Click on **USERS** and then add the `core` user to this team, as shown in the following screenshot:

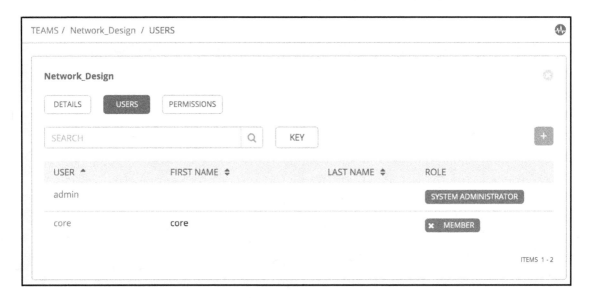

6. Repeat the preceding steps to create a `noc` user, and assign them to the `Network_Operation` team.

7. For the `Network_Design` team, assign the **Project Admin**, **Credential Admin**, and **Inventory Admin** permissions to the organization, as shown in the following screenshot:

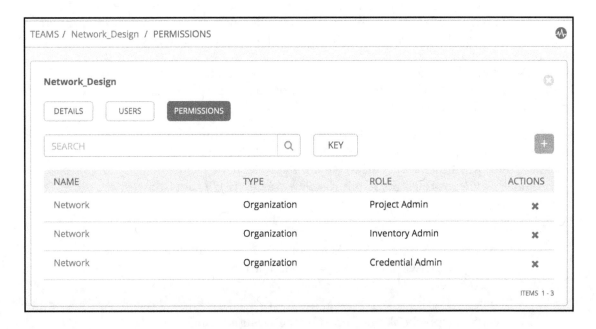

How it works...

One of the main features in AWX is its RBAC, which is achieved by different objects within AWX. These objects are mainly the organization, users, and teams. Since AWX should be the automation framework at an enterprise scale, different teams within the organization need to co-exist in AWX. Each of these teams manages its own devices and maintains its own playbooks, to manage its managed infrastructure. In AWX, the **Organization** is our method to differentiate these different organizations within the enterprise. In our sample example, we have created a **Network** organization to group all the teams and users responsible for the network infrastructure.

Within the Organization, we have different users with different roles, who should have different levels of access to our central automation AWX framework. In order to simplify assigning the correct role to each user, we use the concept of **Teams** in order to group users with similar privileges/roles. So, in our case, we created two **Teams**: the Network_Design and Network_Operation teams. The roles and privileges for these two teams are described as follows:

- The Network_Design team is responsible for creating the playbooks and creating the network inventories, along with the correct credentials to access these devices.
- The Network_Operation team has the privilege to view these inventories and to execute the playbook developed by the **Design** team.

These different constructs work together to build a fine-grained RBAC for each user, utilizing the AWX framework.

Since we have assigned to the Network_Design team the **Project Admin**, **Inventory Admin**, and **Credential Admin** roles, all the users within this team are able to create/edit/delete and use all these objects within the **Network** organization only.

See also...

For more information regarding RBAC and how to use users and **Teams**, please check the following links for Ansible Tower:

- https://docs.ansible.com/ansible-tower/latest/html/userguide/organizations.html
- https://docs.ansible.com/ansible-tower/latest/html/userguide/users.html

- https://docs.ansible.com/ansible-tower/latest/html/userguide/teams.html

Creating a network inventory on AWX

In this recipe, we will outline how to create a network inventory in AWX. Inventories are fundamentals as they describe our network infrastructure and provide us with the capability to group our network devices efficiently.

Getting ready

AWX must be installed and reachable, and the user accounts must be deployed, as outlined in the previous recipe.

How to do it...

1. Create a new inventory called `mpls_core` by navigating to the **INVENTORIES** tab on the left navigation bar, as shown in the following screenshot:

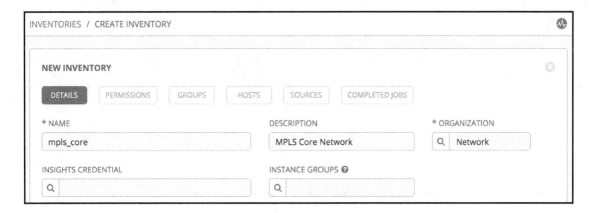

2. Create a new group called `junos`, as shown in the following screenshot:

3. Create the `iosxr`, `pe`, and `P` groups, using a similar approach. The final group structure under the mpls_core inventory should be similar to the one shown in the following screenshot:

4. Create the `mxpe01` host device under the **HOSTS** tab, and create the `ansible_host` variable under the **VARIABLES** section, as shown in the following screenshot:

5. Repeat the same process to create the remaining hosts.
6. Go to the `junos` group that we have created and add the corresponding hosts, as shown in the following screenshot:

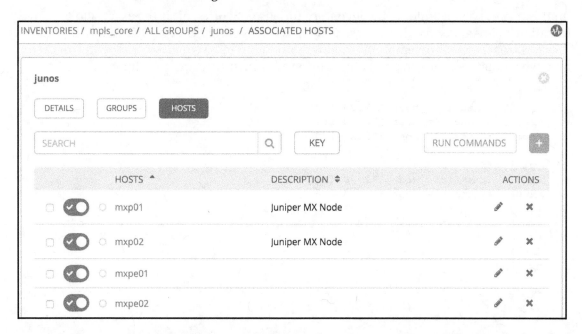

7. Repeat this for all the remaining groups.
8. After creating the `mpls_core` inventory, we will grant read access to the `Network_Operation` group for this inventory, as shown in the following screenshot:

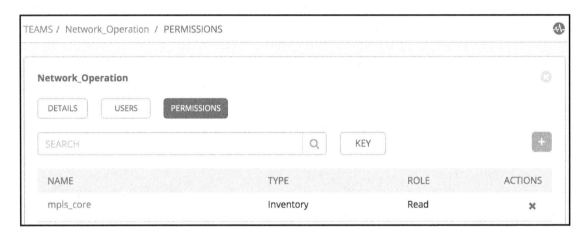

How it works...

In this recipe, we are building the inventory for our network. This is the exact step of defining an inventory file that we use with all our Ansible playbooks. The following code block shows the static inventory file that we normally define when we work with Ansible, and we outline how we can define the same exact structure using inventories in AWX:

```
[pe]
mxpe01      ansible_host=172.20.1.3
mxpe02      ansible_host=172.20.1.4
xrpe03      ansible_host=172.20.1.5

[p]
mxp01       ansible_host=172.20.1.2
mxp02       ansible_host=172.20.1.6
[junos]
mxpe01
mxpe02
mxp01
mxp02

[iosxr]
xrpe03
```

We can define variables for our inventory on the group or host level. In our case, we are defining the `ansible_host` variable for each host, in order to tell AWX how to reach each host in our inventory.

We update the permissions on our inventory so that the operations team has read access to it, in order to view its components. Since the design team has the inventory admin privilege, the design team has full administrative rights on all the inventories created within the network organization. The permissions on our inventory can be viewed as shown in the following screenshot:

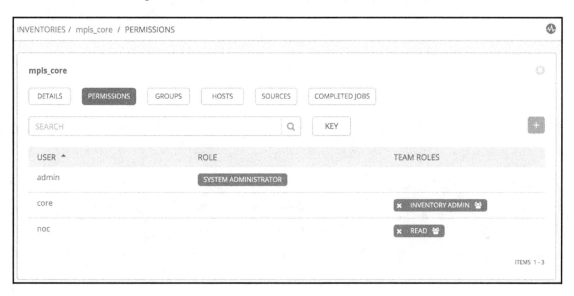

Managing network credentials on AWX

In order for AWX to start to interact with our infrastructure and run the required playbook, we need to define the correct network credentials to log in to our network infrastructure. In this recipe, we outline how to create the required network credentials in order for AWX to log in to network devices and start executing playbooks on our managed network inventory. We will also outline how we can use RBAC within AWX to make it easy to share this sensitive data between different teams within the organization.

Getting ready

AWX must be installed and reachable, and the User accounts must be deployed, as outlined in the previous recipe.

How to do it...

1. From the **CREDENTIALS** tab in the left navigation bar, create the login credentials required to access the network devices. We will use the **Machine** credential type since we will access the devices using new connection modules such as network_cli, NETCONF, or httpapi. Specify the username and password used to log in to the devices:

2. Update the permissions for the credentials that we have created so that the
   `Network_Design` team is the **credential Administrator** and the
   `Network_Operation` team has read-only access. Here is how the permissions on
   the credential are applied:

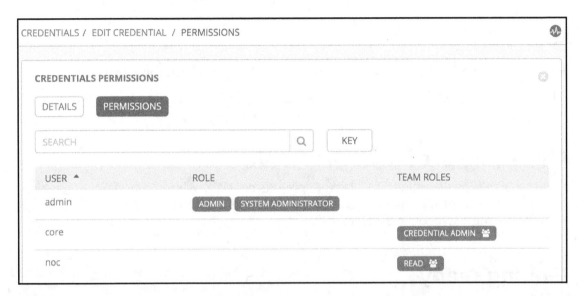

How it works...

In this recipe, we created the network credentials needed to access our network devices, and we specified the username and password required to log in to the devices on the AWX GUI interface. When we entered the password on the AWX interface, it was encrypted and then stored on the PostgreSQL database in an encrypted format that we can't view in plaintext. This provides extra security in terms of password handling within the AWX framework and also provides a simple procedure to share and utilize sensitive information within the organization, so the `Admin` or authorized user can create and edit the credential and can grant user permissions on those credentials to the required users/teams. These users only use the credentials but they don't have any admin rights to view or change them. This greatly simplifies password management when compared with using Ansible and `ansible-vault`.

AWX provides different credential types to access different resources such as physical infrastructure, cloud providers, and **version control systems** (**VCS**). In our case, we use the **Machine** credential type, since we are connecting to our network infrastructure using SSH with a username and password.

See also...

For more information regarding AWX credentials, please check the following URL:

```
https://docs.ansible.com/ansible-tower/latest/html/userguide/credentials.html
```

Creating projects on AWX

In this recipe, we will outline how to create projects on AWX. A project in AWX is an object that represents an Ansible playbook (or playbooks), with all the related files and folders required for this playbook to execute.

Getting ready

AWX must be installed and reachable, and the User accounts must be deployed, as outlined in the previous recipe.

How to do it...

1. Create a new directory, `awx_sample_project`, to hold all the files and folders for our AWX project.

2. Create a `group_vars/all.yml` playbook with the following content:

```
p2p_ip:
    xrpe03:
      - {port: GigabitEthernet0/0/0/0, ip: 10.1.1.7/31 , peer: mxp01,
pport: ge-0/0/2, peer_ip: 10.1.1.6/31}
      - {port: GigabitEthernet0/0/0/1, ip: 10.1.1.13/31 , peer:
mxp02, pport: ge-0/0/2, peer_ip: 10.1.1.12/31}
```

3. Create a `group_vars/iosxr.yml` playbook with the following content:

```
ansible_network_os: iosxr
ansible_connection: network_cli
```

4. Create a `group_vars/junos.yml` playbook with the following content:

```
ansible_network_os: junos
ansible_connection: netconf
```

5. Create a `pb_deploy_interfaces.yml` playbook with the following content:

```
---
- name: get facts
  hosts: all
  gather_facts: no
  tasks:
    - name: Enable Interface
      iosxr_interface:
        name: "{{ item.port }}"
       enabled: yes
      loop: "{{ p2p_ip[inventory_hostname] }}"
    - name: Configure IP address
      iosxr_config:
        lines:
          - ipv4 address {{ item.ip | ipaddr('address') }}
{{item.ip | ipaddr('netmask') }}
        parents: interface {{ item.port }}
      loop: "{{ p2p_ip[inventory_hostname] }}"
```

6. Create a `pb_validate_interfaces.yml` playbook with the following content:

```yaml
---
- name: Get IOS-XR Facts
  hosts: iosxr
  gather_facts: no
  tasks:
    - iosxr_facts:
     tags: collect_facts
    - name: Validate all Interfaces are Operational
      assert:
        that:
          - ansible_net_interfaces[item.port].operstatus == 'up'
      loop: "{{ p2p_ip[inventory_hostname] }}"
    - name: Validate all Interfaces with Correct IP
      assert:
        that:
          - ansible_net_interfaces[item.port].ipv4.address ==
item.ip.split('/')[0]
      loop: "{{ p2p_ip[inventory_hostname] }}"
```

7. Our new folder will have the following directory structure:

```
.
├────── group_vars
│       ├────── all.yml
│       ├────── iosxr.yml
│       └────── junos.yml
├────── pb_deploy_interfaces.yml
└────── pb_validate_interface.yml
```

8. On your GitHub account, create a new public repository named `awx_sample_project`:

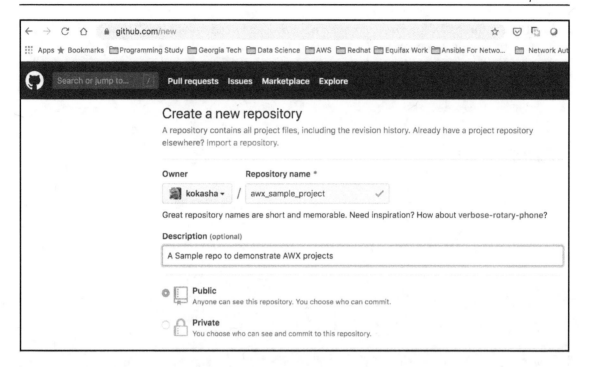

9. Inside our `awx_sample_repo` project folder, initialize a Git repository and link it to the GitHub repository that we created in the previous step, as shown in the following code block:

```
git init
git commit -m "Initial commit"
git add remote origin git@github.com:kokasha/awx_sample_project.git
git push origin master
```

10. On the AWX interface, create a new project based on Git, as shown in the following screenshot:

How it works...

One of the main goals of AWX is to simplify how to collaborate with Ansible playbooks, as well as to simplify how to run and execute Ansible playbooks. In order to achieve these goals, the best and most common approach to work with Ansible playbooks within AWX is using AWX projects stored and tracked in Git version control. This approach allows us to separate code development for our Ansible playbooks (which is stored and versioned using Git) and playbook execution (which will be handled by AWX).

We follow the same logic for developing a project with Ansible by creating a folder to hold all our folders and files that are part of our project. This includes `group_vars` and `host_vars` folders to specify our variables, and we also define the different playbooks needed for our project. We keep all these files and folders in a Git repository and host them on a Git VCS such as GitHub or GitLab.

In order for AWX to start using the playbooks that we have developed, we create a new project within AWX and we choose for it to be based on Git, and we provide the URL for the Git repository that houses this project. We also supply any additional information needed, such as which branch to use; and if this is a private Git repository, we supply the credentials needed to access it.

Once we complete this step, the AWX interface will fetch all the content for this Git repository and download it to this location—by default, `/var/lib/awx/projects`. At this stage, we have all the content for this repository locally stored on the AWX node, to start running our playbooks against our network nodes.

See also...

For more information regarding AWX projects, please check the following URL:

- `https://docs.ansible.com/ansible-tower/latest/html/userguide/projects.html`

Creating templates on AWX

In this recipe, we will outline how to combine inventories, credentials, and projects in order to create templates in AWX. Templates in AWX allow us to create a standard running environment for our Ansible playbooks, which can be executed by different users according to their roles.

Getting ready

The AWX interface must be installed and credentials, inventories, and projects must be created, as outlined in the previous recipes.

How to do it...

1. Create a new template in AWX called `provision_interfaces`, and assign to it the inventory and credentials that we created. We will use the `awx_sample_project` directory, as shown in the following screenshot:

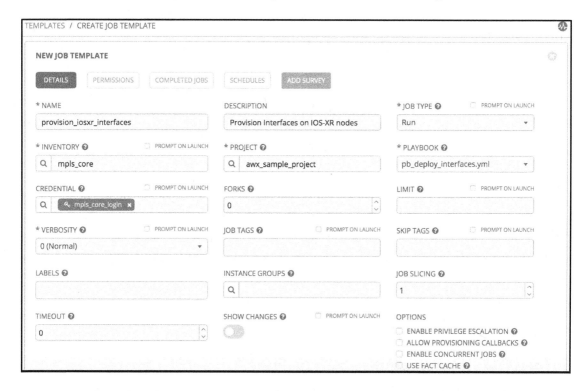

2. We update the permissions for this template so that the `Network_Design` team is `ADMIN` and `Network_Operation` team has the **EXECUTE** role, as shown in the following screenshot:

3. Use the same procedures again to create a template called
   `interface_validation,` using the `pb_validate_interfaces.yml` playbook.

How it works...

In this recipe, we outlined how we combine all the different parts that we have previously
configured in order to execute our playbooks on AWX. AWX uses templates in order to
create this standard execution environment, which we can use in order to run our Ansible
playbooks from AWX.

We created the template with a given name, and we specified the different parameters in
order to create this environment to execute our playbook, as follows:

- We provided the inventory against which we want to execute our playbooks.
- We provided all the required credentials that we need in order to execute our
  playbooks (this can be one or multiple credentials).
- We provided the project from which we will choose the playbook to run.
- We selected the playbook from this project.

There are other optional parameters that we can specify in our templates, such as the following:

- Whether to run this playbook or use **check** mode when we execute this playbook.
- Whether we want to provide a limit on our inventory in order to target a subset of it.
- Any Ansible tags we want to specify.

Finally, we can tailor the permissions for this template for all the users within the organization, and, in our case, we provide the **ADMIN** role for the Network_Design team and the **EXECUTE** role for the Network_Operation team. In this case, the Network_Operation team can execute this playbook, while the Network_Design team has the ability to edit and change the different parameters for this template.

Once we save this template, we can launch a job from it and monitor its result from the **JOBS** tab on the left side in the navigation bar:

We can also see the details for this playbook run as we do normally in Ansible by clicking on the respective job, as shown in the following screenshot:

See also...

For more information regarding AWX templates and the different options available to customize the templates, please check the following URL:

https://docs.ansible.com/ansible-tower/latest/html/userguide/job_templates.html

Creating workflow templates on AWX

In this recipe, we will outline how to create more complex templates on AWX using workflow templates, in order to run multiple playbooks to achieve a common goal. This is an advanced feature, whereby we combine multiple templates in AWX to achieve the task.

Getting ready

AWX templates are configured as outlined in the previous chapter.

How to do it…

1. From the **TEMPLATES** tab, create a **NEW WORKFLOW JOB TEMPLATE**, as shown in the following screenshot:

2. Using the **WORKFLOW VISUALIZER**, create the workflow outlined in the following screenshot:

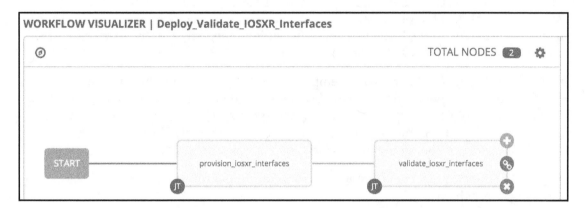

3. Assign the correct permission on the workflow template, as shown in the following screenshot:

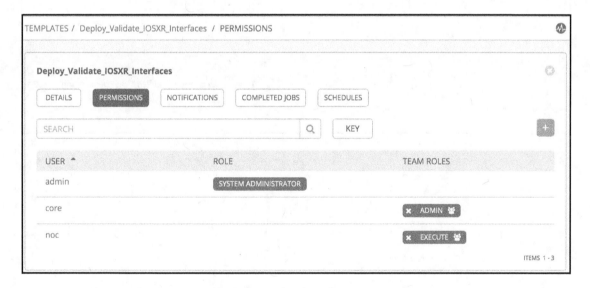

How it works...

If our automation task requires multiple playbooks to run in order to achieve our target, we can use the workflow template feature in AWX to orchestrate between multiple templates in order to achieve this goal. The templates can be combined together based on different criteria regarding the success and failure of the tasks contained in the workflow template.

In our example, we use the workflow template in order to provision the interface on the IOS-XR nodes; then, we validate that all the configuration is applied correctly and that the current network state is as we desire. We combine the `provision_interface` template and the `validate_interfaces` template in order to achieve this. We start by provisioning the interface, and, on the success of this task, we run the validation playbook.

We can check the status of the combined workflow in the **JOBS** tab, as shown in the following screenshot:

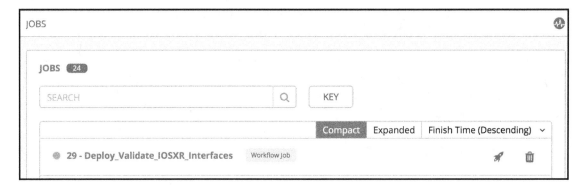

Further, we can go into the details of this workflow by clicking on the workflow name in the **JOBS** tab and viewing the details of each task in this workflow:

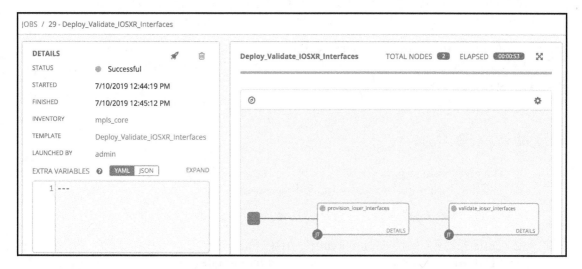

See also...

For more information regarding AWX workflow templates, please check the following URL:

- https://docs.ansible.com/ansible-tower/latest/html/userguide/workflow_
  templates.html

Running automation tasks using the AWX API

In this recipe, we will outline how to initiate jobs on AWX, using the AWX API. One of the main features in AWX is that it provides a powerful API in order to interact with the AWX system, to query all the objects within AWX, and to execute automation tasks from the AWX framework, such as templates and workflow templates. We can also use the API to list all the users/teams, and all the different resources available and configured on the AWX interface.

Getting ready

The AWX interface must be installed and reachable, and the templates and workflow templates must be configured as outlined in the previous chapters.

In order to execute the command to interact with the AWX API, we will use the `curl` command to initiate HTTP requests to the AWX endpoint. This requires cURL to be installed on the machine.

How to do it...

1. Start by exploring the AWX API by listing all the resources available through this API, as shown in the following code snippet:

    ```
    curl -X GET  http://172.20.100.110/api/v2/
    ```

2. Collect all the job templates configured on the AWX interface with the following REST API call, and get the ID for each job template:

    ```
    curl -X GET --user admin:password
    http://172.20.100.110/api/v2/job_templates/ -s | jq
    ```

3. Launch a job template configured on the AWX interface with the following REST API call. In this example, we are launching job_Templates with ID = 7:

    ```
    curl -X POST --user admin:password
    http://172.20.100.110/api/v2/job_templates/7/launch/ -s | jq
    ```

4. Get the status of the job launched from the preceding API call with the following call. ID=35 is retrieved from the previous API call for launching the job template:

    ```
    curl -X GET --user admin:password
    http://172.20.100.110/api/v2/jobs/35/ | jq
    ```

5. Collect all workflow templates configured on the AWX interface with the following API call, and record the ID for each one:

    ```
    curl -X GET --user admin:password
    http://172.20.100.110/api/v2/workflow_job_templates/ -s | jq
    ```

6. Launch the workflow job template using the ID retrieved from the previous API call:

```
curl -X POST --user admin:password
http://172.20.100.110/api/v2/workflow_job_templates/14/launch/ -s |
jq
```

How it works...

AWX provides a simple and powerful REST API to retrieve and inspect all the objects and components of the AWX system. Using this API, we can interact with the AWX interface to launch automation tasks, as well as to retrieve the status of execution of these tasks. In this recipe, we outlined how we can interact with the AWX API using the cURL command-line tool; how we can use other tools such as Postman to interact with the API; and also, how we could use any programming language, such as Python or Go, to build more sophisticated scripts and applications, in order to consume the AWX API. In all our examples, we are using the jq Linux utility in order to output the JSON data returned from each API call in a nice format.

We start by exploring all the endpoints published through the AWX API by inspecting this http://<AWX Node IP>/api/v2/ **Uniform Resource Identifier** (**URI**), which returns all the endpoints available through this API. The following is a snippet of this output:

```
$ curl -X GET http://172.20.100.110/api/v2/ -s | jq
{
  "ping": "/api/v2/ping/",
  "users": "/api/v2/users/",
  "projects": "/api/v2/projects/",
  "project_updates": "/api/v2/project_updates/",
  "teams": "/api/v2/teams/",
  "credentials": "/api/v2/credentials/",
  "inventory": "/api/v2/inventories/",
  "groups": "/api/v2/groups/",
  "hosts": "/api/v2/hosts/",
  "job_templates": "/api/v2/job_templates/",
  "jobs": "/api/v2/jobs/",
}
```

We then list all the job templates configured on the AWX interface by hitting the corresponding API endpoint. This API call is using the `GET` method, and it must be authenticated; that is why we use the `--user` option to pass in the username and password for the user. The following snippet outlines some of the returned values from this call:

```
$ curl -X GET --user admin:password
http://172.20.100.110/api/v2/job_templates/ -s | jq
    {
        "id": 9,
        "type": "job_template",
        "url": "/api/v2/job_templates/9/",
        "created": "2019-12-18T22:07:15.830364Z",
        "modified": "2019-12-18T22:08:12.887390Z",
        "name": "provision_interfaces",
        "description": "",
        "job_type": "run",
< --- Output Omitted  -- >
    }
```

This API call returns a list of all the job templates configured on the AWX interface; however, the most important item we care about is the `id` field for each job template. This is a unique primary key for each job template within the AWX database that identifies each job template; using this `id` field, we can start to interact with each job template, and in the examples outlined in this receipe, we launch a job template by using a `POST` request to this specific job template.

Once we launch the job template, this triggers a job on the AWX node, and we get the corresponding job ID as a result of the `POST` request that we have triggered. Using this job ID, we can check the status of the job that was executed by using a `GET` request to the Jobs API endpoints and supplying the corresponding job ID. We use a similar approach to launch workflow templates, only using a different URI endpoint for the workflows.

There's more...

In order to list and launch a specific job template or a workflow template, we can use the name of the template in the API call instead of using the `id` field. For example, the API call to launch the `provision_interfaces` job template in our sample is shown in the following code snippet:

```
$ curl -X POST --user admin:password
http://172.20.100.110/api/v2/job_templates/provision_interfaces/launch/ -s
| jq
{
  "job": 3,
  "ignored_fields": {},
  "id": 3,
  "type": "job",
< --- Output Omitted  -- >
  "launch_type": "manual",
  "status": "pending",
< --- Output Omitted  -- >
}
```

The same process can be followed to invoke a workflow template, using its name as the parameter.

See also...

For more information regarding the AWX API, please check the following URL:

- https://docs.ansible.com/ansible-tower/latest/html/towerapi/index.html

13
Advanced Techniques and Best Practices for Ansible

In this chapter, we will explore some advanced features and techniques that we can use in Ansible, along with some best practices, in order to build clearer and more robust Ansible playbooks for network automation. All of these techniques can be used with all the code from the previous chapters.

The recipes covered in this chapter are as follows:

- Installing Ansible in a virtual environment
- Validating YAML and Ansible playbooks
- Calculating the execution time for Ansible playbooks
- Validating user input using Ansible
- Running Ansible in `check` mode
- Controlling parallelism and rolling updates in Ansible
- Configuring fact caching in Ansible
- Creating custom Python filters for Ansible

Technical requirements

All the code that we describe in this chapter can be found through this URL: `https://github.com/PacktPublishing/Network-Automation-Cookbook/tree/master/ch13_ansible_best_practice`.

You will need the following for this chapter:

- Ansible machine running CentOS 7
- Ansible 2.9
- Python 3.6.8

Installing Ansible in a virtual environment

In this recipe, we will outline how to install Ansible in a Python virtual environment in order to have an isolated and contained environment for developing and running our playbooks.

Getting ready

Python 3 must be already installed on your Linux machine.

How to do it...

1. Create a new Python virtual environment called dev, and activate it as follows:

```
$ python3 -m venv dev
$ source dev/bin/activate
```

2. Install Ansible in this new virtual environment, as follows:

```
$ (dev) $ pip3 install ansible==2.9
```

How it works...

As outlined in the first chapter of this book, we can install Ansible using one of these two methods:

- Using the package manager on our Linux machine
- Using the Python PIP package manager

In both these options, we are running Ansible using system-level Python. This means that when we install any other packages or scripts required for our automation, such as **Amazon Web Services** (**AWS**) or Azure packages, we are installing/upgrading these packages on the system level. In some cases, we might install a package that conflicts with an existing package on our system, and it might impact other scripts. Python virtual environments are mainly built for this use case. The virtual environment provides an isolated runtime environment where we install our Python packages totally separately from the system-level packages. Thus, we can run different versions of the same package (Ansible, for example) in a totally isolated and independent manner.

In this recipe, we outline how to create a new Python virtual environment using the `venv` Python module. We use the `python` command with the `-m` option to invoke the `venv` module, which allows us to create a new virtual environment. We use the `venv` Python module to create a new virtual environment called `dev`, which will create the `dev` folder to house our new virtual environment.

In order to start using this new virtual environment, we need to activate it. We use the `source` command to run the activate script located in the `dev` folder (`~/dev/bin/activate`). This script will activate the virtual environment and will place us inside this newly created environment. We can verify that our current Python executable is located within this new environment and not related to system-level Python, as shown in the following code snippet:

```
(dev)$ which python
~/dev/bin/python

(dev)$ python --version
Python 3.6.8
```

Once we are inside our virtual environment, we use the `python-pip` command in order to install Ansible within our virtual environment. We can verify that Ansible is installed and is using our new virtual environment as shown in the following code block:

```
(dev)$ ansible --version
ansible 2.9
  config file = None
  configured module search path =
['/home/vagrant/.ansible/plugins/modules',
'/usr/share/ansible/plugins/modules']
  ansible python module location = /home/vagrant/dev/lib64/python3.6/site-
packages/ansible
  executable location = /home/vagrant/dev/bin/ansible
  python version = 3.6.8 (default, Aug  7 2019, 17:28:10) [GCC 4.8.5
20150623 (Red Hat 4.8.5-39)]
```

At this stage, we have installed Ansible in this virtual environment. However, by default, when Ansible is run, it will try to use the system-level Python located in `/usr/bin/python`. In order to override this behavior and force Ansible to use our new virtual environment, we need to set a variable for all our hosts to use this new virtual environment, which we can do in our inventory file, as shown in the following code snippet:

```
$ cat hosts
[all:vars]
ansible_python_interpreter=~/dev/bin/python
```

Validating YAML and Ansible playbooks

In this recipe, we will outline how to validate YAML files and Ansible playbooks using the `Yamllint` and `ansible-lint` tools, in order to make sure that our YAML documents are valid with the correct syntax, as well as validating our Ansible playbooks.

Getting ready

Python and PIP package manager must be already installed on your Linux machine, and Ansible must also be installed.

How to do it...

1. Install `yamllint`, as shown in the following code snippet:

```
$ sudo pip3 install yamllint
```

2. Install `ansible-lint`, as shown in the following code snippet:

```
$ sudo pip3 install ansible-lint
```

3. Change to the directory of your Ansible project, as follows:

```
$ cd ch13_ansible_best_practice
```

4. Run `yamllint`, as shown in the following code snippet:

```
# run yamllint on all files in this folder
$ yamllint
```

5. Run `ansible-lint`, as shown in the following code snippet:

```
# run ansible-lint on this specific ansible-playbook
$ ansible-lint pb_build_datamodel.yml
```

How it works...

We use YAML documents to declare our network topology and the different parameters that we need in order to run our playbooks or generate the configuration for our devices. Since we are going to edit these files regularly to update our network topology and add new services, we need to ensure that all the changes to these files are validated and that the syntax of these files is correct before we import/use these files in our playbooks. One of the most used tools to validate YAML files is the `Yamllint` program, which reads YAML documents and analyzes them for syntax errors and best practice formats, outputting the result of the analysis. We install this tool using the PIP package manager.

In our example, we have a typical Ansible project, with the directory structure shown in the following screenshot:

```
[vagrant@centos7 ch13_ansible_best_practice]$ tree
.
├── ansible.cfg
├── group_vars
│   ├── all.yml
│   ├── iosxr.yml
│   └── junos.yml
├── hosts
├── net_data
│   ├── common.yml
│   └── network_topology.yml
├── pb_generate_net_data.yml
└── roles
    └── build_datamodel
        ├── tasks
        │   └── main.yml
        └── templates
            ├── bgp.j2
            └── infra.j2
```

We analyze all the YAML documents in this folder by running `Yamllint`, as outlined in the preceding section. The following screenshot outlines the output of the `Yamllint` command on the Ansible project folder:

```
[vagrant@centos7 net_automation_cookbook]$ yamllint ch13_ansible_best_practice/
ch13_ansible_best_practice/pb_build_datamodel.yml
  1:4       error      wrong new line character: expected \n  (new-lines)
  4:17      warning    truthy value should be one of [false, true]   (truthy)
  7:7       error      wrong indentation: expected 8 but found 6  (indentation)
  9:19      warning    truthy value should be one of [false, true]   (truthy)
  13:19     warning    truthy value should be one of [false, true]   (truthy)
  20:1      error      too many blank lines (1 > 0)  (empty-lines)

ch13_ansible_best_practice/group_vars/junos.yml
  1:1       warning    missing document start "---"  (document-start)
  3:1       error      too many blank lines (1 > 0)  (empty-lines)

ch13_ansible_best_practice/group_vars/all.yml
  1:1       warning    missing document start "---"  (document-start)
```

The preceding output outlines the problems that the `Yamllint` command found in all the YAML files in this folder, and it provides a very clear output regarding the problems identified in each file. These problems can be identified as errors or warnings, and this affects the return code for the `Yamllint` command.

So, in cases where all the problems in the files are designated as a `warning`, the return code is `0`, which means that the YAML documents are valid. However, they have some minor problems that should be fixed:

```
# no errors or only warning
$ echo $?
0
```

If the problems are identified as an `error`, the return code is not `0`, which means that the YAML document has a major problem that needs to be fixed:

```
# errors are present
$ echo $?
1
```

The return code is critical since it signifies whether the `Yamllint` command was successful or not, and this is critical in building **continuous integration/continuous deployment (CI/CD)** pipelines to automate the provisioning of the infrastructure. One of the steps in the pipeline will be to lint all YAML files in order to make sure that the files are correct, and if the `Yamllint` command succeeds, it will have a return code of `0`.

The `Yamllint` command catches all the syntax errors in the YAML documents. However, `ansible-lint` provides a more comprehensive check on the `ansible-playbook` code specifically and verifies that the playbook adheres to good coding practices. It is very useful to run since it can be used to validate the correct style for playbooks and Ansible roles, and will prompt for any problem in the playbooks.

When we run the `ansible-lint` command for our playbook, we can see that it catches the following error:

```
[vagrant@centos7 ch13_ansible_best_practice]$ ansible-lint pb_build_datamodel.yml
[502] All tasks should be named
pb_build_datamodel.yml:7
Task/Handler: file state=directory path=group_vars
```

The output is very descriptive as it outlines that the task at line 7 within the playbook doesn't have a name, and this doesn't adhere to Ansible best practices. The return code for the command is 2, and this signals that the command has failed. Once we correct this problem, there will be no errors displayed, and the return code will be 0.

There's more...

The `Yamllint` program can be customized by including a `yamllint` file within the project directory structure that includes the rules that need to be modified. So, in our example, when we run the `yamllint` command, we can see that one of the problems outlined is that the line length is > 80 characters, and this is an error as per the default rules with which `yamllint` complies:

```
[vagrant@centos7 ch13_ansible_best_practice]$ yamllint net_data/
net_data/common.yml
  1:1       warning  missing document start "---"  (document-start)
  16:13     error    no new line character at the end of file  (new-line-at-end-of-file)

net_data/network_topology.yml
  1:1       warning  missing document start "---"  (document-start)
  1:6       error    wrong new line character: expected \n  (new-lines)
  3:81      error    line too long (99 > 80 characters)  (line-length)
  4:81      error    line too long (99 > 80 characters)  (line-length)
  6:81      error    line too long (99 > 80 characters)  (line-length)
  7:81      error    line too long (99 > 80 characters)  (line-length)
  7:100     error    no new line character at the end of file  (new-line-at-end-of-file)
```

We can modify our file and try to change the length of the lines that `yamllint` is complaining about, or we can specify that this should not be a problem and only a `warning` should be triggered. We use the latter approach, and we create the `.yamllint` file inside our directory and add the following rule:

```
---
extends: default
rules:
  line-length:
    level: warning
```

So, when we run the `yamllint` command again on our folder, we can see that all the previous messages for line length have changed to warnings:

```
[vagrant@centos7 ch13_ansible_best_practice]$ yamllint net_data/
net_data/common.yml
  1:1       warning  missing document start "---"  (document-start)
  16:13     error    no new line character at the end of file  (new-line-at-end-of-file)

net_data/network_topology.yml
  1:1       warning  missing document start "---"  (document-start)
  1:6       error    wrong new line character: expected \n  (new-lines)
  3:81      warning  line too long (99 > 80 characters)  (line-length)
  4:81      warning  line too long (99 > 80 characters)  (line-length)
  6:81      warning  line too long (99 > 80 characters)  (line-length)
  7:81      warning  line too long (99 > 80 characters)  (line-length)
  7:100     error    no new line character at the end of file  (new-line-at-end-of-file)
```

For `ansible-lint`, we can check all the current rules that `ansible-lint` consults in order to validate a given playbook or role, using the following commands:

```
$ ansible-lint -L
$ ansible-lint -T
```

The `-L` option will output all the rules and a short description of each of these rules.

The `-T` option will output all the rules/tags used by `ansible-lint`.

We can run our `ansible-lint` command to ignore a specific rule/tag, as shown in the following code snippet:

```
$ ansible-lint -x task pb_build_datamodel.yml
```

This will cause `ansible-lint` to ignore all the rules with the `task` tag; this way, we can influence which rules are applied by `ansible-lint` to validate our playbooks.

See also...

- For more information regarding `yamllint`, please use the following URL: `https://yamllint.readthedocs.io/en/stable/`.
- For more information regarding the configuration file used by `yamllint` and how to customize it, please use the following URL: `https://yamllint.readthedocs.io/en/stable/configuration.html`.
- For more information regarding `ansible-lint`, please use the following URL: `https://docs.ansible.com/ansible-lint/`.

Calculating the execution time for Ansible playbooks

In this recipe, we will outline how to get the time that various tasks within an Ansible playbook take to execute. This can help us understand which specific task or role is taking the largest portion of time during a playbook run, and can help us to optimize our playbooks.

How to do it...

1. Update the `ansible.cfg` file to include the following line:

   ```
   [defaults]
   < --- Output Omitted for brevity ---->
   callback_whitelist=timer, profile_tasks, profile_roles
   ```

2. List all the tasks in the `ansible-playbook` code for reference:

   ```
   $ ansible-playbook pb_generate_config.yml --list-tasks
   ```

3. Run the Ansible playbook:

   ```
   $ ansible-playbook pb_generate_config.yml
   ```

How it works...

Ansible provides multiple callback plugins that we can use in order to add new behavior to Ansible when responding to events. One of the most useful callback plugins is the `timer` plugin; it provides the capability to measure the execution time for the tasks and roles within an Ansible playbook. We can enable this functionality by whitelisting these plugins in the `ansible.cfg` file:

- `Timer`: This plugin provides a summary of the execution time for the playbook.
- `Profile_tasks`: This provides us with a summary of the execution time of each task within a playbook.
- `Profile_roles`: This provides us with a summary of the time taken for each role within a playbook.

We list all the tasks within a playbook using the `--list-tasks` option in order to verify all the tasks that will be executed in our playbook. Here is a snippet of the tasks within our sample playbook:

```
playbook: pb_generate_config.yml

  play #1 (all): Generate Device Config TAGS: []
    tasks:
      generate_config : Create Temp Directory    TAGS: []
      generate_config : Generate System Configuration    TAGS: []
      generate_config : Interface Configuration TAGS: []
      generate_config : OSPF Configuration        TAGS: []
      generate_config : MPLS Configuration        TAGS: []
      Create Configs Folder      TAGS: []
      Remove Old Assembled Config        TAGS: []
      Assemble The Final configuration   TAGS: []
      Remove Temp Folder         TAGS: []
```

We then run the playbook and check the newly added detailed execution summary, as outlined in the following screenshot:

```
Monday 14 October 2019  00:48:16 +0000 (0:00:00.162)       0:00:10.317 ********
===============================================================================
generate_config ------------------------------------------------------- 8.05s
file ------------------------------------------------------------------- 1.15s
assemble --------------------------------------------------------------- 1.03s

total ------------------------------------------------------------------ 10.23s
Monday 14 October 2019  00:48:16 +0000 (0:00:00.162)       0:00:10.317 ********
===============================================================================
generate_config : Generate System Configuration ----------------------- 2.08s
generate_config : Interface Configuration ------------------------------ 1.67s
generate_config : MPLS Configuration ----------------------------------- 1.54s
generate_config : OSPF Configuration ----------------------------------- 1.53s
generate_config : Create Temp Directory -------------------------------- 1.24s
Assemble The Final configuration --------------------------------------- 1.03s
Remove Old Assembled Config -------------------------------------------- 0.84s
Remove Temp Folder ----------------------------------------------------- 0.16s
Create Configs Folder -------------------------------------------------- 0.14s
Playbook run took 0 days, 0 hours, 0 minutes, 10 seconds
```

The first part of the summary outlines the execution time for the role (`generate_config`), as well as the different modules, using the `post_task` section (we use only the `file` and `assemble` modules in the `post_task` section). The next part of the summary outlines the execution time for each task within our playbook (including a breakdown for tasks within the role). Finally, we get a summary of the overall execution time for our playbook as a whole, in a single line.

See also...

For more information regarding callback plugins, `profile_tasks` and `profile_roles` plugins, and the `timer`, please consult the following URLs:

- https://docs.ansible.com/ansible/latest/plugins/callback/timer.html
- https://docs.ansible.com/ansible/latest/plugins/callback/profile_tasks.html
- https://docs.ansible.com/ansible/latest/plugins/callback/profile_roles.html

Validating user input using Ansible

In this recipe, we will outline how to validate input data using Ansible. We rely heavily on the information that we either retrieve from the network or declare in `host` or `group` variables, in order to execute different tasks in Ansible such as generating configuration or provisioning devices. Before we start to use this information, we need to be able to validate the structure and validity of this data before further processing our playbooks.

How to do it...

1. Create an `ACLs` definition in `ACLs.yml`, as shown in the following code block:

```
---
ACLs:
  INFRA_ACL:
    - src: 10.1.1.0/24
      dst: any
      dport: ssh
      state: present
    - src: 10.2.1.0/24
      dst: any
```

```
            app: udp
            dport: snmp
            state: present
```

2. Create a new validation task in the `validate_acl.yml` file, as shown in the following code block:

```
---
- include_vars: ACLs.yml
- name: Validate ACL is Defined
  assert:
    that:
      - ACLs is defined
      - "'INFRA_ACL' in ACLs.keys()"
      - ACLs.INFRA_ACL|length > 0
- name: Validate Rules are Valid
  assert:
    that:
      - item.src is defined
      - item.dst is defined
      - item.src | ipaddr
  loop: "{{ ACLs.INFRA_ACL }}"
```

3. Create a new playbook to create **access control lists (ACLs)** and push-to-network devices, as shown in the following code block:

```
---
- name: Configure ACL on IOS-XR
  hosts: all
  tasks:
    - name: Validate Input Data
      import_tasks: validate_acls.yml
      run_once: yes
      delegate_to: localhost
      tags: validate
    - name: Create ACL Config
      template:
        src: acl.j2
        dest: acl_conf.cfg
      delegate_to: localhost
      run_once: yes
    - name: Provision ACLs
      iosxr_config:
        src: acl_conf.cfg
        match: line
```

How it works...

In this example playbook, we want to push ACL configuration to our infrastructure. We generate the configuration using the `template` module, and we push the configuration using the `iosxr_config` module. All our ACL definition is declared in the `ACLs.yml` file. We would like to validate the input data contained within our `ACLs.yml` file since this is the data that we rely on in order to generate our configuration.

We create a `validate_acl.yml` tasks file that has multiple tasks to validate the structure and the content of the data that we will use to generate our configuration. We start by importing our data using the `include_vars` parameter and then we define two main tasks to validate our data:

- The first task is validating that the required data structure is present and that the data structure is in the correct format that we expect.
- The second task is validating the contents of each firewall rule.

In all these validation tasks, we are using the `assert` module in order to test and validate our conditional statements and we can define much more comprehensive checking on the input data structure to cover all the possibilities for our data.

Using this approach, we can validate the validity of our input data and make sure that our data is sane in order to be processed by subsequent tasks within the playbook.

Running Ansible in check mode

In this recipe, we will outline how to run our Ansible playbooks in dry-run mode. This mode is also called `check` mode and, in this mode, Ansible will not perform any changes on the remotely managed nodes. We can consider this as a simulation run for our playbook that will make us understand which changes will be made by Ansible, if we execute the playbook in `check` mode.

How to do it...

1. Update our ACL declaration in the `ACLs.yml` file with the new entry, as shown in the following code snippet:

```
---
ACLs:
  INFRA_ACL:
```

```
< --- Output Omitted for brevity -- >
    - src: 10.3.2.0/24
      dst: 10.2.2.0/24
      dport: dns
      state: present
```

2. Run the `pb_push_acl.yml` provision playbook using `check` mode, as shown in the following code snippet:

```
$ ansible-playbook pb_push_acl.yml -l den-core01  --check
```

How it works...

When we run the playbook using the `check` mode, no changes are done on the remote systems, and we can see the output from the playbook run, as shown in the following screenshot:

```
PLAY [Configure ACL on IOS-XR] ***********************************************************************

TASK [Create ACL Config] *****************************************************************************
changed: [den-core01 -> localhost]

TASK [Provision ACLs] ********************************************************************************
ok: [den-core01]

PLAY RECAP *******************************************************************************************
den-core01                 : ok=2    changed=1    unreachable=0    failed=0    skipped=0    rescued=0    ignored=0
```

This output outlines that the configuration file we generate for our ACL will be changed (a new rule will be added); however, the provision ACLs task is not reporting any change. This is because the configuration file didn't change since we are running our playbook in `check` mode, so in this case, this task is still using the unmodified configuration file, so no changes will be implemented.

We can also check the changes that will occur using the `--diff` flag when running the playbook, as shown in the following code snippet:

```
$ ansible-playbook pb_push_acl.yml -l den-core01  --check --diff
```

We obtain the following output when we use the `--diff` flag, and it outlines the changes that will take place on our configuration file:

```
PLAY [Configure ACL on IOS-XR] ************************************************************

TASK [Create ACL Config] ******************************************************************
--- before: acl_conf.cfg
+++ after: /home/vagrant/.ansible/tmp/ansible-local-24442_dsTkh/tmpV7waBS/acl.j2
@@ -2,4 +2,5 @@
 ipv4 access-list INFRA_ACL
  10 permit tcp 10.1.1.0/24 any eq ssh
  20 permit udp 10.2.1.0/24 any eq snmp
+ 30 permit tcp 10.3.2.0/24 10.2.2.0/24 eq dns
 !

changed: [den-core01 -> localhost]

TASK [Provision ACLs] *********************************************************************
ok: [den-core01]

PLAY RECAP ********************************************************************************
den-core01                 : ok=2    changed=1   unreachable=0   failed=0   skipped=0   rescued=0   ignored=0
```

There's more...

We can use `check` mode as a switch to run or skip tasks. So, in some cases when we are running in `check` mode, we would not like to connect to the device and push any configuration on the device, since nothing will be changed. Using `check` mode, we can build our playbooks to skip these tasks, as shown in the following code block:

```
- name: Configure ACL on IOS-XR
  hosts: all
  serial: 1
  tags: deploy
  tasks:
    - name: Backup Config
      iosxr_config:
        backup:
      when: not ansible_check_mode
    - name: Deploy ACLs
      iosxr_config:
        src: acl_conf.cfg
        match: line
      when: not ansible_check_mode
```

In our `tasks`, we added the `when` directive, and we are checking the value for the `ansible_check_mode` parameter. This parameter is set to `true` when we run our playbook in `check` mode. Thus, on each task, we are checking whether the `check` mode is set, and, if so, we will skip these tasks during the playbook run. If the playbook is run in normal mode (without `check` mode), these tasks will be executed normally.

See also...

For more information regarding running our playbooks in `check` mode, please consult the following URL: `https://docs.ansible.com/ansible/latest/user_guide/playbooks_checkmode.html`.

Controlling parallelism and rolling updates in Ansible

By default, Ansible runs tasks in parallel. In this recipe, we will outline how to control the parallel execution of Ansible and how we can modify this default behavior. We will also explore the concept of rolling updates and how to utilize them in Ansible.

How to do it...

1. Update the `ansible.cfg` file to control parallel execution, as shown in the following code snippet:

   ```
   [defaults]
   forks=2
   ```

2. Update the `pb_push_acl.yml` file to set up rolling updates for the configuration push on the network devices, as shown in the following code block:

   ```
   - name: Configure ACL on IOS-XR
     hosts: all
     serial: 1
     tags: deploy
     tasks:
       - name: Backup Config
         iosxr_config:
           backup:
       - name: Deploy ACLs
         iosxr_config:
           src: acl_conf.cfg
           match: line
   ```

How it works...

Ansible, by default, works by executing each task across all the devices identified in a playbook in parallel. By default, for each task, Ansible will fork five parallel threads (called forks) and execute these threads in parallel across five nodes in the inventory. Once these tasks finish, it will target the remaining devices in the inventory in a batch of five nodes. It performs this on each task executed in the playbook. Using the `forks` keyword in the `ansible.cfg` file, we can modify the default `fork` value that Ansible is using and control the number of parallel nodes that Ansible targets during each task execution. This can speed up our playbook execution; however, it requires more resources in terms of memory and CPU power on the Ansible control node.

> When using a large number of forks, be advised that any `local_action` steps can fork a Python interpreter on your local machine, so you may wish to keep `local_action` or `delegated` steps limited in number or in separate plays. For further information, see https://www. ansible.com/blog/ansible-performance-tuning.

The other option that we can modify to control playbook execution is that, by default, Ansible runs each task across all nodes identified in the playbook, and it will only step from one task to the other once all the nodes have completed the previous task. We might want to modify this behavior in multiple situations, such as pushing the configuration to network devices or upgrading network devices. We might want to execute a playbook on each node in a serial fashion—this means that each node (or group of nodes) is picked up by Ansible and the playbook is executed on it; once this batch is finished, another batch is selected, and the playbook is run again. This approach allows us to deploy our changes in a rolling manner, and if one of our nodes has failed, we can stop the playbook execution. This configuration is controlled using the `serial` keyword in the playbook. It instructs Ansible to start the play with the number of hosts identified by the `serial` option, executes the whole tasks on this batch, then rolls over and selects another batch, and executes the complete playbook on that batch, and so on.

See also...

For more information about Ansible forks and rolling updates, please consult the following URL: https://docs.ansible.com/ansible/latest/user_guide/playbooks_delegation. html.

Configuring fact caching in Ansible

In this recipe, we will outline how to set up and configure fact caching in Ansible. This is an important feature that can help us in optimizing and speeding the execution time of our playbooks when we require facts to be collected from our infrastructure.

How to do it...

1. Update the `ansible.cfg` file to enable fact caching, and set up the required folder to store the cache:

```
[defaults]
< --- Output Omitted for brevity -->
fact_caching=yaml
fact_caching_connection=./fact_cache
```

2. Create a new `pb_get_facts.yml` playbook to collect facts from the network using different approaches:

```
---
- name: Collect Network Facts
  hosts: all
  tasks:
    - name: Collect Facts Using Built-in Fact Modules
      iosxr_facts:
        gather_subset:
          - interfaces
    - name: Collect Using NAPALM Facts
      napalm_get_facts:
        hostname: "{{ ansible_host }}"
        username: "{{ ansible_user }}"
        password: "{{ ansible_ssh_pass }}"
        dev_os: "{{ ansible_network_os }}"
        filter:
          - interfaces
    - name: Set and Cache Custom Fact
      set_fact:
          site: Egypt
          cacheable: yes
```

3. Run the new Ansible playbook on a single node from our inventory:

```
$ ansible-playbook pb_validate_from_cache.yml -l den-core01
```

How it works...

Ansible is a powerful tool to collect information about the operational state of our infrastructure, and we can use this information in generating configuration, building reports, and also to validate the state of our infrastructure. In cases where the state of our infrastructure is highly stable, we might not need to collect the network facts from our devices during every playbook run. In these cases, we might opt to use fact caching in order to speed up the execution of our playbooks. We read the facts (network state) of our devices from a stored location on the Ansible control node, instead of connecting to the devices and collecting the information from the live network.

Fact caching is enabled in the `ansible.cfg` file, and in this file, we also set the backend type that we will use to store the fact data. There are multiple options, ranging from YAML or JSON files to storing this data into `redis` or `Memcached` databases. In our example, for simplicity, we will use YAML files to store the facts collected from the devices. We also specify the folder location to store this information.

Once we have performed these steps, we can run our playbook to collect network facts. In this sample playbook, we are using different modules (approaches), as follows:

- `iosxr_facts`: This is a built-in module within Ansible networking modules to collect facts from IOS-XR devices (for most networking equipment, there is a fact collection module for each vendor supported by Ansible).
- `napalm_get_facts`: This is a custom module from **Network Automation and Programmability Abstraction Layer with Multivendor support** (**NAPALM**) that needs to be installed to collect facts as well; however, it is not part of the core Ansible modules.
- `set_fact`: We use the `set_fact` module to set a custom fact during the playbook run, and we use the `cacheable` option to instruct the module to write this new cached variable into our cache.

Once we run the playbook, we can check that the new folder is created and a new YAML file for each node within our inventory is stored in this location. All the facts collected by these modules are saved in these YAML files, as shown in the following screenshot:

```
[vagrant@centos7 ch13_ansible_best_practice]$ grep 'ansible_*\|napalm*\|site' fact_cache/den-core01
ansible_net_all_ipv4_addresses:
ansible_net_all_ipv6_addresses: []
ansible_net_api: cliconf
ansible_net_gather_subset:
ansible_net_hostname: den-core01
ansible_net_image: bootflash:disk0/xrvr-os-mbi-6.1.2/mbixrvr-rp.vm
ansible_net_interfaces:
ansible_net_model: IOS XRv
ansible_net_python_version: 2.7.5
ansible_net_system: iosxr
ansible_net_version: 6.1.2[Default]
napalm_interfaces:
site: Egypt
```

There's more...

Once we have configured fact caching, we can start to use the Ansible variables declared in our cache in any other playbook, as shown in the following code example:

```
---
- name: Validate Cache Data
  vars:
    ansible_connection: local
  hosts: all
  tasks:
    - name: Validate all Interfaces
      assert:
        that:
          - item.value.operstatus == 'up'
      with_dict: "{{ ansible_net_interfaces }}"
    - name: Validate Custom Fact
      assert:
        that:
          - site == 'Egypt'
```

In the preceding playbook, we are utilizing the variables collected from the cache (ansible_net_interfaces, in this example) and running the tasks against the devices in the inventory. We need to consider that, by default, the entries in the cache are valid only for a specific amount of time, controlled by the timeout value for our cache to ensure that any outdated state in our cache will not be considered. This value is controlled by the fact_caching_timeout option, which can be set in the ansible.cfg file.

See also...

For more information regarding Ansible fact caching, please consult the following URLs:

- `https://docs.ansible.com/ansible/latest/plugins/cache.html`
- `https://docs.ansible.com/ansible/latest/plugins/cache/yaml.html`

Creating custom Python filters for Ansible

Ansible provides a rich set of filters from Jinja2, as well as some additional built-in filters to manipulate data; however, in some cases, you may find that there is no filter available to satisfy your requirements. In this recipe, we will outline how to build custom filters in Python to extend Ansible functionality to manipulate data.

How to do it...

1. In the project directory (`ch13_ansible_best_practice`), create a new folder, `filter_plugins`.

2. Create a new Python script called `filter.py` under the `filter_plugins` folder, with the following content:

```python
class FilterModule(object):
    def filters(self):
        return {
            'acl_state': self.acl_state
        }
    def acl_state(self,acl_def):
        for acl_name, acl_rules in acl_def.items():
            for rule in acl_rules:
                rule['state'] = rule['state'].upper()
        return acl_def
```

3. Create a new Ansible playbook, `pb_test_custom_filter.yml`, with the following content:

```yaml
---
- name: Test Custom Filter
  hosts: all
  vars:
    ansible_connection: local
  tasks:
```

```
- name: Read ACL data
  include_vars: ACLs.yml
  run_once: yes
- name: Apply Our Custom Filter
  set_fact:
    standard_acl: "{{ ACLs | acl_state }}"
  run_once: yes
- name: Display Output After Filter
  debug: var=standard_acl
```

How it works...

We can extend the `filter` library provided by Ansible and create a custom filter using Python. In order to implement our custom filter, we create a folder called `filter_plugins` under our project directory, and we create a Python script with any name (we used `filter.py` in our example).

 The custom Python filters must be placed in a folder called `filter_plugins` in order for Ansible to pick up these filters and process them.

Inside this Python script, we create a Python class called `FilterModule`. Inside this class, we declare a function named `filters` that returns a dictionary of all our custom filters that we define. We then start to create our filter by declaring a function called `acl_state` that takes the `acl_def` variables (which is our ACLs' definition that we pass in our playbook). In this example, we are simply taking the definition of our ACL state and changing it to uppercase. We then return the newly modified ACL definition.

We create an Ansible playbook as normal, and we read our ACL definition from the `ACLs.yml` file. Then, we create a new task to set a custom fact using the `set_fact` module, and we pass our ACLs' data structure to our custom filter that we have created (`acl_state`). We save the return value from our custom filter to a new variable called `standard_acl`, and we use the `debug` module in the next task to output the value of this new variable.

The following snippet outlines the new value for our ACL and how the state parameter within our ACL definition has changed to uppercase:

```
ok: [str-core02] => {
    "standard_acl": {
        "INFRA_ACL": [
            {
                "dport": "ssh",
                "dst": "any",
                "src": "10.1.1.0/24",
                "state": "PRESENT"
            },
            {
                "app": "udp",
                "dport": "snmp",
                "dst": "any",
                "src": "10.2.1.0/24",
                "state": "PRESENT"
            },
            {
                "app": "udp",
                "dport": "dns",
                "dst": "10.2.2.0/24",
                "src": "10.3.2.0/24",
                "state": "PRESENT"
            }
        ]
    }
}
```

There's more...

We outlined how to pass the variable definition to our custom filter in the previous example; however, we can also pass multiple fields to our custom filter in order to have more control over the return value of our filter. In order to outline this, we will create another custom filter that will take the ACL definition along with a field variable, and, based on this field, we will change the value of this field in our ACL definition to uppercase. Here is the modified `filter.py` Python script:

```
class FilterModule(object):

< -- Output Omitted for brevity -- >
    def custom_acl(self, acl_def, field=None):
        for acl_name, acl_rules in acl_def.items():
            for rule in acl_rules:
                if field and field in rule.keys():
                    rule[field] = rule[field].upper()
```

```
        return acl_def
def filters(self):
    return {
        'acl_state': self.acl_state,
        'custom_acl': self.custom_acl
    }
```

Here is the output of the modified tasks within the playbook, using our new custom filter:

```
- name: Apply Our Custom Filter
  set_fact:
    standard_acl: "{{ ACLs | acl_state }}"
    final_acl: "{{ ACLs | custom_acl('dports') }}"
  run_once: yes
- name: Display Output After Filter
  debug: var=final_acl
```

Here is the output for our `final_acl` file after applying the new custom filter:

```
"final_acl": {
    "INFRA_ACL": [
        {
            "dport": "SSH",
            "dst": "any",
            "src": "10.1.1.0/24",
            "state": "present"
        },
        {
            "app": "udp",
            "dport": "SNMP",
            "dst": "any",
            "src": "10.2.1.0/24",
            "state": "present"
        },
        {
            "app": "udp",
            "dport": "DNS",
            "dst": "10.2.2.0/24",
            "src": "10.3.2.0/24",
            "state": "present"
        }
    ]
}
```

The preceding screenshot shows the output after applying the new custom filter.

Other Books You May Enjoy

If you enjoyed this book, you may be interested in these other books by Packt:

Learning Python Networking - Second Edition
José Manuel Ortega, Dr. M. O. Faruque Sarker and Sam Washington

ISBN: 978-1-78995-809-6

- Execute Python modules on networking tools
- Automate tasks regarding the analysis and extraction of information from a network
- Get to grips with asynchronous programming modules available in Python
- Get to grips with IP address manipulation modules using Python programming
- Understand the main frameworks available in Python that are focused on web application
- Manipulate IP addresses and perform CIDR calculations

Azure Networking Cookbook

Mustafa Toroman

ISBN: 978-1-78980-022-7

- Learn to create Azure networking services
- Understand how to create and work on hybrid connections
- Configure and manage Azure network services
- Learn ways to design high availability network solutions in Azure
- Discover how to monitor and troubleshoot Azure network resources
- Learn different methods of connecting local networks to Azure virtual networks

Leave a review - let other readers know what you think

Please share your thoughts on this book with others by leaving a review on the site that you bought it from. If you purchased the book from Amazon, please leave us an honest review on this book's Amazon page. This is vital so that other potential readers can see and use your unbiased opinion to make purchasing decisions, we can understand what our customers think about our products, and our authors can see your feedback on the title that they have worked with Packt to create. It will only take a few minutes of your time, but is valuable to other potential customers, our authors, and Packt. Thank you!

Index

111, 112
  used, for initializing network snapshot 334, 335
  used, for validating user input 433, 434, 435
  variables, using 17, 18
Arista device facts
  gathering 154, 155, 156
Arista devices
  authenticating to 126, 128
  configuration, deploying on 147, 148
  connecting, from Ansible 126, 128
  eAPI, enabling on 128, 130, 131
  generic system options, configuring on 131, 132, 133
  interfaces, configuring on 137, 139
  operational data, retrieving from 157, 159
  overlay BGP EVPN, configuring on 145, 146, 147
  underlay BGP, configuring on 141, 142, 143, 144
  VLANs, configuring on 149, 150, 151
  VXLANs tunnels, configuring on 152, 153, 154
assemble module
  reference link 93
assertions, Batfish Ansible modules
  reference link 340
autonomous system number (ASN) 141
AWS account
  authenticating to 223, 224, 225, 226
AWS endpoints
  reference link 229
AWS SDK
  installing 221, 222
AWS
  resources, decommissioning on 248, 249, 250
AWX API
  reference link 421
  used, for running automation tasks 417, 418, 419, 420
AWX credentials
  reference link 404
AWX installation
  reference link 391
AWX projects
  reference link 409
AWX templates
  reference link 413

AWX workflow templates
  reference link 417
AWX
  installing 386, 387, 389, 390
  network credentials, managing 401, 403
  network inventory, creating on 397, 398, 400, 401
  prerequisites 390
  projects, creating 404, 405, 406, 407, 408, 409
  teams, managing 391, 392, 394, 396
  templates, creating 409, 410, 411, 412, 413
  users, managing 391, 392, 394, 396
  workflow templates, creating 414, 415, 416, 417
Azure account
  authenticating to 256, 257, 258, 259, 260, 261, 262, 263
Azure built-in roles
  reference link 264
Azure NSG module, Ansible
  reference link 278
Azure resource module, Ansible
  reference link 266
Azure resources
  decommissioning, with Ansible 281, 282, 283
Azure route table modules
  reference link 274
Azure SDK
  installing 253, 254
Azure subnets module, Ansible
  reference link 270
Azure virtual network module, Ansible
  reference link 268

B

basic system information
  configuring 50, 51, 52
Batfish
  installing 326
  integrating, with Ansible 327, 328, 329
  network facts, collecting 337, 338, 339
  network snapshot, creating 332, 333
  reference link 327
  used, for validating ACLs 344, 345, 346
  used, for validating traffic forwarding 341, 342, 343

www.ingramcontent.com/pod-product-compliance
Lightning Source LLC
LaVergne TN
LVHW081509050326
832903LV00025B/1427